easy **Writer**

fourth edition

Andrea A. Lunsford
STANFORD UNIVERSITY

with a section for
multilingual writers by

Paul Kei Matsuda
Arizona State University

Christine M. Tardy
DePaul University

A POCKET REFERENCE

BEDFORD/ST. MARTIN'S
Boston ◆ New York

For Bedford/St. Martin's

Senior Developmental Editor: Carolyn Lengel
Production Editor: Ryan Sullivan
Senior Production Supervisor: Dennis J. Conroy
Executive Marketing Manager: John Swanson
Art Director: Lucy Krikorian
Text Design: Anne Carter
Copy Editor: Alice Vigliani
Indexer: Melanie Belkin
Cover Design: Donna Dennison
Composition: Six Red Marbles
Printing and Binding: Quebecor World Eusey Press

President: Joan E. Feinberg
Editorial Director: Denise B. Wydra
Editor in Chief: Karen S. Henry
Director of Development: Erica T. Appel
Director of Marketing: Karen R. Soeltz
Director of Editing, Design, and Production: Marcia Cohen
Assistant Director of Editing, Design, and Production:
   Elise S. Kaiser
Managing Editor: Shuli Traub

Library of Congress Control Number: 2009928651

Manufactured in the United States of America.

4   3   2   1   0   9
f   e   d   c   b   a

For information, write: Bedford/St. Martin's, 75 Arlington
Street, Boston, MA 02116   (617-399-4000)

ISBN-10: 0-312-55425-7
ISBN-13: 978-0-312-55425-5

Acknowledgments

Acknowledgments and copyrights are continued at the back
of the book on page 342, which constitutes an extension of
the copyright page.

How to Use This Book

Whether you're a writing student, an engineer, or a psychologist, chances are that you're called on to write and do research often, maybe even every day. Chances are also good that you often have questions about writing and research. *EasyWriter* aims to provide answers to such questions.

Ways into the book

BRIEF CONTENTS. Inside the front cover you will find a flap listing the book's contents. Once you locate a general topic in the Brief Contents, it will point you to the chapter of the book that contains specific information on the topic.

USER-FRIENDLY INDEX. The index lists everything covered in the book. You can find information by looking up a topic ("articles," for example) or, if you're not sure what your topic is called, by looking up the word you need help with (such as *a* or *the*).

CONTENTS. If you're looking for specific information within a general topic, inside the back cover a brief but detailed table of contents lists chapter titles and major headings.

FIND IT. FIX IT. Following "How to Use This Book," advice on the twenty most common errors provides hand-edited examples and brief explanations to guide you toward recognizing, understanding, and editing the most common errors. This "Find It. Fix It." section includes cross-references to other places in the book where you'll find more detail.

PRACTICAL ADVICE ON RESEARCH AND DOCUMENTATION. Source maps walk you step by step through the processes of selecting, evaluating, and citing sources. Documentation models are easy to find in four color-coded sections—one each for MLA, APA, *Chicago*, and CSE styles.

REVISION SYMBOLS. If your instructor uses revision symbols to mark your drafts, consult the list of symbols on the inside back cover and its cross-references to places in the book where you'll find more help.

GLOSSARIES. The Glossary of Terms, on blue-green pages (pp. 319–30) at the back of the book, provides definitions of grammatical terms, including every term in boldface type in the book. The Glossary of Usage, on yellow pages (pp. 331–41), gives help with troublesome words (*accept* and *except*, for example).

Ways to navigate the pages

The descriptions below correspond to the numbered elements on the sample page opposite.

❶ GUIDES AT THE TOP OF EVERY PAGE. Headers tell you what chapter or subsection you're in, the chapter number and section letter, and the page number. Icons that link to the name of the section (sunglasses for *Sentence Style*, for example) also appear at the top of the page.

❷ HAND-EDITED EXAMPLES. Most examples are hand-edited in blue, allowing you to see the error and its revision at a glance. Blue pointers and boldface type make examples easy to spot on the page.

❸ FOR MULTILINGUAL WRITERS BOXES. Advice for multilingual writers appears in a separate section (Chapters 33–37) and in boxed tips throughout the book. You can find a list of topics covered, including language-specific tips, on p. 361.

❹ CROSS-REFERENCES TO THE WEB SITE. The *EasyWriter* Web site expands the book's coverage. The cross-references to the Web site point you to practical online resources — from a tutorial on avoiding plagiarism to grammar exercises, model essays, and links to other Web resources. Inside the front cover, you can find a directory for the model student essays and other coverage on the Web site.

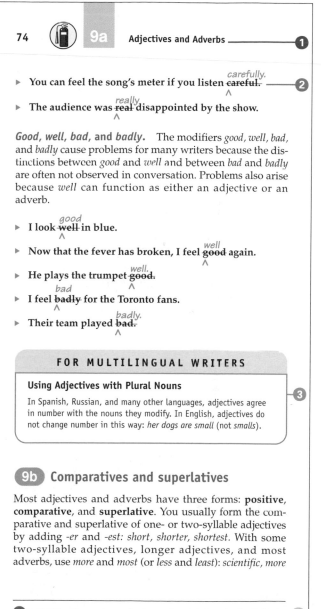

74 **9a** Adjectives and Adverbs _____ ❶

▶ You can feel the song's meter if you listen ~~careful.~~ —— ❷
  carefully.
  ∧

▶ The audience was ~~real~~ disappointed by the show.
  really
  ∧

Good, well, bad,* and *badly. The modifiers *good, well, bad,*
and *badly* cause problems for many writers because the distinctions between *good* and *well* and between *bad* and *badly*
are often not observed in conversation. Problems also arise
because *well* can function as either an adjective or an
adverb.

▶ I look ~~well~~ in blue.
  good
  ∧

▶ Now that the fever has broken, I feel ~~good~~ again.
  well
  ∧

▶ He plays the trumpet ~~good.~~
  well.
  ∧

▶ I feel ~~badly~~ for the Toronto fans.
  bad
  ∧

▶ Their team played ~~bad.~~
  badly.
  ∧

FOR MULTILINGUAL WRITERS

Using Adjectives with Plural Nouns

In Spanish, Russian, and many other languages, adjectives agree —— ❸
in number with the nouns they modify. In English, adjectives do
not change number in this way: *her dogs are small* (not *smalls*).

9b Comparatives and superlatives

Most adjectives and adverbs have three forms: **positive**,
comparative, and **superlative**. You usually form the comparative and superlative of one- or two-syllable adjectives
by adding *-er* and *-est: short, shorter, shortest*. With some
two-syllable adjectives, longer adjectives, and most
adverbs, use *more* and *most* (or *less* and *least*): *scientific, more*

---

bedfordstmartins.com/easywriter For exercises, go to **Exercise Central** and —— ❹
click on **Adjectives and Adverbs.**

Find It. Fix It.

Surface errors—grammar, punctuation, word choice, and other small-scale matters—don't always disturb readers. Whether your instructor marks an error in any particular assignment will depend on personal judgments about how serious and distracting it is and about what you should be focusing on in the draft. In addition, not all surface errors are consistently viewed as errors: some of the patterns identified in my research are considered errors by some instructors but stylistic options by others. Such differing opinions don't mean that there is no such thing as correctness in writing—only that *correctness always depends on some context*, on whether the choices a writer makes seem appropriate to readers.

Research reveals a number of changes that have occurred in student writing over the past twenty-five years. First, writing assignments in first-year composition classes now focus less on personal narrative and much more on research essays and argument. As a result, students are now writing longer essays than they did in the 1980s and working much more often with sources, both print and nonprint. Thus it's no surprise that students today are struggling with the conventions for using and citing sources.

What else has changed? For starters, wrong-word errors are *by far the most common* errors among first-year student writers today. Twenty years ago, spelling errors were most common by a factor of more than three to one. The use of spell checkers has reduced the number of spelling errors in student writing—but spell checkers' suggestions may also be responsible for some (or many) of the wrong words students are using.

All writers want to be considered competent and careful. You know that your readers judge you by your control of the conventions you have agreed to use, even if the conventions change from time to time. To help you in producing writing that is conventionally correct, you should become familiar with the twenty most common error patterns among U.S.

⬤ bedfordstmartins.com/easywriter For advice on learning from your own most common writing problems, go to **Writing Resources** and click on **Taking a Writing Inventory**.

college students today, listed here in order of frequency. A brief explanation and examples of each error are provided in the following sections, and each error pattern is cross-referenced to other places in this book where you can find more detailed information and additional examples.

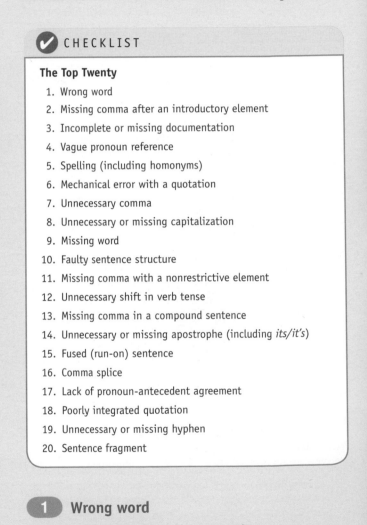

✓ CHECKLIST

The Top Twenty

1. Wrong word
2. Missing comma after an introductory element
3. Incomplete or missing documentation
4. Vague pronoun reference
5. Spelling (including homonyms)
6. Mechanical error with a quotation
7. Unnecessary comma
8. Unnecessary or missing capitalization
9. Missing word
10. Faulty sentence structure
11. Missing comma with a nonrestrictive element
12. Unnecessary shift in verb tense
13. Missing comma in a compound sentence
14. Unnecessary or missing apostrophe (including *its/it's*)
15. Fused (run-on) sentence
16. Comma splice
17. Lack of pronoun-antecedent agreement
18. Poorly integrated quotation
19. Unnecessary or missing hyphen
20. Sentence fragment

1 Wrong word

▸ Religious texts, for them, take ~~prescience~~ over other kinds of sources.
        precedence

Prescience means "foresight," and *precedence* means "priority."

▶ The child suffered from a severe *allegory* to peanuts.
  ^ *allergy*

  Allegory is a spell checker's replacement for a misspelling of
  allergy.

▶ The panel discussed the ethical implications *of* ~~on~~ the
  ^
  situation.

Wrong-word errors can involve using a word with the wrong
shade of meaning, using a word with a completely
wrong meaning, or using a wrong **preposition** or another
wrong word in an idiom. Selecting a word from a thesaurus without knowing its meaning or allowing a spell checker
to correct spelling automatically can lead to wrong-word
errors, so use these tools with care. If you have trouble with
prepositions and idioms, memorize the standard usage. (See
Chapter 32 on word choice and Chapter 37 on prepositions
and idioms.)

2 Missing comma after an introductory element

▶ Determined to get the job done, we worked all weekend.
  ^

▶ Although the study was flawed, the results may still be
  ^
  useful.

Readers usually need a small pause—signaled by a
comma—between an introductory word, **phrase**, or **clause**
and the main part of the **sentence**. Use a comma after every
introductory element. When the introductory element is
very short, you don't always need a comma, but including
it is never wrong. (See 19a.)

3 Incomplete or missing documentation

▶ Satrapi says, "When we're afraid, we lose all sense of
  analysis and reflection." *(263).*
  ^

  The page number of the print source for this quotation must
  be included.

▶ **According to one source, James Joyce wrote two of the**
("100 Best").
five best novels of all time.
   ^

   The source mentioned should be identified (this online source
   has no author or page numbers).

Cite each source you refer to in the text, following the
guidelines of the documentation style you are using. (The
preceding examples follow MLA style—see Chapter 42; for
other styles, see Chapters 43–45.) Omitting documentation
can result in charges of plagiarism. (See Chapter 40.)

4 Vague pronoun reference

POSSIBLE REFERENCE TO MORE THAN ONE WORD

▶ **Transmitting radio signals by satellite is a way of**

   overcoming the problem of scarce airwaves and limiting
   the airwaves
   how ~~they~~ are used.
      ^

   In the original sentence, _they_ could refer to the signals or to
   the airwaves.

REFERENCE IMPLIED BUT NOT STATED
                              a policy
▶ **The company prohibited smoking, ~~which~~ many**
                                      ^
   employees resented.

   What does _which_ refer to? The editing clarifies what employees
   resented.

A **pronoun** should refer clearly to the word or words it
replaces (called the _antecedent_) elsewhere in the sentence or
in a previous sentence. If more than one word could be the
antecedent, or if no specific antecedent is present, edit to
make the meaning clear. (See Chapter 11.)

5 Spelling (including homonyms)

          Reagan
▶ **Ronald ~~Regan~~ won the election in a landslide.**
         ^
   Everywhere
▶ **~~Every where~~ we went, we saw crowds of tourists.**
   ^

The most common misspellings today are those that spell checkers cannot identify. The categories that spell checkers are most likely to miss include homonyms, compound words incorrectly spelled as separate words, and proper **nouns**, particularly names. After you run the spell checker, proofread carefully for errors such as these—and be sure to run the spell checker to catch other kinds of spelling mistakes.

6 Mechanical error with a quotation

▶ "I grew up the victim of a disconcerting confusion,"/
  Rodriguez says (249).

  The comma should be placed *inside* the quotation marks.

Follow conventions when using quotation marks with commas (19h), colons, and other punctuation. Always use quotation marks in pairs, and follow the guidelines of your documentation style for block quotations. Use quotation marks for titles of short works (23b), but use italics for titles of long works (27a).

7 Unnecessary comma

BEFORE CONJUNCTIONS IN COMPOUND CONSTRUCTIONS THAT ARE NOT COMPOUND SENTENCES

▶ This conclusion applies to the United States/ and to the
  rest of the world.

  No comma is needed before *and* because it is joining two phrases that modify the same verb, *applies*.

WITH RESTRICTIVE ELEMENTS

▶ Many parents/ of gifted children/ do not want them to
  skip a grade.

  No comma is needed to set off the restrictive phrase *of gifted children*, which is necessary to indicate which parents the sentence is talking about.

Do not use commas to set off **restrictive elements** that are necessary to the meaning of the words they modify. Do not use a comma before a **coordinating conjunction** (*and, but, for, nor, or, so, yet*) when the conjunction does not join parts of a **compound sentence** (error 13). Do not use a comma before the first or after the last item in a series, between a **subject** and **verb**, between a verb and its **object** or **complement**, or between a **preposition** and its object. (See 19i.)

8 Unnecessary or missing capitalization

▶ Some ~~Traditional~~ Chinese ~~Medicines~~ containing
   traditional   medicines
   ~~Ephedra~~ remain legal.
  ephedra^

Capitalize proper nouns and proper adjectives, the first words of sentences, and important words in titles, along with certain words indicating directions and family relationships. Do not capitalize most other words. When in doubt, check a dictionary. (See Chapter 25.)

9 Missing word

▶ The site foreman discriminated women and promoted
                              against^
  men with less experience.

Proofread carefully for omitted words, including prepositions (37a), parts of two-part verbs (37b), and correlative **conjunctions**. Be particularly careful not to omit words from quotations.

10 Faulty sentence structure

▶ ~~The information which~~ high school athletes are
               High^
  presented with ~~mainly includes~~ information on what
  credits needed to graduate, ~~and thinking about the~~
      they^
  ~~college~~ which ~~athletes are trying~~ to play for, and apply.
   colleges to try^   how to^

A sentence that starts out with one kind of structure and then changes to another kind can confuse readers. Make sure that each sentence contains a subject and a verb, that subjects and **predicates** make sense together (14b), and that comparisons have clear meanings (14d). When you join elements (such as subjects or verb phrases) with a coordinating conjunction, make sure that the elements have parallel structures (see Chapter 17).

11   Missing comma with a nonrestrictive element

▶ **Marina, who was the president of the club, was first to speak.**

The clause *who was the president of the club* does not affect the basic meaning of the sentence: Marina was first to speak.

A **nonrestrictive element** gives information not essential to the basic meaning of the sentence. Use commas to set off a nonrestrictive element (19c).

12   Unnecessary shift in verb tense

▶ **Priya was watching the great blue heron. Then she**
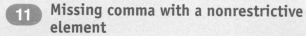
slips and falls into the swamp.

Verbs that shift from one **tense** to another with no clear reason can confuse readers (18a).

13   Missing comma in a compound sentence

▶ **Meredith waited for Samir, and her sister grew impatient.**

Without the comma, a reader may think at first that Meredith waited for both Samir and her sister.

A **compound sentence** consists of two or more parts that could each stand alone as a sentence. When the parts are joined by a coordinating conjunction, use a comma before the conjunction to indicate a pause between the two thoughts (19b).

14 Unnecessary or missing apostrophe (including *its*/*it's*)

▸ Overambitious parents can be very harmful to a ~~childs~~ *child's*
well-being.

▸ The car is lying on ~~it's~~ *its* side in the ditch. ~~Its~~ *It's* a white 2004
Passat.

To make a noun **possessive**, add either an apostrophe and an
-s (*Ed's book*) or an apostrophe alone (*the boys' gym*). Do *not* use
an apostrophe in the **possessive pronouns** *ours*, *yours*, and
hers. Use *its* to mean *belonging to it*; use *it's* only when you
mean *it is* or *it has*. (See Chapter 22.)

15 Fused (run-on) sentence

▸ Klee's paintings seem simple *but* they are very sophisticated.

▸ *Although she* ~~She~~ doubted the value of meditation she decided to
try it once.

A **fused sentence** (also called a *run-on*) joins clauses that
could each stand alone as a sentence with no punctuation or
words to link them. Fused sentences must either be divided
into separate sentences or joined by adding words or punctuation. (See Chapter 12.)

16 Comma splice

▸ I was strongly attracted to her, *for* she was beautiful and funny.

▸ We hated the meat loaf *that* the cafeteria served ~~it~~ every
Friday.

A **comma splice** occurs when only a comma separates
clauses that could each stand alone as a sentence. To correct a
comma splice, you can insert a semicolon or period, connect
the clauses with a word such as *and* or *because*, or restructure
the sentence. (See Chapter 12.)

17 Lack of pronoun-antecedent agreement

▸ ~~Every student~~ must provide their own ~~uniform.~~

All students *uniforms.*

▸ Each of the puppies thrived in ~~their~~ new home.

its

Pronouns must agree with their antecedents in **gender** (male or female) and in **number** (**singular** or **plural**). Many **indefinite pronouns**, such as *everyone* and *each*, are always singular. When a singular antecedent can refer to a man or a woman, either rewrite the sentence to make the antecedent plural or to eliminate the pronoun, or use *his or her, he or she*, and so on. When antecedents are joined by *or* or *nor*, the pronoun must agree with the closer antecedent. A **collective noun** such as *team* can be either singular or plural, depending on whether the members are seen as a group or as individuals. (See 11b.)

18 Poorly integrated quotation

▸ A 1970s study of what makes food appetizing "Once it became apparent that the steak was actually blue and the fries were green, some people became ill" (Schlosser 565).

showed how color affects taste:

▸ "Dumpster diving has serious drawbacks as a way of life" (~~Eighner~~ 383). Finding edible food is especially tricky.

According to Lars Eighner,

Quotations should fit smoothly into the surrounding sentence structure. They should be linked clearly to the writing around them (usually with a signal phrase) rather than dropped abruptly into the writing. (See 40a.)

19 Unnecessary or missing hyphen

▸ This paper looks at fictional and real life examples.

A compound adjective modifying a noun that follows it requires a hyphen.

▸ The buyers want to fix up the house and resell it.

A two-word verb should not be hyphenated.

A **compound adjective** that appears before a noun needs a hyphen. However, be careful not to hyphenate two-word verbs or word groups that serve as subject complements. (See Chapter 28.)

20 Sentence fragment

NO SUBJECT

▶ Marie Antoinette spent huge sums of money on herself and her favorites. ~~And~~ *Her extravagance* helped bring on the French Revolution.

NO COMPLETE VERB

▶ The old aluminum boat *was* sitting on its trailer.

BEGINNING WITH A SUBORDINATING WORD

▶ We returned to the drugstore, ~~Where~~ *where* we waited for our buddies.

A **sentence fragment** is part of a sentence that is written as if it were a complete sentence. Reading your draft out loud, backwards, sentence by sentence, will help you spot sentence fragments. (See Chapter 13.)

FOR MULTILINGUAL WRITERS

Language-Specific Tips

Is your first language Arabic? Chinese? Spanish? something else? See the directory for multilingual writers at the back of the book to find tips about predictable error patterns in other languages.

bedfordstmartins.com/easywriter For practice identifying and correcting these writing problems, click on **The Top Twenty**. For additional exercises, click on **Exercises**.

diagrams, 56
dialects, regional, 149
diction. *See* word choice
different from, different than, 334
Digg, 182
digital object identifier (DOI), 269, 270, 273
direct address, commas with, 112
direct discourse, 103–4
directness in writing, strategies for, 13
direct objects
  defined, 322
  and transitive verb, 63, 161, 173–74
direct questions, question mark with, 118
direct quotations, quotation marks, 121
disciplines, writing in, 47–51
  assignments, analyzing, 47
  evidence in, 48–50
  humanities, 48–49
  natural and applied sciences, 50
  social sciences, 49–50
  terminology and style of, 47–48
discourse, direct and indirect, 103–4
discreet, discrete, 334
disinterested, uninterested, 334
disruptive modifiers, 77
dissertations, citing, 244, 277
distinct, distinctive, 334
documentation, missing or incomplete, 3–4
documentation style
  APA style, 253–82
  Chicago style, 283–300
  CSE style, 301–17
  for humanities, 49
  MLA style, 206–52
  for natural and applied science, 50
  for social sciences, 49
document design, 51–58. *See also* formatting
  arguments, 34–35
  color, 53–54
  design principles, 51–53
  headings, 55
  line spacing, 54
  margins and white space, 53
  pagination, 54
  paper, 54
  and rhetorical situation, 15
  type size and fonts, 54
  visuals, 55–58
  for Web texts, 41
doesn't, don't, 334
dots. *See* ellipses

doublespeak, 152
drafting
  guidelines for, 20
  multilingual writers, review by native speaker, 204
  research writing, 202–3
due to, because of, 333

each, every, 163
each other, one another, 334
-ed, -d endings, past tense and past participle, 61
editing
  commas, 107
  hyphens, 140
  pronouns, 80
  questions for, 23
  research project, 204
  for subject-verb agreement, 68
  troubleshooting writing. *See* Find It. Fix It.
  verbs, 63
effect, affect, 331
e.g. (for example), 134
either . . . or, 101–2
electronic communication, 39–46
  discussion forums, 39
  email, 39
  multimedia presentations, 41–46
  texting, 39
  Web logs (blogs) and social networking sites, 40
  Web texts, 40–41
electronic sources
  APA in-text citation, 257–58
  APA list of references, 269–76
  Chicago style, 289–93
  CSE style, 310–14
  MLA in-text citation, 212
  MLA works cited list, 229–38
elicit, illicit, 335
ellipses
  period with, 129–30
  quotations, omissions in, 129–30, 193, 199
elliptical constructions, pronoun case in, 81
email
  academic English, use in, 39
  business writing, 50–51
emigrate from, immigrate to, 335
emotional appeals
  creating, 33
  identifying, 28
emphasis
  dashes for, 127
  italics for, 137–38
end punctuation, 117–19

English language, varieties of, 148–49, 159
enough, some, 163
enthused, enthusiastic, 335
equally as good, 335
-er, -est ending, 75, 319
errors, common. *See* Find It. Fix It.
-es ending, present tense, subject-verb agreement with, 71
essays. *See also* arguments, title, quotation marks for, 123
et al. (and others), 134, 217, 287
etc. (and so forth), 134
ethical appeals
   creating, 31–32
   identifying, 28
euphemisms, avoiding, 152
evaluating sources, 184–89
every, each, 163
every day, everyday, 335
every one, everyone, 335
evidence
   in arguments, 29–30
   choosing, 19, 143–44
   and critical reading, 26
   for disciplines, 48
   for humanities assignments, 49
   for natural and applied science assignments, 50
   for social science assignments, 49–50
except, accept, 331
exclamation points
   with quotation marks, 113, 124
   uses of, 118–19
explanatory notes, MLA style, 214
expletives
   avoiding, 99–100
   defined, 322
explicit, implicit, 335

Facebook
   citing, 238, 293
   writing guidelines, 40
family relationships, capitalizing, 133
farther, further, 335
few, many, 163
fewer, less, 335
field research, 182–83
figurative language, 153–54
figures
   APA style, 254
   Chicago style, 284, 298
   CSE style, 301
   MLA style, 207, 213, 249
finalize, 335
Find It. Fix It., 1–10
   apostrophe, unnecessary or missing, 8, 119–20

capitalization, unnecessary or missing, 6, 130–33
commas, missing after introductory element, 3, 107
commas, missing in compound sentences, 7, 107–8
commas, missing with nonrestrictive elements, 7, 108–9
commas, unnecessary, 5–6, 113–14
comma splice, 8, 85–87
documentation, missing or incomplete, 3–4, 200
fused (run-on) sentences, 8, 85–87
hyphens, unnecessary or missing, 9–10, 139–40
pronoun-antecedent agreement, lack of, 9, 82–84
pronoun reference, vague, 4, 83–84
quotations, mechanical error with, 5, 123–25
quotations, poorly integrated, 9, 198
sentence fragments, 10, 87–90
sentence structure, faulty, 6–7, 159–61
spelling errors, 4–5, 154–55
verb tense, shifts, 7, 102–3
words, missing, 6, 171–74
wrong-word errors, 2–3, 150–54
firstly, secondly, etc., 335
first person, 103, 326
flaming, 39
flaunt, flout, 335
folders, for drafts, 21
fonts. *See also* type size, serif and sans serif, 54
footnotes
   APA style, 259
   MLA style, 214
   numbers and quotation marks, 124
foreign words
   italics for, 137
   use in writing, 17
formality
   appropriate levels of, 150–52
   and rhetorical situation, 16
formatting. *See also* document design
   APA style, 253–54, 263, 280–82
   Chicago style, 283–84, 297–300
   CSE style, 301–2, 315–17
   MLA style, 206–7, 218, 225, 247–52
former, latter, 335
fractions
   hyphens in, 139

numbers in, 135
subject-verb agreement with, 70
fragments. *See* sentence fragments
freewriting, to explore topic, 18
fused (run-on) sentences, 322
 revising, 8, 85–87
future perfect progressive tense,
 64
future perfect tense, 64
future progressive tense, 64
future tense, 63

gender
 defined, 322
 pronoun-antecedent agreement,
 9, 82
 sexist nouns, alternatives to,
 146
 sexist pronouns, 83, 146
general statements, and paragraph development, 21
general words, 153
genres. *See also* writing projects
 in business writing, 50
 defined, 158, 322
 features of, 159
 in humanities, 49
 in natural and applied sciences,
 50
 and rhetorical situation, 15
 in social sciences, 49
 U.S. academic genres, 159–60
gerunds
 defined, 322
 forming, 160, 169
 versus infinitives, 168–70
 possessive case with, 79
good, well, 74, 335
good and, 336
Google searches, 181–82
grant proposals, documentation
 style, 50

handouts, for oral presentations,
 43
hanged, hung, 336
he, generic use, revising, 83
headings
 APA style, 254
 business writing, 51
 Chicago style, 283
 CSE style, 301
 MLA style, 207
 parallelism, 101
 type size and style, 55
 wording of, 55
her/his, 336
herself, himself, myself, yourself, 336
he/she, 336
himself, herself, myself, yourself, 336

his/her, 336
historical sources, 179
hopefully, 336
however, 86, 112, 116
humanities
 assignments, types of, 49
 documentation style, 49
 evidence and sources, 49
hyphens, 139–40
 common errors, 9–10
hypothesis, forming, 177

Ibid. (in the same place), 285
i.e. (that is), 134
illusion, allusion, 332
immigrate to, emigrate from, 335
impact, 336
imperative mood, 66, 322
imply, infer, 336
in, 173
indefinite articles, 164–66, 323
indefinite pronouns
 list of, 70
 pronoun-antecedent agreement
 with, 9, 83
 subject-verb agreement with, 70
independent clauses
 conjunctive adverb to link,
 86, 116
 coordinating conjunctions
 between, 107, 115
 dash to link, 87
 defined, 85, 320, 323
 main idea in, 96
 semicolon with, 86, 108, 115–16
 sentence fragments and, 87
indexes, library resource, 180–81
indicative mood, 66, 323
indirect discourse, 104, 323
indirect objects, defined, 323
indirect questions, period in,
 117, 323
indirect quotations
 citing, 211, 257
 quotation marks, unnecessary,
 124
infer, imply, 336
infinitive phrases, 323
infinitives
 defined, 323
 forming, 160, 169
 versus gerunds, 168–70
 for multilingual writers, 168–70
 split, 77, 329
inside of, outside of, 336
intensifiers, 323
interact, interface, 336
interface, interact, 336
interjections, 323
 commas with, 112

Internet addresses, slashes in, 129
Internet research, 181–82
   authoritative sources, 182
   bookmarking, 182
   keyword searches, 181
   sources, evaluating, 188–89
interviews in field research,
      182–83
in-text citations
   APA style, 255–58
   Chicago style, 284–85
   CSE style, 302–3
   MLA style, 207–13
intransitive verbs, 63, 323
introductions
   of arguments, 34
   oral presentations, 41
   plan for writing, 19
   research project, 203
introductory elements, commas
      with, 3, 107
irregardless, regardless, 336
irregular verbs, 61–62
   defined, 323
   list of, 61–62
is when, is where, 93, 336
it
   indefinite use of, 84
   vague use of, 84
italics, uses of, 136–38
items in a series
   colon preceding, 117, 128
   commas, unnecessary, 6, 114
   commas in, 111
   parallelism, 100–101
   semicolon in, 116
it is, at beginning of sentence,
      99–100
its, it's, 8, 120, 337

jargon, avoiding, 151
journals
   APA style
      online, 269
      print, 266–68
   articles, evaluating, 186–87
   Chicago style
      online, 289
      print, 288–89
   CSE style
      online, 311
      print, 306–7
   MLA style
      online, 232, 234
      print, 225–29
   scholarly sources, 178–79
just as . . . so, 102

keywords and phrases
   in oral presentations, 42

   for paragraph coherence, 21
   of specialized vocabularies,
      47–48
keyword searches
   Boolean operators in, 180, 320
   defined, 323
   Internet research, 181
   library resources, 180
kind, sort, type, 337
kind of, sort of, 337

lab notebooks, 50
lab reports, 50
language, building common
      ground with, 145–46
later, latter, 337
latter, former, 335
lay, lie, 63, 337
least, less, 75
leave, let, 337
lend, loan, 337
less, fewer, 335
less, least, 75
let, leave, 337
letters, business writing, 50–51
letters as letters, italics for, 137
letters to the editor, citing, 228,
      233, 268
liable, likely, apt, 332
librarians, reference, 179
Library of Congress online, 182
Library of Congress Subject
      Headings (LCSH), 180
library research, 179–81
   keyword searches, 180
   sources, types of, 180–81
lie, lay, 63, 337
likely, liable, apt, 332
limiting modifiers, 76–77
linking verbs
   defined, 324
   with modifiers, 73–74
   subject complement following,
      71–72
list of references
   APA style, 259–78
   CSE style, 303–14
lists
   colon preceding, 117, 128
   parallelism, 101
   parentheses in, 126
lists, online discussion, writing
      guidelines, 39
literally, 337
little, much, 163
loan, lend, 337
logical appeals
   creating, 32
   identifying, 28–29
loose, lose, 337

lose, loose, 337
lots, lots of, 337

magazines
APA style, 268
Chicago style, 289
CSE style, 307
MLA style, 228, 232
popular sources, 178–79
main verbs, 324
man, mankind, 337
many, few, 163
maps, 56
margins
for APA style, 253
for *Chicago* style, 283
for CSE style, 301
in document design, 53
for MLA style, 206
may, can, 333
may be, maybe, 338
media, 338
media, and rhetorical situation,
15
memos, 50–51
metaphors, 154
misplaced modifiers, 76–77, 324
mixed metaphors, 154
MLA (Modern Language Association) style, 206–52, 280–82
explanatory and bibliographic
notes, 214
for humanities, 49
in-text citations
electronic sources, 212–13
print sources, 207–12
list of works cited, 214–45
author listings, 217–19
books, 219–25
directory to, 214–16
electronic sources, 229–38
formatting, 218
multimedia sources, 238–43
other sources, 243–44
print periodicals, 225–29
long quotations, format for,
122, 206
manuscript format, 206–7
poetry, quoting, 122–23
signal verbs, tense of, 198, 208
sources without models, citing,
219, 240
student research essay example,
247–52
visuals, labeling, 200, 207,
212–13, 249
*MLA Handbook for Writers of
Research Papers,* Seventh
Edition, 301–17
modal auxiliaries, defined, 320

modifiers, 77–78
adjectives and adverbs, 73–74
dangling, 78, 322
disruptive, 77
limiting, 76–77
misplaced, 76–78, 324
placement in sentences, 76–78
squinting, 77, 329
vague, 99
money, numbers in, 135
mood of verbs, 66, 324, 329
moral, morale, 338
more, most, 75
most, more, 75
much, little, 163
multilingual writers
adjectives with plural nouns, 75
articles, 164–66
capitalization, 132
conditional sentences, 170–71
count and noncount nouns,
162
determiners, 163–64
draft, review by native speaker,
204
English, global varieties of, 149
fancy language, avoiding, 152
foreign words, using, 17
gerunds, 168–70
plagiarism as cultural concept,
202
prepositions, 171–73
quoting in English, 124
search engines, use of, 160
sentence length, judging, 86
sentence structure, basic,
160–61
sentence structure, tips for
learning, 159–60
sources, identifying, 197
thesis, stating, 18
two-word verbs, 173–74
U.S. academic genres, 158–60
verb phrases, forming, 166–68
multimedia presentations, Power-
Point, 43–46
multivolume works, citing, 210,
224, 263, 288
musical works
citing, 241
italics for, 136
myself, yourself, himself, herself, 336

natural and applied sciences
assignments, types of, 50
documentation style, 50
evidence and sources, 50
N.B. (note well), 134
n.d. (no date), 258, 272, 276
neither . . . nor, 102

newspapers
  Chicago style, 289
  CSE style
    online, 311
    print, 307
  MLA style, online, 232
  online sources for, 182
  print articles, citing, 228, 268
  title, italics for, 136
noncount nouns
  article, none with, 165
  defined, 162, 324
  determiners with, 164
  for multilingual writers, 162
nonrestrictive elements
  commas with, 7, 108–10
  defined, 108, 324
  identifying, 108–9
  phrases as, 110
nor, or, 338
NOT, Boolean operator, 180, 320
not . . . but, 102
Notes. See also footnotes
  Chicago style, 284, 285
  MLA style, 214
notes and bibliographic entries,
    272
  Chicago style, 286–96
note-taking, 192–97
  abbreviations in, 134
  general guidelines, 192
  paraphrasing, 193–95
  quotations, 192–93
  summarizing, 195–96
not only . . . but also, 102
noun phrases, 88, 326
nouns
  collective, 9, 69–70, 82–83, 324
  common, 131, 324
  compound, 120, 138
  count and noncount, 162, 164,
    324
  defined, 324
  possessive, forming, 8
  possessive case, 120
  proper, 131, 324
  sexist, alternatives to, 146
N.p. (no publisher), 234–35, 238
n. pag. (no page numbers), 229,
    232
number
  defined, 325
  pronoun-antecedent agreement,
    9, 82
  subject-verb agreement, 67
number, amount, 332
the number of, a number of, at
    beginning of sentence, 70
numbers
  compound, hyphens in, 139

as terms, italics for, 137
words or figures, use of, 135–36

object complements, defined, 321
objective case, 79
object of sentence
  defined, 325
  direct objects, 63, 161, 173–74
  in English language, 161
  indirect object, 323
object of the preposition, 172, 325
observation, field research, 183
off, of, 338
OK, O.K., okay, 338
on, 173
on account of, 338
one another, each other, 334
one of the, subject-verb agreement
    with, 71
online sources. *See* electronic
    sources
only one of the, subject-verb agree-
    ment with, 71
OR, Boolean operator, 180, 320
or, nor, 338
oral presentations
  delivery, tips for, 43–44
  introduction and conclusion,
    importance of, 41
  PowerPoint, 43–46
  practicing, 43
  purpose and audience, 41
  text for use during, 42
  visuals, integrating in, 42
organization
  of arguments, 34
  for oral presentations, 42
  for paragraph coherence, 21
  and rhetorical situation, 15–16
outlines, parallelism, 101
outside of, inside of, 336
owing to the fact that, 338

page numbers
  APA style, 253
  Chicago style, 283
  CSE style, 301
  MLA style, 206
paragraphs, 21–22
parallelism, 100–102
  for paragraph coherence, 21
paraphrasing
  guidelines for, 193–95
  integrating in writing, 199
  plagiarism, 201
  present tense, using, 64
  unacceptable, examples of,
    194–95
parentheses, 125–26
  in Boolean searches, 180

other punctuation with, 126
parenthetical citations, MLA
     style, 208–13
parenthetical expressions
   bracketed material in, 126
   commas with, 112
participial phrases, commas with,
     110
participles
   defined, 325
   past, forming, 60–62, 325
particles, adverbial, 173, 319
parts of speech, 325
passive voice
   versus active voice, 100
   and *be*, 167–68
   consistency in use, 103
   defined, 65, 325, 330
past participle
   forming, 61
   irregular verbs, 61–62
past perfect progressive tense, 64
past perfect tense, 64, 325
past progressive tense, 63
past tense, 61–63
per, 338
percent, *percentage*, 338
percentages, 135
perfect progressive tenses, 64,
     325–26
perfect tenses, forming, 64, 325,
     326
periodicals, citing
   APA style, 266–69
   Chicago style, 288–89
   CSE style, 306–9
   MLA style, 225–29
periods, 117–18
   with ellipses, 129–30
   with parentheses, 126
   with quotation marks, 123
person
   defined, 103, 326
   pronoun-antecedent agree-
        ment, 82
   shifts in, 103
   subject-verb agreement, 67
personal opinion, and stance, 15
personal pronouns
   as direct object, 174
   uses of, 80
photographs as visuals, 56
phrasal verbs. *See* two-word
     verbs
phrase fragments, 88–89
phrases
   comma with, 106–10
   defined, 88, 326
   infinitive, 323
   noun, 88, 326

participial, 325, 326
prepositional, 173, 326, 327
restrictive and nonrestrictive,
     110
signal, 198
verb, 166–68, 326
wordy, avoiding, 99
place names, commas with, 112
plagiarism, avoiding, 201–2
planning
   organizing writing, 19–20
   for research, 177
   Web texts, 40
plays
   italics for, 136
   MLA style, 210–11
plenty, 338
plurals
   adjectives with, for multilin-
        gual writers, 75
   count and noncount nouns, 162
   defined, 326
   nouns, determiners with, 164
   plural forms, singular meaning,
        words with, 71–72, 162
   possessive case, 120–21
plus, 338
poetry
   quoting, 122–23
   slashes for line divisions,
        128–29
   title, italics for, 136
   title, quotation marks for, 123
point of view. *See* person
pompous language, avoiding, 151
popular sources, 178–79
portfolio
   choosing writings for, 24
   cover letter, 24
possessive case
   apostrophe, forming with, 8,
        119–20
   defined, 79, 119, 326
possessive pronouns
   defined, 327, 328
   its, 120
postal abbreviations, state names,
     118
posting, online. *See* online
     posting
PowerPoint
   student example, 45–46
   writing guidelines, 43
precede, *proceed*, 338
predicates, 327
   compound, 89, 327
   faulty predication, 93
prefixes
   defined, 327
   hyphen with, 139

prepositional phrases
    defined, 173, 326, 327
    fragments, 88
prepositions
    defined, 327
    gerunds with, 170
    for multilingual writers, 171–73
    object of, 172, 325
    two-word verbs, 173–74, 326
present participle, 325
present perfect progressive tense,
        64
present perfect tense, 64, 327
present progressive tense, 63, 327
present tense
    forming, 63
    special use of, 64–65
    subject-verb agreement with, 71
pretty, 338
primary sources, types of, 48, 178
principal, principle, 339
progressive tenses, forming,
        63–64, 167–68, 325, 327
projects, writing. *See* writing
        projects
pronoun-antecedent agreement,
        9, 82–84
pronoun case, 79–82
    in compound structures, 81
    in elliptical constructions, 81
    before gerunds, 79
    objective, 79
    possessive, 79
    in subject complements, 79
    subjective, 79
pronoun reference, vague, 4,
        83–84
pronouns, 78–84
    agreement. *See* pronoun-
        antecedent agreement
    antecedents of, 78–79, 82
    case. *See* pronoun case
    editing, 80
    indefinite, 70, 83
    personal, 80, 174
    possessive, 120, 327, 328
    relative, 71, 328
    sexist, 83, 146
proofreading, research project,
        204
proper adjectives, capitalizing,
        6, 131
proper nouns, capitalizing, 6,
        131, 324
proximity, in document design, 51
punctuation
    apostrophes, 119–21
    brackets, 126–27
    colons, 128
    commas, 107–14

    dashes, 127
    ellipses, 129–30
    end, 117–19
    exclamation points, 118–19
    parentheses, 125–26
    periods, 117–18
    question marks, 118
    quotation marks, 121–25
    semicolons, 115–17
    slashes, 128–29
purpose for writing, 14

qualifiers, in arguments, 29–30
question marks
    with quotation marks, 113, 124
    use of, 118
questions
    direct, 118
    to explore topic, 18
    indirect, 117
    research, 177
    tag, 112
quotation, quote, 339
quotation marks, 121–25
    in Boolean searches, 180
    comma with, 113, 123
    common errors, 5, 124–25
    with definitions, 123
    direct quotations, 121
    other punctuation with, 123–24
    single, 122
    for titles of works, 5, 123
quotations. *See also* quotation
        marks
    bracketed material in, 126–27,
        193, 199
    direct, 121
    indirect, 124
    integrating in writing, 9, 198
    long, style for, 122, 198, 206,
        253, 283
    note-taking guidelines, 192–93
    omissions, ellipses for, 129–30,
        193, 199
    in paraphrase, 193–94
    poetry, quoting, 122–23
    present tense, using, 64
    signal phrases to introduce,
        198

race and ethnicity, assumptions
        about, 146–47
raise, rise, 63, 339
rarely ever, 339
readers. *See* audience
reading, critically. *See* critical
        reading
real, really, 339
reason is . . . because, 93, 339
reason why, 339

recordings. *See* sound recordings
references, list of. *See* list of references
reference works, types of, 181
reflecting, questions for, 23–24
regardless, irregardless, 336
regular verbs, 61, 328
relative pronouns, 71
repetition
    in document design, 52
    for paragraph coherence, 21
reports, 51
research, 176–204
    and evidence, 19
    field research, 182–83
    Internet research, 181–82
    library research, 179–81
    sources, types of, 178–79
research writing
    context, considering, 176
    drafting, 202–3
    editing and proofreading, 204
    hypothesis, forming, 177
    introduction and conclusion, 203
    note-taking, 192–97
    plagiarism, avoiding, 201–2
    planning, 177
    process of, 202–4
    research question, 177
    revising and reviewing, 203
    titles, 203
    working thesis, 177
respectfully, respectively, 339
restrictive elements
    commas with, 5–6, 108–10, 113–14
    identifying, 108–9
    phrases as, 110
résumé, 51
reviewing
    questions for, 22
    research project, 203
revising
    questions for, 22
    research project, 203
rhetorical situations, 12–17
    assignments and purposes, 14
    audience, 14–15
    language and style, 16–17
    medium, genre, formats for, 15–16
    portfolio, choosing writings for, 24
    stance and tone, 15
    visuals, choosing, 16
rise, raise, 63, 339
run-on sentences. *See* fused (run-on) sentences

salutation of letter, colon in, 128
sans serif fonts, 54
scholarly sources, 178–79
sciences. *See* natural and applied sciences
scientific writing
    passive voice, using, 65
    present tense, using, 64
search engines, grammar usage, verifying with, 160
searches, online. *See* keyword searches
secondary sources, 178
secondly, firstly, etc., 335
second person, 103, 326
semicolons, 115–17
    in items in a series, 116
    linking clauses with, 86, 108, 115–16
    misused, 116–17
    with quotation marks, 124
sentence errors
    commas splices, 8, 85–87
    comparisons, unclear, 94
    compound structures, inconsistency, 93
    faulty predication, 93
    faulty structure, 6–7, 93
    fused (run-on) sentences, 8, 85–87
    sentence fragments, 10, 87–90, 92
    shifts, 103–4
    subordination, excessive, 97–98
sentence fragments, 87–90
    clause fragments, 89–90
    compound predicate, 89
    phrase, 88–89
    revising, 10, 88–90, 92
sentences
    capitalization, 130–31
    compound, 328
    conciseness, 98–100
    conditional, 170–71
    consistency and completeness, 93–94
    coordination, 94–95
    length, judging, 86
    parallelism, 100–102
    style and rhetorical situation, 16
    subordination, 95–98
sentence structure, tips for multilingual writers, 159–60
series. *See* items in a series
serif fonts, 54
set, sit, 63, 339
several, both, 163
sexist nouns, alternatives to, 146
sexist pronouns
    masculine, revising, 83, 146

sexist pronouns *(continued)*
  and pronoun-antecedent agree-
    ment, 83
she/he, 336
shifts
  between direct and indirect
    discourse, 103–4
  in person, 103
  in tone and diction, 104
  verb tense, 7, 102–3
  in voice, 103
short stories, title, quotation
    marks for, 123
sic, 127
signal phases, to introduce quota-
    tions, 198
signal verbs
  list of, 198
  tense and documentation style,
    198–99, 255
signpost language, for oral pre-
    sentations, 42
similes, 153–54
simple predicates, 327
simple tense, 328
since, 339
singular, defined, 328
sit, set, 63, 339
slang, 150–51
  quotation marks, avoiding, 125
slides, PowerPoint, 43–46
so, 339
social bookmarking sites, 182
social networking sites
  posting, citing, 238, 293
  writing guidelines, 40
social sciences
  assignments, types of, 49
  documentation style, 49
  evidence and sources, 49–50
software
  citing, 276
  italics for, 137
some, enough, 163
someplace, 339
some time, sometime, sometimes, 340
songs, title, quotation marks for, 123
sort, type, kind, 337
sort of, kind of, 337
sound recordings
  citing, 240, 278
  italics for, 137
sources
  acknowledging, requirements
    for, 200
  annotating, 196
  effective use, guidelines for,
    190–91
  evaluating, guidelines for,
    184–85

historical, 179
for humanities assignments, 49
identifying, 197
integrating in writing, 197–200
Internet research, 181–82
library resources, 179–81
list, preparing, 203–4
for natural and applied science
    assignments, 50
primary and secondary, 48, 178
reading and interpreting,
    185–89
scholarly and popular, 178–79
for social science assignments,
    49–50
synthesizing, 192
using effectively, 190–91
specific words, 153
speeches, citing, 241
spell checkers
  common errors with, 3–5,
    154–55
  tips for use, 155
split infinitives, 77, 329
squinting modifiers, 77, 329
-s ending
  plural forms, singular meaning
    words, 72
  possessive case, 120–21
  present tense, subject-verb
    agreement with, 71
stance
  determining, 15
  of sources, 184–85
state names, postal abbreviations,
    118
stationary, stationery, 340
stereotyping, avoiding in writing,
    145–47
style
  for business writing, 51
  and culture, 144–45
  of disciplines, 48
  and rhetorical situation, 16–17
subject complements
  and linking verbs, 71
  pronoun case with, 79
subjective case, 79
subjects
  compound, 68–69
  consistency and completeness,
    92–94
  in English language, 161
  simple, 68
  -verb agreement. *See* subject-
    verb agreement
subject-verb agreement, 67–73
  be in spoken form, 72
  and collective noun subjects,
    69–70

and compound subjects, 69
editing for, 68
and indefinite pronoun subjects, 70
and linking verbs, 71
with subject following verb, 72
with subjects with plural forms,
71
with titles, 72
and verb tense, 67
who, which, that as subjects, 71
with words as words, 72
words between subject and
verb, ignoring, 68
subjunctive mood, 66–67
subordinate clauses. *See* dependent clauses
subordinating conjunctions
dependent clauses, starting
with, 87, 89–90, 94–95
to distinguish main ideas, 95–97
list of, 89, 96
subordination in sentences, 95–98
subsequently, consequently, 334
suffixes, hyphen with, 139
summary
integrating in writing, 199
note-taking guidelines, 195–96
present tense, using, 64
superlatives
adjectives and adverbs, 74–75,
319
double, 75
superscript, reference to notes,
214, 259, 284, 302
supposed to, used to, 340
sure, surely, 340
surface errors, 1
surveys, field research, 183
syntax, 329
synthesizing, 192

tables, 50–51, 56
APA style, 254, 281
Chicago style, 284
CSE style, 301
MLA style, 200, 207, 213
tag questions, commas with, 112
take, bring, 333
television
series, italics for, 137
title of episode, quotation
marks for, 123
tense of verbs. *See* verb tenses
texting, level of formality, 39
than, then, 340
that
subject-verb agreement with,
71
vague use of, 84

that, which, 340
the, 164–65
theirselves, 340
then, than, 340
therefore, 86
there is, there are, at beginning of
sentence, 72, 99–100
thesaurus, 3
thesis
argumentative thesis, 30–31
defined, 330
working thesis, 18–19
they, indefinite use of, 84
thinking critically. *See* critical
thinking
third person, 103, 326
this, that, 163
this, vague use of, 84
time of day
abbreviating, 134
colon in, 128
numbers in, 136
titles of persons
abbreviating, 133
capitalizing, 132
titles of works
capitalizing, 132
italics for, 136–37
quotation marks for, 5, 123
research project, 203
subject-verb agreement with,
72
to, too, two, 340
tone
defined, 330
determining, factors in, 15
and disciplines, 48
shifts in, 104
topic selection, 1
exploring, strategies for, 17–18
questions for, 14
Top Twenty (common errors). *See*
Find It. Fix It.
Toulmin's framework for arguments, 29–30
transitional words and phrases
commas with, 112
in sentence fragments, 89
transitions
commas, 112
defined, 330
and directness, 13
for paragraph coherence, 21
transitive verbs, 63
defined, 63, 330
and direct object, 63, 161,
173–74
translations, citing, 223, 263
Twitter, writing guidelines, 40
two, to, too, 340

two-word verbs
  hyphens, unnecessary, 9–10,
    139–40
  for multilingual writers, 173–74
type, sort, kind, 337
type size
  for college writing, 54
  for headings, 55

uninterested, disinterested, 334
unique, 340
unity, paragraphs, 20
us, we, pronoun case with, 82
U.S. academic style, elements
    of, 13
used to, supposed to, 340

verbal phrases, fragments, 88–89
verbals
  gerunds, 168–70
  infinitives, 160, 168–70
  participles, 60–62
verb phrases
  forming, 166–68, 326
  for multilingual writers, 166–68
verbs, 61–67. *See also* subject-verb
    agreement
  auxiliary, 166–68
  editing, 63
  intransitive, 63, 323
  irregular, 61–62, 323
  lie, lay, 63
  linking, 71, 324
  mood, 66
  regular, 61, 328
  rise, raise, 63
  signal, 198
  sit, set, 63
  strong, in sentences, 99
  transitive, 63, 161, 330
  two-word verbs, 9–10, 139–40,
    173–74
  voice, 65
verb tenses, 63–65
  and documentation style,
    198–99
  forming, 63–64
  of irregular verbs, 61–62
  perfect, 64, 325, 326
  progressive, 63–64, 167–68, 325
  of regular verbs, 66–67
  sequence of, 65
  shifts in, 7, 102–3
  and subject-verb agreement,
    67
very, 340
visuals, 56, 199
  altering, 57–58
  APA style, 254
  in arguments, 31–32

Chicago style, 283–84
copyrighted, permissions for, 200
CSE style, 301
evaluating, questions for, 26–28,
    57
to explore topic, 18
integrating in writing, 199–200
MLA style, 200, 207, 212–13, 249
numbering and captions, 57–58,
    200, 254
in oral presentations, 42
and rhetorical situation, 16,
    55–56
slides. *See* PowerPoint
sources for, 57
types of, 56
using, guidelines for, 58
for Web texts, 41
voice, 65. *See also* active voice;
    passive voice
shifts in, 103

warrants, in arguments, 29–30, 330
way, ways, 341
we, us, pronoun case with, 82
Web, research on. *See* Internet
    research
Web browsers, bookmarking, 182
Web logs (blogs), 40
Web sites. *See also* electronic
    sources
  APA style, 269, 272–76
  Chicago style, 292, 294–95
  CSE style, 311
  italics for, 137
  MLA style, 234–36
Web texts, writing guidelines,
    40–41
well, good, 74, 335
where, 341
whether . . . or, 102
which
  subject-verb agreement with, 71
  vague use of, 84
which, that, 340
white space, in document design,
    53
who, subject-verb agreement
    with, 71
who, whoever, whom, whomever,
    pronoun case with, 80
who's, whose, 341
whose, who's, 341
word choice, 150–55
  denotation and connotation,
    152–53
  empty words, eliminating, 99
  figurative language, 153–54
  formality, level of, 150–52
  general and specific words, 153

redundant words, avoiding, 98
shifts in, 104
wrong-word errors, 2–3
word order, in sentences, 161
word-processing programs
dash in, 127
spell checkers, errors of, 4–5,
154–55
words as words
italics for, 137
subject-verb agreement with, 72
working thesis
features of, 18
forming, 177
parts of, 18
in plan for writing, 19
works cited, list of, MLA style,
214–45
writing
assumptions, avoiding, 145–47
changes related to, 1
communicating across cultures,
143–45
portfolios, 24
process of writing. *See* writing
process
writing situation. *See* rhetorical
situation
writing process
collaborating, 25

drafting, 20
editing, 23
evidence and research, 19
paragraphs, 21–22
planning, 19
reflecting, 23–24
reviewing, 22
revising, 22
topics, exploring, 17–18
topic selection, 14
working thesis, 18
writing projects
academic style. *See* academic
writing
arguments, 28–38
business writing, 50–51
disciplines, writing in, 47–51
electronic communication,
38–41
oral and multimedia presentations, 41–47
research projects. *See* research
writing
Web texts, 40–41
wrong-word errors, causes of, 2–3

yet, but, 333
you, indefinite use of, 84
your, you're, 341
yourself, myself, himself, herself, 336

For Multilingual Writers

Throughout *EasyWriter*, boxed tips offer help on the following topics for writers whose first language is not English.

- Bringing in Other Languages   *17*
- Stating a Thesis   *18*
- Using Adjectives with Plural Nouns   *75*
- Judging Sentence Length   *86*
- Quoting in American English   *124*
- Learning English Capitalization   *132*
- Recognizing Global Varieties of English   *149*
- Avoiding Fancy Language   *152*
- Identifying Sources   *197*
- Thinking about Plagiarism as a Cultural Concept   *202*
- Asking a Native Speaker to Review Your Draft   *204*

Writing

Writing

Sentence Grammar

Sentence Style

Punctuation/ Mechanics

Language

Multilingual Writers

Research

Documentation

1   A Writer's Choices

You send a text message to your best friend confirming weekend plans. Later on, you put together an analysis of cost-cutting possibilities for the manager of the company you're working for. And later still, just before calling it a day, you pull out the notes you took on your biology experiment and write up the lab report that is due tomorrow. In between, you probably do a lot of other writing as well—notes, lists, blog entries, and so on.

These are the kinds of writing most of us do every day, more or less easily, yet each demands that we make various important choices. In your text message, you probably use a kind of shorthand, not bothering to write complete sentences or even entire words. For your boss, however, you probably choose to be more formal and "correct." And for your lab report, you probably choose to follow the format your instructor has demonstrated. In each case, the choices you make are based on your **rhetorical situation**—the entire context for the writing.

Rhetorical situations include many elements: assignment and purpose; topic; audience; stance and tone; medium, genre, and format; and visuals. Writers should make careful choices about all these elements in order to communicate effectively.

1a   Academic writing

Expectations about academic writing vary considerably from field to field (see Chapter 5), but becoming familiar with widespread conventions will prepare you well for writing in most academic contexts.

Establishing authority.   Most instructors expect you to begin to establish your own authority—to become a constructive critic who can analyze and interpret the work of others. These practices can help you establish authority:

- Assume that your opinions count (as long as they are informed rather than tossed out with little thought) and that your audience expects you to present them in a well-reasoned manner.
- Show your familiarity with the ideas and works of others, both from the assigned course reading and from good points your instructor and classmates have made.

Being direct and clear.   Research for this book confirms that readers depend on writers to organize and present their material—using sections, paragraphs, sentences, arguments, details, and source citations—to aid understanding. Good academic writing prepares readers for what is coming next, provides definitions, and includes topic sentences. To achieve directness in your writing, try the following strategies:

- State your main point early and clearly.

- Avoid overqualifying your statements. Instead of writing *I think the facts reveal*, come right out and say *The facts reveal.*

- Avoid digressions. If you use an anecdote or example from personal experience, be sure it relates directly to the point you are making.

- Use appropriate evidence, such as examples and concrete details, to support each point.

- Make obvious and clear transitions from point to point. The first sentence of a new paragraph should reach back to the paragraph before and then look forward to what comes next.

- Follow logical organizational patterns.

- Design and format the project appropriately for the audience and purpose you have in mind (see Chapter 5).

✔ CHECKLIST

U.S. Academic Style

- Consider your purpose and audience carefully, making sure that your topic is appropriate to both. (1b–d)
- State your **claim** or **thesis** explicitly, and support it with evidence and authorities of various kinds. (Chapter 3)
- Carefully document all of your sources. (Chapters 42–45)
- Make explicit links between ideas.
- Use the appropriate level of formality. (Chapter 32a)
- Use conventional formats for academic genres.
- Use conventional grammar, spelling, punctuation, and mechanics. (Chapters 7–28)
- Use an easy-to-read type size and typeface, conventional margins, and double spacing. (Chapter 6)

1b Assignments and purposes

If you have a specific writing assignment, what does it ask you to do? Look for words such as *define, explain, prove,* and *survey.* Keep in mind that these words may differ in meaning from discipline to discipline or from job to job.

What information do you need to complete the assignment? Think about whether you will need to do research or find (or create) graphics and visual information.

Keep in mind the assignment's specific requirements for length, genre, medium, format, organization, and deadline.

Consider the primary purpose for writing—is it to explain, summarize, or persuade? to respond to a question, learn about a topic, or make recommendations? to express certain feelings? If you are unclear about the primary purpose, talk with the person who gave you the assignment.

1c Topic

To choose a topic, try answering the following questions:

- Is the topic interesting and important to you?
- Is the topic focused enough for you to write about it in the time and space allowed?
- Do you have some ideas about how to pursue the topic?

Once you have a topic in mind, ask yourself a few more questions:

- What do you know about the topic?
- What seems important—or unimportant—about it?
- What do you expect to conclude about the topic? (Remember that you may change your mind.)
- What do you need to find out about the topic?

For information on exploring a topic, see 2a.

1d Audience

- What audience do you most want to reach—people who are already sympathetic to your views? people who disagree with your views? members of a group you belong to? members of a group you don't belong to?
- In what ways are the members of your audience different from you? from one another? Consider such factors as education, age, gender, occupation, region, social class,

ethnic and cultural heritage, politics, religion, marital status, and sexual orientation.

- What assumptions can you legitimately make about your audience? What might they value—brevity, originality, conformity, honesty, wit, seriousness, thrift? How can you appeal to their values?

- What sorts of information and evidence will your audience find most compelling—quotations from experts? personal experiences? photographs? diagrams or charts?

- What responses do you want as a result of what you write? How can you make clear what you want to happen? (For more on audience, see 29d.)

1e Stance and tone

Knowing your own stance—where you are coming from—can help you think about ways to get your readers to understand and perhaps share your views. What is your overall attitude toward the topic—approval? disapproval? curiosity? indifference? What social, political, religious, or other factors account for your attitude? You should also be aware of any preconceptions about your topic that may affect your stance.

Your purpose, audience, and stance will help to determine the tone your writing should take. Should it be humorous? serious? impassioned? helpful? Think about ways to show that you are knowledgeable and trustworthy.

1f Media, genre, and formats

- What medium is most appropriate for your project—print, or something else? (For more on writing for other media, see Chapter 4.)

- What genre (or form) does your task call for—a report? a review? an essay? a letter? a Web site? a speech? a multimedia presentation?

- If you are creating a document, what formats or design conventions are appropriate? Find out which formats are most often used in similar situations. If you are unsure about what format to use, ask your instructor or supervisor for guidance.

- What organizational patterns are most appropriate for your topic, purpose, and audience? Will you use chronological order or some other order, such as

problem-solution or cause-effect? Should you use headings and subheadings to help readers follow your organization? (For more on headings, see 6c.)

1g   Visuals

Pay special attention to how the look of your writing fits its purpose and intended audience, and to how well your text and visuals work together. Think carefully about when to emphasize words and when to emphasize visuals.

- Does your topic call for visuals? If so, what kind? Visuals should add meaning or clarity, not just decoration.
- Choose visuals that can help you capture your readers' interest, emphasize a point you have already made in your text, present information that is difficult to convey in words, or communicate with audiences who have different language skills and abilities.
- Place each visual as near as possible to the text it illustrates.
- Remember to introduce each visual clearly: *As the map to the right depicts . . .*
- Comment on the significance or effect of each visual: *Figure 1 corroborates the claim made by geneticists: while the human genome may be mapped, it is far from understood.*
- Does the particular visual you are considering convey the tone you want to achieve? Is that tone appropriate for your audience, purpose, and topic?
- What will your audience expect this writing to look like? (For more on designing documents, see Chapter 6.)

1h   Language and style

- What level of formality is most appropriate—extremely informal, as in an email to a friend? moderately formal, as in a letter to someone you know only slightly? very formal, as in legal or institutional documents? (See 32a.)
- What forms of address are most appropriate for your audience? Will they appreciate jargon or slang? Are words from another language or other varieties of English appropriate? (See Chapter 31.)
- What kind of sentence style will be most appropriate—short, straightforward sentences that convey information clearly and concisely? longer descriptive sentences that create a picture in readers' minds or evoke emotional

responses? lists of phrases to give directions? brief **sentence fragments** to get a point across quickly and informally?

FOR MULTILINGUAL WRITERS

Bringing in Other Languages

Even when you write in English, you may want to include words, phrases, or passages in another language. If so, consider whether your readers will understand that language and whether you need to provide a translation, as in this example from John (Fire) Lame Deer's "Talking to the Owls and Butterflies":

> Listen to the air. You can hear it, feel it, smell it, taste it. *Woniya waken*—the holy air—which renews all by its breath. *Woniya, woniya waken*—spirit, life, breath, renewal—it means all that.

In this instance, more than one translation is necessary because the phrase Lame Deer is discussing has multiple meanings in English.

---

2 Exploring, Planning, and Drafting

One student defines drafting as the time in a writing project "when the rubber meets the road." As you explore your topic, decide on a thesis, organize materials to support that central idea, and sketch out a plan, you have already begun the drafting process.

2a Exploring a topic

Among the most important parts of the writing process are choosing a topic (see 1c), exploring what you know about it, and determining what you need to find out. These strategies can help you explore your topic:

- Brainstorm. Try out ideas, alone or with another person. Jot down key words and phrases about the topic, and see what they prompt you to think about next.

---

bedfordstmartins.com/easywriter To see student drafts, click on **Student Writing**.

- Freewrite without stopping for ten minutes or so to see what insights or ideas you come up with.

- Draw or make word pictures about your topic.

- Try clustering —writing your topic on a sheet of paper, then writing related thoughts near the topic idea. Circle each idea or phrase, and draw lines to show how ideas are connected.

- Ask questions about the topic: *What is it? What caused it? What is it like or unlike? What larger system is the topic a part of? What do people say about it?* Or choose the journalist's questions: *Who? What? When? Where? Why? How?*

2b Developing a working thesis

Once you have explored your topic, craft a working thesis that includes two parts: a topic, which states what you are writing about, and a comment, which makes an important point about the topic.

TOPIC   COMMENT

▶ The existence of global warming is questioned by politicians more often than by scientists.

TOPIC   COMMENT

▶ The current health care crisis arises from three major causes.

A successful working thesis has three characteristics:

1. It is potentially interesting to the intended audience.
2. It is as specific as possible.
3. It limits the topic enough to make it manageable.

FOR MULTILINGUAL WRITERS

Stating a Thesis

In some cultures, it is considered rude to state an opinion outright. In the United States, however, academic and business practices require writers to make key positions explicitly clear.

2c Gathering evidence and doing research

What kinds of evidence will be most persuasive to your audience and most effective in the field you are working in—historical precedents? expert testimony? statistical data? experimental results? personal anecdotes? Knowing what kinds of evidence count most in a particular field or with particular audiences will help you make appropriate choices.

If the evidence you need calls for research, determine what research you need to do:

- Make a list of what you already know about your topic.

- Keep track of where information comes from so you can return to your sources later.

- What else do you need to know, and where are you likely to find good sources of information? Consider library resources, authoritative online sources, field research, and so on.

(For more on research, see Chapters 38–41.)

2d Planning and drafting

Sketch out a rough plan for organizing your writing, as in the following example:

WORKING THESIS

   Increased motorcycle use demands reorganization of parking lots.

INTRODUCTION

   — Give background and overview of the current situation
      (motorcycle use is up).

   — State my purpose (to offer solutions to the problem identified
      in the thesis).

BODY

   — Describe the current situation (tell about my research in area
      parking lots).

   — Describe the problem in detail (report on statistics; cars vs.
      cycles).

   — Present two possible solutions (enlarge lots, or reallocate
      space).

CONCLUSION

— Recommend against first solution because of cost and space limitations.

— Recommend second solution, and summarize its benefits.

Once you have come up with a plan, these guidelines can help you complete a draft:

• Keep all information close at hand and arranged in the order of your plan.

• Before beginning, create a folder for your project and, within it, create two subfolders—one labeled "sources" and the other labeled "drafts." As you write, save your work into the "drafts" folder. Choose a file name that you will recognize instantly, and include the draft number in the file name: *human genome draft 1.* As you revise, save a copy of each new draft and change the draft number (*human genome draft 2*). Also back up your work.

• Try to write in stretches of at least thirty minutes; writing will get easier as you go along.

• Don't get bogged down with details such as word choice or mechanics.

• Remember that a draft is never perfect. Concentrate on getting all your ideas down.

• Stop writing at a logical place, one where you know what will come next. Doing so will make it easier to resume writing later.

2e Developing paragraphs

The three qualities essential to most academic paragraphs are unity, development, and coherence.

Unity.   An effective paragraph focuses on one main idea. You can achieve unity by stating the main idea clearly in one sentence—the topic sentence—and relating all other sentences in the paragraph to that idea. Like a thesis (see 2b), the topic sentence includes a topic and a comment on that topic. A topic sentence often begins a paragraph, but it may come at the end—or be implied rather than stated directly.

Development.   In addition to being unified, a paragraph should hold readers' interest and explore its topic fully,

> ✅ CHECKLIST
>
> **Strong Paragraphs**
>
> Most readers of English have certain expectations about paragraphs:
>
> - Paragraphs begin and end with important information.
> - The opening sentence is often the topic sentence that tells what the paragraph is about.
> - The middle of the paragraph develops the idea.
> - The end may sum up the paragraph's contents, closing the discussion of an idea and anticipating the paragraph that follows.
> - A paragraph makes sense as a whole; the words and sentences are clearly related.
> - A paragraph relates to other paragraphs around it.

using whatever details, evidence, and examples are necessary. Without such development, a paragraph may seem lifeless and abstract.

Most good academic writing backs up general ideas with specifics. Shifting between the general and the specific is especially important at the paragraph level. If a paragraph contains nothing but specific details, its meaning may not be clear—but if a paragraph makes only general statements, it may seem boring or unconvincing.

Coherence.   A paragraph has coherence—or flows—if its details fit together in a way that readers can easily follow. The following methods can help you achieve paragraph coherence:

- ORGANIZATION. When you arrange information in a particular order, you help readers move from one point to another. Many paragraphs also follow a general-to-specific or specific-to-general pattern.

- REPETITION. Repeating key words and phrases—or pronouns that refer to them, or synonyms—not only links sentences but also suggests the importance of those words and phrases, contributing to coherence.

- PARALLEL STRUCTURES. Structures that are grammatically similar, or parallel, are another effective way to bring coherence to a paragraph. (See Chapter 17.)

- **TRANSITIONS.** Transitional words and phrases, such as *after all*, *for example*, and *however*, bring coherence to a paragraph by helping readers follow the progression of one idea to the next.

The same methods you use to create coherent paragraphs can be used to link paragraphs so that a whole piece of writing flows smoothly. You can create links to previous paragraphs by repeating or paraphrasing key words and phrases and by using parallelism and transitions.

2f Reviewing

Ask classmates or your instructor to respond to your draft, answering questions like these:

- What do you see as the major point, claim, or thesis?
- How convincing is the evidence? What can I do to support my thesis more fully?
- What points are unclear? How can I clarify them?
- How easy is it to follow my organization? How can I improve?
- What can I do to make my draft more interesting?

2g Revising

Revising means using others' comments along with your own analysis of the draft to make sure it is as complete, clear, and effective as possible. These questions can help you revise:

- How does the draft accomplish its purpose?
- Does the title tell what the draft is about?
- Is the thesis clearly stated, and does it contain a topic and a comment?
- How does the introduction catch readers' attention?
- Will the draft interest and appeal to its audience?
- How does the draft indicate your stance on the topic?
- What are the main points that illustrate or support the thesis? Are they clear? Do you need to add material to the points or add new points?
- Are the ideas presented in an order that will make sense to readers?
- Are the points clearly linked by logical transitions?

- Have you documented your research appropriately?

- How are visuals and other sources (if any) integrated into your draft? Are they clearly labeled and referred to in the draft? Have you commented on their significance?

- How does the draft conclude? Is the conclusion memorable?

2h Editing

Once you are satisfied with your revised draft's big picture, edit your writing to make sure that every detail is as correct as you can make it.

- Read your draft aloud to make sure it flows smoothly and to find typos or other mistakes.

- Are your sentences varied in length and in pattern or type?

- Have you used active verbs and effective language?

- Are all sentences complete and correct?

- Have you used the spell checker—and double-checked its recommendations?

- Have you chosen an effective design and used white space, headings, and color appropriately?

- Have you proofread one last time, going word for word?

(For more on troubleshooting your writing, see "Find It. Fix It." on pp. 1–10.)

2i Reflecting

Thinking back on what you've learned helps make that learning stick. Whether or not your instructor requires you to write a formal reflection on a writing course or piece of writing, make time to think about what you have learned from the experience.

Your development as a writer. The following questions can help you think about your writing:

- What lessons have you learned from the writing? How will they help you with future writing projects?

- What aspects of your writing give you most confidence? What needs additional work, and what can you do to improve?

- What confused you during this writing? How did you resolve your questions?

- How has this piece of writing helped you clarify your thinking or extend your understanding?
- Identify a favorite passage of your writing. What pleases you about it? Can you apply what you learn from this analysis to other writing situations?
- How would you describe your development as a writer?

Portfolios. You may want (or be required) to select samples of writing for inclusion in a portfolio.

- Consider your purpose and audience to make good choices about what to include and about whether the portfolio should be print or electronic.

- Choose pieces that show your strengths as a writer, and decide how many to include.

- Consider organization. What arrangement will make most sense to readers?

- Think about what layout and design will present your work most effectively.

- Edit and proofread each piece, and get responses from peers or an instructor.

A student's portfolio cover letter. The following is the first paragraph of a reflective statement written by student James Kung to accompany the portfolio for his first-year composition course.

"Writing is difficult and takes a long time." This simple yet powerful statement has been uttered so many times in our class that it has become our motto. In just ten weeks, my persuasive writing skills have improved dramatically, thanks to many hours spent writing, revising, polishing, and (when I wasn't writing) thinking about my topic. These improvements are clearly illustrated by the drafts, revisions, and other materials included in my course portfolio.

James Kung's letter goes on to analyze his revisions and the benefits of his writing process. He concludes with information about his future plans and a signature.

bedfordstmartins.com/easywriter To read James Kung's complete reflective statement, click on **Student Writing**.

2j Collaborating

Writers often work together to come up with ideas, to respond to one another's drafts, or even to coauthor texts. Here are some strategies for working with others:

- Establish ground rules for the collaboration. Be sure every writer has an equal opportunity—and responsibility—to contribute.

- Exchange contact information, and plan face-to-face meetings (if any).

- Pay close attention to each writer's views. Expect disagreement, and remember that the goal is to argue through all possibilities.

- If you are preparing a collaborative document, divide up the drafting duties and set reasonable deadlines. Work together to iron out the final draft, aiming for consistency of tone. Proofread together, and have one person make corrections.

- Give credit where credit is due. In team projects, acknowledge all members' contributions as well as any help you receive from outsiders.

3 Critical Thinking and Argument

In one sense, all language has an argumentative edge: even when you greet friends, you want to convince them that you are genuinely glad to see them. In much academic and professional writing, however, **argument** is more narrowly defined as a text—verbal, visual, or both—that makes a claim and supports it fully. Reading critically is essential to understanding such arguments.

3a Reading critically

Reading critically means asking questions about the meaning of the text and how that meaning is presented, or about the author and his or her purpose for creating the text. A critical reader does not simply accept what the author says; instead, a critical reader analyzes why the text is convincing (or not convincing).

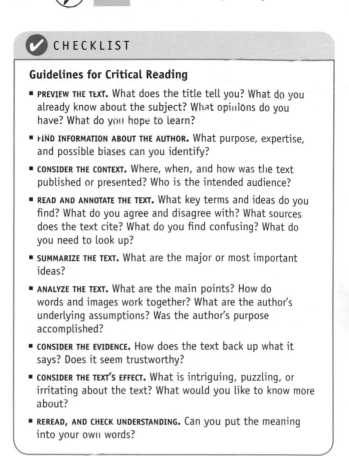

✓ CHECKLIST

Guidelines for Critical Reading

- **PREVIEW THE TEXT.** What does the title tell you? What do you already know about the subject? What opinions do you have? What do you hope to learn?

- **FIND INFORMATION ABOUT THE AUTHOR.** What purpose, expertise, and possible biases can you identify?

- **CONSIDER THE CONTEXT.** Where, when, and how was the text published or presented? Who is the intended audience?

- **READ AND ANNOTATE THE TEXT.** What key terms and ideas do you find? What do you agree and disagree with? What sources does the text cite? What do you find confusing? What do you need to look up?

- **SUMMARIZE THE TEXT.** What are the major or most important ideas?

- **ANALYZE THE TEXT.** What are the main points? How do words and images work together? What are the author's underlying assumptions? Was the author's purpose accomplished?

- **CONSIDER THE EVIDENCE.** How does the text back up what it says? Does it seem trustworthy?

- **CONSIDER THE TEXT'S EFFECT.** What is intriguing, puzzling, or irritating about the text? What would you like to know more about?

- **REREAD, AND CHECK UNDERSTANDING.** Can you put the meaning into your own words?

3b Thinking critically about visuals

Being visually literate—being able to read an image and understand how it aims to persuade or manipulate—is crucial to becoming a critical thinker. Visual literacy requires you to analyze images and the arguments they contain. Thinking about the following elements of a visual text can help:

DESIGN

- What do you notice first? Why is your attention drawn to that spot, and what effect does this have on your response?

- How does the composition affect the message? Why are some elements in the foreground and others in the background? Why might the composition be arranged as it is? What effect do the designer's choices have on the way you feel about the design?

- How does the use of color enhance or conflict with the images and words? Is color used for highlighting? Is the use of color appropriate?

- If the visual contains both words and images, how do the two relate? How well do they work together? If no words appear, is the message clear without them? Why or why not?

- Is any part of the composition repeated? If so, is the repetition effective?

CREATOR

- Who created the visual? What other work has the creator done?

- What attitude does he or she seem to have toward this work? What effect is the visual supposed to have on others?

CONTENT

- What is the subject? How well do visuals explain the subject?

CONTEXT

- Where and in what form did the visual originally appear?

- What can you infer about the message from the visual's original context?

AUDIENCE

- Who is the intended audience? Does it include you? If so, does the visual affect you the way its creator intended?

- What assumptions does the visual make about the audience's values?

• Why do you think this visual was created? Does it achieve its purpose?

OVERALL IMPRESSION

• What works and what doesn't work in this visual?

• What overall impression does the visual create, and how?

Think about these questions as you look at the accompanying advertising parody, which was created by the nonprofit group Adbusters. What conclusions can you draw about this visual?

3c Identifying basic appeals in an argument

Identify emotional appeals. Emotional appeals stir our emotions and remind us of deeply held values. In analyzing any argument, look for what the writer or creator is doing to tug on the audience's emotions.

Identify ethical appeals. Ethical appeals support the credibility, moral character, and goodwill of the argument's creator. To find these appeals, ask yourself what the creator is doing to show that he or she has done homework on the subject and is knowledgeable and credible about it. What kind of character does he or she build, and how? Most important, ask if the creator of the argument seems trustworthy and has the best interests of the audience in mind.

Identify logical appeals. Logical appeals are often thought to be the most persuasive to Western audiences—as some say, "The facts don't lie" (although facts can certainly be manipulated). In addition to checking the facts of any argument, then, look for firsthand evidence drawn from observations, interviews, surveys or questionnaires, experiments, and personal experience, as well as second-

> ✅ CHECKLIST
>
> **Analyzing Verbal and Visual Arguments**
>
> - What cultural contexts—the time and place the argument was written; the economic, social, and political events surrounding the argument; and so on—inform the argument? What do they tell you about where the writer or creator is coming from?
> - What is the main issue of the argument?
> - What emotional, ethical, or logical appeals is the argument making? Are the appeals reasonable and fair? (See 3c.)
> - How has the writer or creator established credibility?
> - What sources does the argument rely on? How current and reliable are they? Are some perspectives left out, and if so, how does this exclusion affect the argument?
> - What claim does the argument make, and how solid is the supporting evidence?
> - How has the writer or creator used visuals and design to support the argument? How well do words and images work together to make a point? (See 3b.)
> - What overall impression does the argument create? Are you convinced?

hand evidence from authorities, precedents, the testimony of others, statistics, and other research sources. As you evaluate these sources, ask how trustworthy they are and whether all terms are clearly defined.

3d Analyzing the elements of an argument

According to philosopher Stephen Toulmin's framework for analyzing arguments, most arguments contain common features: a **claim** (or claims); reasons for the claim; stated or unstated assumptions that underlie the argument (Toulmin calls these *warrants*); **evidence** such as facts, authoritative opinion, examples, and statistics; and **qualifiers** that limit the claim in some way.

Suppose you read a brief argument about providing sex education in schools. The diagram that follows shows how you can use the elements of argument for analysis.

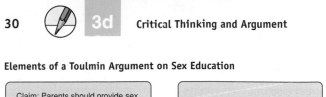
Elements of a Toulmin Argument on Sex Education

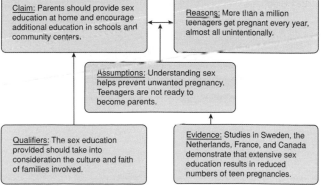

Claim: Parents should provide sex education at home and encourage additional education in schools and community centers.

Reasons: More than a million teenagers get pregnant every year, almost all unintentionally.

Assumptions: Understanding sex helps prevent unwanted pregnancy. Teenagers are not ready to become parents.

Qualifiers: The sex education provided should take into consideration the culture and faith of families involved.

Evidence: Studies in Sweden, the Netherlands, France, and Canada demonstrate that extensive sex education results in reduced numbers of teen pregnancies.

3e Making an argument

Chances are you've been making convincing arguments since early childhood. But if family members and friends are not always easy to convince, then the job of making effective arguments to those unfamiliar with you presents even more challenges. It is especially difficult to argue constructively with complete strangers in cyberspace.

Arguable statements. An arguable statement must meet three criteria:

1. It should seek to convince readers of something, to change their minds, or to urge them to do something.
2. It should address a problem that has no obvious or absolute solution or answer.
3. It should present a position that readers can have varying perspectives on.

ARGUABLE STATEMENT	Video games lead to violent behavior.
UNARGUABLE STATEMENT	Video games earn millions of dollars every year.

Argumentative thesis or claim. To move from an arguable statement to an argumentative thesis, begin with an arguable statement:

ARGUABLE STATEMENT   Pesticides should be banned.

Attach at least one good reason.

REASON   because they endanger the lives
                                of workers

You now have a working argumentative thesis.

ARGUMENTATIVE THESIS   Because they endanger the lives
                                of workers, pesticides should be
                                banned.

Develop the underlying assumption that supports your
argument.

ASSUMPTION   Workers have a right to a safe
                                working environment.

Identifying this assumption will help you gather evidence
in support of your argument. Finally, consider whether you
need to qualify your claim in any way.

Ethical appeals.   To make any argument effective, you
need to establish your credibility. Here are some good ways
to do so:

- Demonstrate that you are knowledgeable about the issues
  and topic.
- Show that you respect the views of your audience and
  have their best interests at heart.
- Demonstrate that you are fair and evenhanded.

Visuals can also make ethical appeals. A logo, seal, or slogan
(such as the logo of the Environmental Protection Agency
that follows) may suggest that a government agency's
reports and Web sites are believable because they are backed
by the authority of the federal government.

A Visual That Makes an Ethical Appeal

♻EPA United States Environmental Protection Agency

A Visual That Makes a Logical Appeal

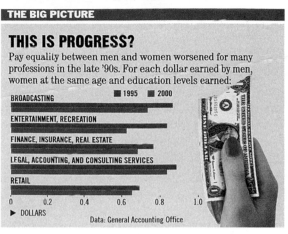

THE BIG PICTURE

THIS IS PROGRESS?

Pay equality between men and women worsened for many professions in the late '90s. For each dollar earned by men, women at the same age and education levels earned:

■ 1995 ■ 2000

BROADCASTING

ENTERTAINMENT, RECREATION

FINANCE, INSURANCE, REAL ESTATE

LEGAL, ACCOUNTING, AND CONSULTING SERVICES

RETAIL

0   0.2   0.4   0.6   0.8   1.0

▶ DOLLARS

Data: General Accounting Office

Logical appeals.   Audiences almost always want proof—logical reasons that back up your argument. You can create good logical appeals in the following ways:

- Provide strong examples that are representative and that clearly support your point.
- Introduce precedents—particular examples from the past—that support your point.
- Use narratives or stories in support of your point.
- Cite authorities and their testimony, as long as each authority is timely and is genuinely qualified to speak on the topic.
- Establish that one event is the cause—or the effect—of another.

Visuals that make logical appeals can be useful in arguments, since they present factual information that can be taken in at a glance. Consider how long it would take to explain all the information in the graph above by using words alone.

Emotional appeals.   Audiences can feel manipulated when an argument tries too hard to appeal to pity, anger, or fear. You can appeal to the hearts as well as to the minds of your audience with the ethical use of strong emotional appeals:

- Introduce a powerful text that supports your point.
- Use detailed description and concrete language to make your points more vivid.
- Use figurative language—metaphors, similes, analogies, and so on—to make your point both lively and memorable.

Visuals that make emotional appeals can add substance to your argument as long as you test them with potential readers to check whether they interpret the visual the same way you do. The following image of coffins returning from Iraq might strike some viewers as making an antiwar argument, but others may view it as an argument about patriotism or about respect for sacrifice.

A Visual That Makes an Emotional Appeal

3f   Organizing an argument

Although there is no universally "ideal" organizational framework for an argument, the following pattern (often referred to as the classical system) has been used throughout the history of the Western world:

INTRODUCTION

- Gets readers' attention and interest
- Establishes your qualifications to write about your topic
- Establishes common ground with readers
- Demonstrates fairness
- States or implies your argumentative thesis

BACKGROUND

- Presents any necessary background data or information, including pertinent personal narratives or stories

LINES OF ARGUMENT

- Present good reasons and evidence (including logical and emotional appeals) in support of your thesis, usually in order of importance
- Demonstrate ways your argument is in readers' best interest

CONSIDERATION OF ALTERNATIVE ARGUMENTS

- Examines alternative or opposing points of view
- Notes advantages and disadvantages of alternative views
- Explains why one view is better than other(s)

CONCLUSION

- May summarize the argument briefly
- Elaborates on the implication of your thesis
- Makes clear what you want readers to think and do
- Makes a strong ethical or emotional appeal in a memorable way

3g   Designing an argument

Most arguments today are carefully designed to make the best use of space, font style and type size, color, and visu-

als. The following tips can help you design a document that will add to the ethical, logical, and emotional appeals you are making:

- Check out any conventions that may be expected in the kind of argument you are writing. Look for examples of similar arguments, or ask your instructor for information about such conventions.
- Consider using a special design element to emphasize an important point. For example, you might put essential evidence in a carefully labeled sidebar or box.
- Choose colors carefully, keeping in mind that colors call up many responses: red may mean war, for example, or blue may mean purity.

3h A student's argument essay

In this essay, Teal Pfeifer argues that images in the media affect how women see themselves, and she offers a solution to a problem. Her essay has been excerpted to show some key parts of her argument as well as her good use of reasons, evidence, and appeals to logic and emotion.

Teal Pfeifer

Professor Rashad

English 102

13 April 2008

Devastating Beauty

Collarbones, hipbones, cheekbones—so many bones. She looks at the camera with sunken eyes, smiling, acting beautiful. Her dress is Versace, or Gucci, or Dior, and it is revealing, revealing every bone and joint in her thin, thin body. She looks fragile and beautiful, as if I could snap her in two. I look at her and feel the soft cushion of flesh that surrounds my own joints; then I look away and wonder what kind of self-discipline it takes to become beautiful like this.

By age seventeen a young woman has seen an average of 250,000 ads featuring a severely underweight woman whose body type is, for most people, unattainable by any means, including extreme ones such as anorexia, bulimia, and drug use ("The Skinny on Media"). The media promote clothing, cigarettes, fragrances, and

even food with images like these, and the women in these images are a smaller size than ever before. In 1950, the White Rock Mineral Water girl was 5′4″ tall and weighed 140 pounds; now she is 5′10″ tall and weighs only 110 pounds, signifying the growing deviation between the weight of models and that of the normal female population (Pipher 184).

This media phenomenon has had a major effect on the female population as a whole, both young and old. Five to ten million women in America today suffer from an eating disorder related to poor self-image, and yet advertisements continue to prey on insecurities fueled by a woman's desire to be thin. Current estimates reveal that "80 percent of women are dissatisfied with their appearance" and "45 percent of those are on a diet on any given day" ("Statistics"). Yet even the most stringent dieting will generally fail to create the paper-thin body so valued in the media, and continuing efforts to do so can lead to serious psychological problems such as depression.

While many women express dissatisfaction with their bodies, they are not the only victims of the emaciated images so frequently presented to them. Young girls are equally affected by these images, if not more so. Eighty percent of girls under age ten have already been on a diet and expressed the desire to be thinner and more beautiful (*Slim Hopes*). Thus from a young age, beauty is equated with a specific size. The message girls get is an insidious one: in order to be your best self, you should wear size 0 or 1. The pressure only grows more intense as girls grow up. According to results from the Kaiser Family Foundation Survey "Reflections of Girls in the Media," 16 percent of ten- to seventeen-year-old girls reported that they had dieted or exercised to look like a TV character. Yet two-thirds of teenage girls acknowledged that these thin characters were not an accurate reflection of "real life" (qtd. in Dittrich, "Children").

It is tragic to see so much of the American population obsessed with weight and reaching an ideal that is, for the most part, ultimately unattainable. Equally troubling is the role magazines play in feeding this obsession. When a researcher asked female

students from Stanford University to flip through several magazines containing images of glamorized, super-thin models, 68 percent of the women felt significantly worse about themselves after viewing the magazine models (qtd. in Dittrich, "Media"). Another study showed that looking at models on a long-term basis leads to stress, depression, guilt, and lowered self-worth (qtd. in Dittrich, "Media").

How can we reject images that are so harmful, especially to young women? Perhaps the most effective way to rid the print medium of emaciated models and eliminate the harmful effects they cause is to mount a boycott. If women stopped buying magazines that target them with such harmful advertising, magazines would be forced to change the kinds of ads they print. Such a boycott would send a clear message: women and girls reject the victimization that takes place every time they look at a skeletally thin model and then feel worse about themselves. Consumers can ultimately control what is put on the market: if we don't buy, funding for such ads will dry up fast.

In the past, boycotts have been effective tools for social change. Rosa Parks, often identified as the mother of the modern-day civil rights movement, played a pivotal role in the Montgomery bus boycott in December 1955. When Parks refused to give up her seat to a white rider, she was arrested, and this incident inspired the boycott. For more than a year, African Americans in Montgomery chose to walk instead of ride the buses. The boycott was eventually successful: segregation on buses was declared illegal by the U.S. Supreme Court.

As a society, we have much to learn from boycotts of the past, and their lessons can help us confront contemporary social ills. As I have shown, body-image dissatisfaction and eating disorders are rising at an alarming rate among young girls and women in American society. The anorexia and bulimia that women suffer from are not only diseases that can be cured; they are also ones that can be prevented—if women will take a solid stand against such advertisements and the magazines that publish them. This is where power lies—in the hands of those who hand over the dollars that

support the glorification of unhealthy and unrealistic bodies. It is our choice to exert this power and to reject magazines that promote such images.

Works Cited

Dittrich, Liz. "About-Face Facts on Children and the Media." *About-Face*. About-Face, 1996-2008. Web. 10 Mar. 2008.

---. "About-Face Facts on the Media." *About-Face*. About-Face, 1996-2008. Web. 10 Mar. 2008.

Pipher, Mary. *Reviving Ophelia: Saving the Selves of Adolescent Girls*. New York: Ballantine, 1994. Print.

"The Skinny on Media and Weight." *Common Sense Media*. Common Sense Media Inc., 27 Sept. 2006. Web. 15 Mar. 2008.

Slim Hopes. Dir. Sut Jhally. Prod. Jean Kilbourne. Media Education Foundation, 1995. Videocassette.

"Statistics." *National Eating Disorders Association*. National Eating Disorders Association, 2006. Web. 14 Mar. 2008.

4 Writing for Other Media

Writing today occurs across a wide range of genres and media—your audience may encounter your work in print, online, as a presentation, or in some other way. But no matter what genre or medium you are writing for, you still need to consider your rhetorical situation—the audience, purpose, and complete context for your writing.

4a Electronic communication

Though much of your electronic communication may be very informal, always remember to consider your audience and situation; texting slang and shortcuts may not be appropriate.

---

bedfordstmartins.com/easywriter For more information on effective electronic communication, go to **Writing Resources** and click on **Online Writing**.

Email.   When contacting an instructor or employer, stick to the conventions of academic English.

- Use a subject line that states your purpose accurately and clearly.

- Take care not to offend or irritate your reader. Tone is difficult to convey in online messages: what you intend as a joke may come across as an insult. Avoid writing messages in ALL CAPS.

- Be pertinent; include only the information readers need.

- Use a more formal tone along with a formal greeting and closing when sending a message to an instructor (*Dear Ms. Aulie* rather than *Hi*).

- Proofread email messages just as you would other writing.

- Consider email permanent and always findable, even if you delete it.

- Conclude your message with your name and email address.

- Make sure that the username on the email account you use for contacting instructors and other authority figures does not present a poor impression. If your username is *Party2Nite*, consider changing it, or use your school email account for academic and professional communication.

Texting.   If someone sends you a text message that includes shortcuts or slang, feel free to reply in the same way. But if you have not been invited to text instructors or employers, stick to more formal methods of communication while keeping messages brief and to the point.

Lists and discussion forums.   Think of academic lists and forums as an extension of class discussion.

- Treat all participants with respect. Avoid unnecessary criticism of spelling or other errors. If you disagree with an assertion of fact, offer what you believe to be the correct information, but don't insult the writer.

- If you think you've been flamed, give the writer the benefit of the doubt. Replying with patience helps you seem mature and credible.

- Reply off-list to the sender of a message if the whole group does not need to read your reply.

- Note that many discussion lists are archived, so more people than you think may be reading your messages. Your postings create an impression of you, so make it a good one.

Web logs (blogs) and social networking spaces.　Blogs and social networking spaces such as Facebook and Twitter allow users to say almost anything about themselves and to comment freely on the postings of others. Such online spaces can also be useful for academic discussion or for posting writing for others' comments.

- These spaces may feel private, but most aren't—don't post anything you don't want everyone (including instructors and potential employers) to see.

- To comment, follow the same conventions you would for commenting on a discussion-list posting.

4b　Web texts

As when you create any piece of writing, plan Web texts with an eye on your deadline and your rhetorical situation, including purpose, audience, topic, and stance. (See Chapter 1.)

Planning Web texts.　These tips can help you think through your Web text:

- Consider the overall impression you want to create—bold? serious? This impression should guide your decisions about text, navigation, visuals, color, links, embedded files, and so on.

- Look at Web sites you admire for ideas on design, navigation, and organization.

- Think of each page as having two main parts: navigation (such as menus or links) and content areas. Make these parts distinct from one another, and make navigation clear to your readers.

- Map or storyboard your Web document. Consider a template for consistent layout of pages or sections.

- Indicate links among pages, and link all sections of the text to the home page. If you decide to link to external sites, plan appropriate placement of those links.

- Put contact information on every page.

- Plan to reassess, revise, and maintain your Web text on an ongoing basis.

Choosing design, visuals, and multimedia.　Follow basic design principles with every writing project (see Chapter 6). The following tips will help you make effective choices about design, visuals, and multimedia:

- Remember that the top left part of a page is where users look first; place the most important content there.

- Plan your use of visuals and audio carefully, and check file size and resolution of images to make sure they will download quickly.

- Integrate visuals and text carefully. Don't use visuals just for decoration.

- Make the relationship between visuals or audio and text clear, either in the text itself or in labels or captions.

- Request permission to use any visuals or sound clips that you have not created yourself unless you find an explicit statement that the information is available for free use. Government documents are in the public domain and thus free for use, but always include source information.

- Remember that visuals and audio are often not accessible to those with disabilities. Test your Web site to see how accessible it is.

4c   Oral and multimedia presentations

More and more students report that formal presentations are becoming part of their work, both in and out of class.

Considering the task, purpose, and audience. Think about how much time you have to prepare; where the presentation will take place; how long the presentation is going to be; whether you will use written-out text or note cards; whether visual aids, handouts, or other accompanying materials are called for; and what equipment you will need. If you are making a group presentation, you will need time to divide duties and to practice with your classmates.

Consider the purpose of your presentation. Are you to lead a discussion? teach a lesson? give a report? engage a group in an activity?

Consider your audience. What do they know about your topic, what opinions do they already hold about it, and what do they need to know to follow your presentation and perhaps accept your point of view?

Emphasizing the introduction and conclusion. Listeners tend to remember beginnings and endings most readily. Consider making yours memorable by using a startling statement, opinion, or question; a vivid anecdote; or a powerful quotation.

Using explicit structure and signpost language. Organize your presentation clearly and carefully, and give an overview of your main points at the outset. (You may wish to reemphasize these points toward the end of the talk.) Then pause between major points, and use signpost language as you move from one idea to the next. Such signposts should be clear and concrete: *The second crisis point in the breakup of the Soviet Union occurred hard on the heels of the first* instead of *Another thing about the Soviet Union's problems* . . . You can also offer signposts by repeating key words and ideas; avoiding long, complicated sentences; and using as many concrete verbs and nouns as possible. If you are talking about abstract ideas, try to provide concrete examples for each.

Preparing the text for ease of presentation. If you decide to speak from a full text of your presentation, use fairly large double- or triple-spaced print that will be easy to read. End each page with the end of a sentence so that you won't have to pause while you turn a page. Whether you speak from a full text, a detailed outline, note cards, or points on flip charts or slides, mark the places where you want to pause, and highlight the words you want to emphasize. (If you are using transparencies or presentation software, print out a paper version and mark it up.)

Integrating visuals. Visual information displayed on PowerPoint slides, posters, or other media during an oral presentation can add interest, clarify points, keep the speaker on track, and help members of the audience who learn better by listening *and* looking. For any visual information you display, remember to follow basic design principles (see Chapter 6), avoiding clutter and making information as legible as possible. In addition, be sure that all the information you show is clear, well organized, and relevant to your presentation. The following tips will ensure that your visuals work for rather than against your presentation.

DISPLAYING WRITTEN INFORMATION

- Ensure that your audience can read any written information you display with your presentation. Choose background and type colors that contrast well for easy reading. A poster heading should be at least 2" high; for text on a PowerPoint slide, use 44- to 50-point type for headings, 30- to 34-point type for subheads.

- Use short phrases or bulleted lists, not paragraphs, to guide your audience through your main points. Less is more when it comes to displaying writing. Use the displayed text to emphasize what you are saying.

USING POWERPOINT SLIDES

- Don't put more words or images on a slide than you need to make your point. Use only a few bullet points (no more than fifty words)—and never read the bullets. Instead, make your words and your slides complement each other.
- Use light backgrounds in a darkened room, dark backgrounds in a lighted one.
- If you include audio or video clips, make sure they are audible.
- Use only visuals that are large and sharp enough to be clearly visible to your audience.

USING HANDOUTS

- Use handouts for text that is too extensive to be presented during your talk.
- Unless you want the audience to look at handouts while you are speaking, distribute them at the end of your presentation.

Practicing your presentation. Leave enough time to practice your presentation—including the use of all visuals—at least twice. You might also record your rehearsals, or practice in front of a mirror or with friends who can comment on content and style.

Timing your run-throughs will tell you whether you need to cut (or expand) material to make the presentation an appropriate length.

Making your presentation. To calm your nerves and get off to a good start, know your material thoroughly and use the following strategies to good advantage before, during, and after your presentation:

- Visualize your presentation with the aim of feeling comfortable during it.
- Consider doing some deep-breathing exercises before the presentation, and concentrate on relaxing; avoid too much caffeine.
- If possible, stand up. Most speakers make a stronger impression standing rather than sitting.

- Pause before you begin, concentrating on your opening lines.
- Face your audience at all times, and make eye contact as much as possible.
- Allow time for the audience to respond and ask questions.
- Thank your audience at the end of your presentation.

4d A student's PowerPoint slides and script (excerpt)

Following are part of a script and the first three slides from a PowerPoint presentation prepared by student Jennifer Bernal in response to an assignment to analyze a graphic novel. The excerpts from her script show highlights that cue slides or remind her what to point out. Note that she cites each source on the slides; her list of sources appears on her final slide, which is not shown here.

[slide 1] Hello, I'm Jennifer Bernal. And I've been thinking about the voice of the child narrator in the graphic novel *Persepolis* by

Slide 1

bedfordstmartins.com/easywriter For additional sample student presentations, click on **Student Writing**.

Marjane Satrapi, an autobiographical narrative of a young girl's coming of age in Iran during the Islamic revolution. My research questions seemed fitting for a child: what? how? why? What is the "child's voice"? How is it achieved? Why is it effective? The child's voice in this book is characterized by internal conflict: the character sometimes sounds like a child and sometimes like an adult. She truly is a child on the threshold of adulthood. I'm going to show how Satrapi expresses the duality of this child's voice, not only through content but also through her visual style.

[slide 2] The main character, Marjane, faces a constant conflict between childhood and adulthood. But the struggle takes place not only between the child and the adults in her society but also between the child and the adult within Marjane herself. For example, Marjane is exposed to many ideas and experiences as she tries to understand the world around her. Here [first image] we see her surprising an adult by discussing Marx. But we also see her being a kid. Sometimes, like all children, she is unthinkingly cruel: here [second image] we see her upsetting another little girl with the horrifying (and, as it turns out, incorrect) "truth" about her father's absence.

Slide 2

Slide 3

The Child's Voice through Visual Style: Repetition

Fig. 3 from Marjane Satrapi, *Persepolis* (New York: Pantheon, 2003) 96.

Figs. 4, 5, 6 - from Satrapi 19, 114, 117.

[slide 3] One reviewer calls Satrapi's style "supernaive." It seems to me that this simple visual style is achieved through repetition and filtering. Let's take a look at this. [point to slide] First, there's *repetition* of elements. We often see the same images being used over and over. Sometimes [point to first image] the repetition suggests the sameness imposed by the repressive government. At other times, similar images are repeated throughout the book for emphasis. For example [point to examples], on several occasions we see her raising her finger and speaking directly to the reader to make an emphatic point. The repetition throughout *Persepolis* makes it look and feel more like a children's book. . . .

5 Writing in the Disciplines

Writing is important in almost every profession, but it works in different ways in different disciplines. You may begin to get a sense of such differences as you prepare assignments for courses in the humanities, social sciences, and natural sciences.

5a Academic work in any discipline

You will need to become familiar with the expectations, vocabularies, styles, methods of proof, and conventional formats used in each field.

Analyze academic assignments and expectations. When you receive an assignment in any discipline, your first job is to make sure you understand what that assignment asks you to do. Whatever your assignment, use the checklist questions below to analyze it.

Understand disciplinary vocabularies. A good way to enter into the conversation of a field or discipline is to study its vocabulary. Highlight key terms in your reading or notes to help you distinguish any specialized terms. If you find only a little specialized vocabulary, try to master the new

---

✔ CHECKLIST

Analyzing an Assignment in Any Discipline

- What is the purpose of the assignment? Does it serve as a basis for class discussion or brainstorming about a topic, or is the purpose to demonstrate your mastery of certain material and your competence as a writer?
- What does the assignment ask you to do—summarize, explain, evaluate, interpret, illustrate, define, or something else?
- Who is the audience? Does it include anyone other than your instructor?
- Do you need clarification of any terms?
- What do you need to know or find out to complete the assignment?
- Do you understand the expectations for background reading and preparation, use of sources, method of organization and development, format, and length?
- Can you find an example of an effective response to a similar assignment?
- Does your understanding of the assignment fit with that of other students? Talking over an assignment with classmates is one good way to test your understanding.

terms quickly by reading your textbook carefully, asking your instructor questions, and looking up key words or phrases.

Identify the style of a discipline. Study writing in the field to identify its stylistic features:

- How would you describe the overall tone of the writing?
- Do writers in the field usually strive for an objective stance? (See 39a.)
- In general, how long are the sentences and paragraphs?
- Are verbs generally active or passive—and why? (See 7e.)
- Do the writers use first person (*I*) or prefer terms such as *one* or *the investigator*? What is the effect of this choice?
- Does the writing integrate visual elements such as graphs, tables, charts, photographs, or maps?
- How is the writing organized? Does it typically include certain features (such as an abstract or a discussion of methods), headings, or other formatting elements?

Understand the use of evidence. As you grow familiar with any area of study, you will develop a sense of what it takes to prove a point in that field. As you read assigned materials, consider the following questions about evidence:

- How do writers in the field use precedent and authority? (See 3c.)
- What use is made of quantitative data (items that can be counted and measured) and qualitative data (items that can be systematically observed)?
- How is logical reasoning used? How are definition, cause and effect, analogy, and example used in this discipline?
- What are the primary materials—the firsthand sources of information—in this field? What are the secondary materials—the sources of information derived from others? (See 38b.)
- How is research used and integrated into the text?

5b Writing in the humanities

When you write for humanities disciplines like English or history, you will usually begin with a close reading of a text and use your analysis of the text to develop a critical thesis. Common assignments in the humanities include summa-

ries, response papers, position papers, critical analyses, and research-based projects.

Documentation style in the humanities.   Modern languages, literature, and philosophy usually ask students to format their assignments according to the style of the Modern Language Association, or MLA (see Chapter 42). History usually asks students to use formats set out by the University of Chicago (*Chicago* style—see Chapter 44). Ask instructors what documentation style they prefer.

Evidence and sources in the humanities.   Evidence for assignments in the humanities often comes from a primary source you are examining, such as a poem, a philosophical treatise, or an artifact such as a painting. Your close reading should yield evidence in support of your thesis. For some assignments, secondary sources such as journal articles or reference works will also provide useful evidence. Ground your analysis of your source(s) in key questions about the work you are examining that will lead you to a thesis.

5c Writing in the social sciences

When you write assignments in the social sciences, you will need to question, analyze, and interpret sources, including both quantitative studies that emphasize statistical evidence and qualitative studies that do not aim for objectivity but rather rely on data such as interviews and observations. Common assignments in the social sciences include reaction papers, position papers, summaries, abstracts, literature reviews, briefs, case studies, and reports.

Documentation styles in the social sciences.   Many instructors in social science classes will ask you to follow the format and documentation style set forth by the American Psychological Association, or APA (see Chapter 43). Social science assignments often prescribe standard features: an abstract, an introduction, a review of the literature, a methods section, a results section, a discussion, and references.

Evidence and sources in the social sciences.   You will need to understand both the quantitative and qualitative evidence used in your sources as well as other evidence

you may create from research you conduct on your own. Summarizing and synthesizing information drawn from sources will be key to your success.

5d   Writing in the natural and applied sciences

Writers in the natural and applied sciences work with evidence that can be observed, verified, and controlled. While you can't avoid interpretation in such writing, you should strive for objectivity and clarity. Common assignments in the natural and applied sciences include lab notebooks, lab reports, research proposals and reports, literature reviews, grant proposals, and multimedia presentations.

Documentation styles in the natural and applied sciences. Many scientific texts follow the guidelines for format and documentation set forth by the Council of Science Editors, or CSE (see Chapter 45). Science articles often include standard features: an abstract, an introduction, a literature review, a materials and methods section, a results and discussion section, and references. Grant proposals commonly include a title page, an introduction, purpose(s) and significance of the proposed study, methods, timeline, budget, and references.

Evidence and sources in the natural and applied sciences. Writers in these fields typically draw on two major sources of evidence: research—including studies, experiments, and analyses—conducted by reputable and credible scientists; and research conducted by the writer. Each source should provide a strong piece of evidence for the writer's project.

5e   Writing for business

In business classes, you will prepare for the kinds of writing you will face in the work world. Common assignments in business include memos, letters, résumés, and reports.

Formats for business writing. Most business writers use conventional formats for email and memos: clear subject

---

bedfordstmartins.com/easywriter To see samples of student writing in many disciplines, go to **Student Writing** and click on **Writing in the Disciplines**.

lines; clear *to, from,* and *date* lines; and brief, concise, point-by-point organization, using headings if necessary to guide readers. Letters often use block format in which all text, including return address, date, and inside address, is aligned to the left margin. An effective résumé begins with your name and contact information and goes on to present subheadings for sections such as career objectives, education, experience, and references.

Most businesses have standard formats that they follow for reports and other longer pieces of writing. Consult your instructor if you need an appropriate model for the type of writing you have been asked to do.

Style in business.   Business writers aim to be clear, concise, and focused on their audiences and to use a somewhat formal, always respectful tone.

6   Designing Documents

Because visual and design elements such as headings, lists, fonts, images, and graphics can help you get and keep a reader's attention, they bring a whole new dimension to writing—what some refer to as *visual rhetoric.*

6a Understanding design principles

Most design experts begin with several very simple principles that guide the design of all texts.

Contrast.   The contrast in a design attracts and guides readers around the document. You may achieve contrast through color, icons, boldface or large type, white space (areas without type or graphics), and so on. Begin with a focal point—the dominant visual or words on the page or screen—and structure the flow of all your other information from this point.

Proximity.   Whether they are text or visuals, parts of a document that are topically related should be physically close (*proximate* to one another).

The Centers for Disease Control and Prevention site uses contrasting colors effectively by placing white type against a dark blue background and dark type against lighter-colored backgrounds. The site also demonstrates proximity, placing each image above its label and supporting text.

The U.S. Postal Service site repeats the red and blue horizontals from the home page, shown here, on many other screens. The site also makes the content's alignment clear by placing information in boxes under three major headings.

Repetition.   Readers are guided in large part by the repetition of key words or design elements. You can take advantage of this principle by using color, type style, and other visual elements consistently throughout the document.

Alignment.   This principle refers to how visuals and text on a page are lined up, both horizontally and vertically. The headline, title, or banner on a document, for example,

should be carefully aligned horizontally so that the reader's eye is drawn easily along one line from left to right. Vertical alignment is equally important. In general, you can choose to align things with the left side, the right side, or the center of a page or screen. Whatever type of alignment you begin with, stick with it. The result will be a cleaner and more organized look.

Overall impression.   Aim for a design that creates the appropriate overall impression or mood for your document. For an academic essay, you will probably make conservative choices that strike a serious scholarly note. In a newsletter for a campus group, you might choose bright colors and arresting images.

6b Choosing appropriate formats

Because writers have so many design possibilities to choose from, it's important to spend some time thinking about the most appropriate format for a document.

Margins and white space.   The margins and other areas of white space in a print or electronic document guide readers around the page. Since the eye takes in only so much data in one movement, very long lines can be hard to read. Set margins so that the average line includes about twelve words (or sixty-five characters). Use white space around graphics, headings, or lists to make them stand out.

Color.   Your use of color should relate to the purpose(s) of your document and its intended audience.

- Use color to draw attention to elements you want to emphasize: headings and subheadings, bullets, text boxes, parts of charts or graphs, and other visuals.

- Be consistent in your use of color; use the same color for all main headings, for example.

- For most documents, keep the number of colors fairly small; too many colors can create a jumbled or confused look. In addition, avoid colors that clash or that are hard on the eyes (certain shades of yellow, for example). Check to make sure that all color visuals and text are legible.

- Remember that when colors are printed or projected, they may not look the same as they do on your computer screen.

- Look for examples of effective use of color. Find color combinations that you think look especially good—and then try them out.

| Certain color combinations clash and are hard to read. | Other combinations are easier on the eyes. |

Paper.   The quality of the paper and the readability of the type affect the overall look and feel of print documents. Although inexpensive paper is fine for your earlier drafts, use 8 1/2" × 11" good-quality white bond paper for your final drafts. For résumés, you may wish to use parchment or cream-colored paper. For brochures and posters, colored paper may be most appropriate. Try to use the best-quality printer available to you for your final product.

Pagination.   Your instructor may ask that you follow a particular format (see Chapters 42–45); if not, beginning with the first page of text, place your last name and the page number in the upper right-hand corner of the page.

Type.   Most personal computers allow writers to choose among a great variety of type sizes and typefaces, or fonts. For most college writing, 10- to 12-point type sizes are best. For print documents, a serif font (as used in the main text of this book) is generally easier to read than a sans serif font, though sans serif is often easier to read online. And although unusual fonts might seem attractive at first glance, readers may find such fonts distracting and hard to read over long stretches of material. Most important, be consistent in the size and style of type you choose.

Spacing.   Final drafts for most of your college writing should be double-spaced, with the first line of paragraphs indented one-half inch or five spaces. Other documents, such as letters, memorandums, lab reports, and Web texts, are usually single-spaced, with no paragraph indentation. Single-spaced text usually adds a blank line between paragraphs instead of indenting paragraphs to make the text easier to read. Other kinds of documents, such as flyers and newsletters, may call for multiple columns of text.

6c Using headings effectively

Headings call attention to the organization of a text and thus aid comprehension. Some kinds of reports have standard headings (like *Abstract* or *Summary*), which readers expect (and writers should therefore provide). If you use headings, you need to decide on type size and style, wording, and placement.

Type size and style. In college papers, you will usually distinguish levels of headings using indents along with type—for example, centered capitals and lowercase boldface for the first-level headings, capitals and lowercase boldface aligned at the left for the second level, capitals and lowercase italics aligned left for the third level, and so on.

First-Level Heading

Second-Level Heading

Third-Level Heading

Consistent headings. Look for the most succinct and informative way to word your headings. Most often, state the topic in a single word, usually a noun (*Toxicity*); in a phrase, usually a noun phrase (*Levels of Toxicity*) or a gerund phrase (*Measuring Toxicity*); in a question that will be answered in the text (*How Can Toxicity Be Measured?*); or in an imperative that tells readers what steps to take (*Measure the Toxicity*). Whichever structure you choose, make sure you use it consistently for all headings of the same level, and remember to position each level of heading consistently throughout your paper.

6d Using visuals effectively

Visuals can help make a point more vividly and succinctly than words alone. In some cases, visuals may even be your primary text.

Selecting visuals. Consider carefully what you want visuals to do for your writing before making your selections. What will your audience want or need you to show? Try to choose visuals that will enhance your credibility, allow you to make your points more emphatically, and clarify your overall text. (See the following table for advice on which visuals are best for particular situations.)

Type of Visual		When to Use It
Pie Chart		Use *pie charts* to compare parts to the whole.
Bar Graph		Use *bar graphs* and *line graphs* to compare one element with another, to compare elements over time, or to show correlations and frequency.
Table		Use *tables* to draw attention to detailed numerical information.
Diagram		Use *diagrams* to illustrate textual information or to point out details of objects or places described.
Map		Use *maps* to show geographical locations and to emphasize spatial relationships.
Cartoon		Use *cartoons* to illustrate a point dramatically or comically.
Photo		Use *photographs* or *illustrations* to show particular people, places, objects, and situations described in the text or to help readers find or understand types of content.

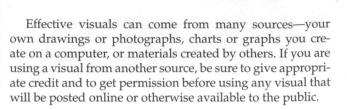
Effective visuals can come from many sources—your own drawings or photographs, charts or graphs you create on a computer, or materials created by others. If you are using a visual from another source, be sure to give appropriate credit and to get permission before using any visual that will be posted online or otherwise available to the public.

Identifying visuals in your writing. Position visuals alongside or after the text that refers to them. Number your visuals (number tables separately from other visuals), and give them informative titles. In some instances, you may need to provide captions to give readers additional data such as source information.

Figure 1. College Enrollment for Men and Women by Age, 2007 (in millions)

Table 1. Word Choice by Race: *Seesaw* and *Teeter-totter,* Chicago, 1986

Analyzing and altering visuals. Technical tools available to writers and designers today make it relatively easy to manipulate visuals. As you would with any source material, carefully assess any visuals you find for effectiveness, appropriateness, and validity:

- Check the context in which the visual appears. Is it part of an official government, school, or library site?
- If the visual is a photograph, are the date, time, place, and setting shown or explained? Is the information about the photo believable?
- If the visual is a chart, graph, or diagram, are the numbers and labels explained? Are the sources of the data given? Will the visual representation help readers make sense of the information, or could it mislead them?
- Is biographical and contact information given for the designer, artist, or photographer?

At times, you may make certain changes to visuals that you use, such as cropping an image to show the most important detail or digitally brightening a dark image. To

ensure that alterations to images are ethical, follow these guidelines:

- Do not attempt to mislead readers. Show things as accurately as possible.
- Tell your audience what changes you have made.
- Include all relevant information about the visual, including the source.

✔ CHECKLIST

Using Visuals Effectively

- Use visuals as a part of your text, never as decoration.
- In print texts, refer to the visual before it actually appears. For example: *As Table 1 demonstrates, the cost of a college education has risen dramatically in the last decade.*
- Tell the audience explicitly what the visual demonstrates, especially if it presents complex information. Do not assume readers will "read" the visual the same way you do; your commentary on it is important.
- Number and title all visuals. Number tables and figures separately.
- Follow established conventions for documenting visual sources, and ask permission for use if necessary. (See 40b.)
- Use clip art sparingly, if at all. Clip art is so easy to cut and paste that you may be tempted to slip it in everywhere, but resist this urge.
- Get responses to your visuals in an early draft. If readers can't follow them or are distracted by them, revise accordingly.
- Do a test-run printout of all visuals just to make sure your printer is adequate for the job.
- Use scanners and image editors to prepare drawings, photographs, or other illustrations for insertion into your document. But remember to do so ethically.

Sentence
Grammar

Writing

Sentence
Grammar

Sentence
Style

Punctuation/
Mechanics

Language

Multilingual
Writers

Research

Documentation

7 Verbs

One famous restaurant in Boston offers to bake, broil, pan-fry, deep-fry, poach, sauté, fricassee, blacken, or scallop any of the fish entrées on its menu. To someone ordering—or cooking—at this restaurant, the important distinctions lie entirely in the **verbs**.

7a Regular and irregular verb forms

The **past tense** and **past participle** of a **regular verb** are formed by adding *-ed* or *-d* to the **base form**.

BASE FORM	PAST TENSE	PAST PARTICIPLE
love	loved	loved
honor	honored	honored
obey	obeyed	obeyed

An **irregular verb** does not follow the *-ed* or *-d* pattern. If you are unsure about whether a verb is regular or irregular, or what the correct form is, consult the following list or a dictionary. Dictionaries list any irregular forms under the entry for the base form.

Some common irregular verbs

BASE FORM	PAST TENSE	PAST PARTICIPLE
arise	arose	arisen
be	was/were	been
beat	beat	beaten
become	became	become
begin	began	begun
bite	bit	bitten, bit
blow	blew	blown
break	broke	broken
bring	brought	brought
build	built	built
burn	burned, burnt	burned, burnt
burst	burst	burst
buy	bought	bought
catch	caught	caught
choose	chose	chosen
come	came	come
cost	cost	cost
cut	cut	cut

60

BASE FORM	PAST TENSE	PAST PARTICIPLE
dig	dug	dug
dive	dived, dove	dived
do	did	done
draw	drew	drawn
dream	dreamed, dreamt	dreamed, dreamt
drink	drank	drunk
drive	drove	driven
eat	ate	eaten
fall	fell	fallen
feel	felt	felt
fight	fought	fought
find	found	found
fly	flew	flown
forget	forgot	forgotten, forgot
freeze	froze	frozen
get	got	gotten, got
give	gave	given
go	went	gone
grow	grew	grown
hang (suspend)[1]	hung	hung
have	had	had
hear	heard	heard
hide	hid	hidden
hit	hit	hit
keep	kept	kept
know	knew	known
lay	laid	laid
lead	led	led
leave	left	left
lend	lent	lent
let	let	let
lie (recline)[2]	lay	lain
lose	lost	lost
make	made	made
mean	meant	meant
meet	met	met
pay	paid	paid
prove	proved	proved, proven
put	put	put
read	read	read

[1]*Hang* meaning "execute by hanging" is regular: *hang, hanged, hanged.*
[2]*Lie* meaning "tell a falsehood" is regular: *lie, lied, lied.*

 bedfordstmartins.com/easywriter For exercises, go to **Exercise Central** and click on **Verbs**.

BASE FORM	PAST TENSE	PAST PARTICIPLE
ride	rode	ridden
ring	rang	rung
rise	rose	risen
run	ran	run
say	said	said
see	saw	seen
send	sent	sent
set	set	set
shake	shook	shaken
shoot	shot	shot
show	showed	showed, shown
shrink	shrank	shrunk
sing	sang	sung
sink	sank	sunk
sit	sat	sat
sleep	slept	slept
speak	spoke	spoken
spend	spent	spent
spread	spread	spread
spring	sprang, sprung	sprung
stand	stood	stood
steal	stole	stolen
strike	struck	struck, stricken
swim	swam	swum
swing	swung	swung
take	took	taken
teach	taught	taught
tear	tore	torn
tell	told	told
think	thought	thought
throw	threw	thrown
wake	woke, waked	waked, woken
wear	wore	worn
win	won	won
write	wrote	written

✓ CHECKLIST

Editing the Verbs in Your Writing

- Check verb endings that cause you trouble. (7a)
- Double-check forms of *lie* and *lay, sit* and *set, rise* and *raise*. (7b)
- Refer to action in a literary work in the present tense. (7c)
- Check that verb tenses in your writing express meaning accurately. (7c and 7d)
- Use passive voice appropriately. (7e)

7b *Lie* and *lay*, *sit* and *set*, *rise* and *raise*

These pairs of verbs cause confusion because both verbs in each pair have similar-sounding forms and somewhat related meanings. In each pair, one verb is **transitive**, meaning that it is followed by a **direct object** (*I lay the package on the counter*). The other is **intransitive**, meaning that it does not have an object (*He lies on the floor unable to move*). The best way to avoid confusing these verbs is to memorize their forms and meanings.

BASE FORM	PAST TENSE	PAST PARTICIPLE	PRESENT PARTICIPLE	-S FORM
lie (recline)	lay	lain	lying	lies
lay (put)	laid	laid	laying	lays
sit (be seated)	sat	sat	sitting	sits
set (put)	set	set	setting	sets
rise (get up)	rose	risen	rising	rises
raise (lift)	raised	raised	raising	raises

▶ The doctor asked the patient to ~~lay~~ *lie* on his side.

▶ She ~~sat~~ *set* the vase on the table.

▶ He ~~rose~~ *raised* himself to a sitting position.

7c Verb tenses

Tenses show when the verb's action takes place. The three **simple tenses** are the **present tense**, the **past tense**, and the **future tense**.

PRESENT TENSE	I *ask, write*
PAST TENSE	I *asked, wrote*
FUTURE TENSE	I *will ask, will write*

More complex aspects of time are expressed through **progressive**, **perfect**, and **perfect progressive** forms of the simple tenses.

PRESENT PROGRESSIVE	she *is asking, is writing*
PAST PROGRESSIVE	she *was asking, was writing*

FUTURE PROGRESSIVE	she *will be asking, will be writing*
PRESENT PERFECT	she *has asked, has written*
PAST PERFECT	she *had asked, had written*
FUTURE PERFECT	she *will have asked, will have written*
PRESENT PERFECT PROGRESSIVE	she *has been asking, has been writing*
PAST PERFECT PROGRESSIVE	she *had been asking, had been writing*
FUTURE PERFECT PROGRESSIVE	she *will have been asking, will have been writing*

The simple tenses locate an action only within the three basic time frames of present, past, and future. Progressive forms express continuing actions; perfect forms express completed actions; perfect progressive forms express actions that continue up to some point in the present, past, or future.

Using the present tense for special purposes. When writing about action in literary works, use the present tense.

▶ Ishmael slowly ~~realized~~ *realizes* all that ~~was~~ *is* at stake in the search for the white whale.

General truths or scientific facts should be in the present tense, even when the **predicate** in the **main clause** is in the past tense.

▶ Pasteur demonstrated that his boiling process ~~made~~ *makes* milk safe.

In general, when you are quoting, summarizing, or paraphrasing a work, use the present tense.

▶ Keith Walters ~~wrote~~ *writes* that the "reputed consequences and promised blessings of literacy are legion."

But when using APA (American Psychological Association) style, report the results of your experiments or another researcher's work in the past tense (*wrote, noted*) or the

present perfect (*has discovered*). (For more on APA style, see Chapter 43.)

▶ Comer (1995) ~~notes~~ ^{noted} that protesters who deprive themselves of food are seen not as dysfunctional but rather
as "caring, sacrificing, even heroic" (p. 5).

7d Verb tense sequence

Careful and accurate use of tenses is important for clear writing. When you use the appropriate tense for each action, readers can follow time changes easily.

▶ By the time he lent her the money, she ^{had} declared bankruptcy.

The revised sentence makes clear that the bankruptcy occurred before the loan.

7e Active and passive voice

Voice tells whether a **subject** is acting (*He questions us*) or being acted upon (*He is questioned*). When the subject is act-ing, the verb is in the **active voice**; when the subject is being acted upon, the verb is in the **passive voice**. Most contem-porary writers use the active voice as much as possible because it makes their prose stronger and livelier. To shift a sentence from passive to active voice, make the performer of the action the subject of the sentence.

▶ ^{My sister took the} ~~The~~ prizewinning photograph ~~was taken by my sister.~~

Use the passive voice when you want to emphasize the recip-ient of an action rather than the performer of the action.

▶ DALLAS, NOV. 22—President John Fitzgerald Kennedy was shot and killed by an assassin today.

—TOM WICKER, *New York Times*

In scientific and technical writing, use the passive voice to focus attention on what is being studied.

▶ The volunteers' food intake was closely monitored.

7f Mood

The **mood** of a verb indicates the writer's attitude toward what he or she is saying. The **indicative mood** states facts or opinions and asks questions: *I did the right thing.* The **imperative mood** gives commands and instructions: *Do the right thing.* The **subjunctive mood** (used primarily in **dependent clauses** beginning with *that* or *if*) expresses wishes and conditions that are contrary to fact: *If I were doing the right thing, I'd know it.*

The present subjunctive uses the base form of the verb with all subjects.

▶ It is important that children *be* psychologically ready for a new sibling.

The past subjunctive is the same as the simple past except for the verb *be,* which uses *were* for all subjects.

▶ He spent money as if he *had* infinite credit.

▶ If the store *were* better located, it would attract more customers.

Because the subjunctive creates a rather formal tone, many people today tend to substitute the indicative mood in informal conversation.

INFORMAL

▶ If the store *was* better located, it would attract more customers.

For academic or professional writing, use the subjunctive in the following contexts:

CLAUSES EXPRESSING A WISH

▶ He wished that his mother ~~was~~ *were* still living nearby.

THAT CLAUSES EXPRESSING A REQUEST OR DEMAND

▶ The plant inspector insists that a supervisor ~~is~~ *be* on site at all times.

IF CLAUSES EXPRESSING A CONDITION THAT DOES NOT EXIST

▶ If marijuana ~~was~~ *were* legalized, the federal government
could earn tax revenue from its sales.

One common error is to use *would* in both clauses. Use the
subjunctive in the *if* clause and *would* in the other clause.

▶ If I ~~would have~~ *had* played harder, I would have won.

---

8 Subject-Verb Agreement

In everyday terms, the word *agreement* refers to an accord
of some sort: you reach an agreement with your boss about
salary; friends agree to go to a movie; the members of a
family agree to share household chores. This meaning covers grammatical **agreement** as well. **Verbs** must agree with
their **subjects** in **number** (singular or plural) and in **person**
(first, second, or third).

To make a verb in the **present tense** agree with a third-
person singular subject, add *-s* or *-es* to the **base form**.

▶ A vegetarian diet *lowers* the risk of heart disease.

To make a verb in the present tense agree with any other
subject, use the base form of the verb.

▶ I *miss* my family.
▶ They *live* in another state.

Have and *be* do not follow the *-s* or *-es* pattern with third-
person singular subjects. *Have* changes to *has*; *be* has irregular forms in both the present tense and the **past tense**.

▶ War *is* hell.
▶ The soldier *was* brave beyond the call of duty.

---

bedfordstmartins.com/easywriter For exercises, go to **Exercise Central** and click on **Subject-Verb Agreement**.

8a   Words between subject and verb

The subject is sometimes separated from the verb by other words. Make sure the verb agrees with the **simple subject** and not with another **noun** that falls in between.

▸ Many books on the best-seller list ~~has~~ *have* little literary

value.

The simple subject is *books*, not *list*.

Be careful when you use *as well as, along with, in addition to, together with,* and similar phrases. They do not make a singular subject plural.

▸ A passenger, as well as the driver, ~~were~~ *was* injured in the

accident.

Though this sentence has a grammatically singular subject, it suggests a plural subject and would be clearer with a compound subject: *The driver and a passenger were injured in the accident.*

8b   Compound subjects

Compound subjects joined by *and* are generally plural.

▸ A backpack, a canteen, and a rifle ~~was~~ *were* issued to each

recruit.

✔ CHECKLIST

Editing for Subject-Verb Agreement

- Identify the subject that goes with each verb to check for agreement problems. (8a)
- Check compound subjects joined by *and, or,* and *nor.* (8b)
- Check collective-noun subjects to determine whether they refer to a group as a single unit or as multiple members. (8c)
- Check indefinite-pronoun subjects. Most take a plural verb. (8d)

When subjects joined by *and* are considered a single unit or refer to the same person or thing, they take a singular verb form.

▶ **The lead singer and chief songwriter** *wants* **to make the new songs available online.**

▶ **Drinking and driving** ~~remain~~ *remains* **a major cause of highway accidents and fatalities.**

In this sentence, *drinking and driving* is considered a single activity, and a singular verb is used.

With subjects joined by *or* or *nor,* the verb agrees with the part closer to the verb.

▶ **Neither my roommate nor my neighbors** *like* **my loud music.**

▶ **Either the witnesses or the defendant** *is* **lying.**

If you find this sentence awkward, put the plural noun closer to the verb: *Either the defendant or the witnesses* <u>are</u> *lying.*

8c Collective nouns as subjects

Collective nouns—such as *family, team, audience, group, jury, crowd, band, class,* and *committee*—and fractions can take either singular or plural verbs, depending on whether they refer to the group as a single unit or to the multiple members of the group. The meaning of a sentence as a whole is your guide.

▶ **After deliberating, the jury** *reports* **its verdict.**

The jury acts as a single unit.

▶ **The jury still** *disagree* **on a number of counts.**

The members of the jury act as multiple individuals.

▶ **Two-thirds of the park** ~~have~~ *has* **burned.**

    Two-thirds refers to the single portion of the park that burned.

▶ **One-third of the student body** ~~was~~ *were* **commuters.**

    One-third here refers to the students who commuted as individuals.

Treat phrases starting with *the number of* as singular and with *a number of* as plural.

SINGULAR	The number of applicants for the internship *was* unbelievable.
PLURAL	A number of applicants *were* put on the waiting list.

8d   Indefinite-pronoun subjects

Indefinite pronouns do not refer to specific persons or things. Most take singular verb forms.

SOME COMMON INDEFINITE PRONOUNS

another	each	much	one
any	either	neither	other
anybody	everybody	nobody	somebody
anyone	everyone	no one	someone
anything	everything	nothing	something

▶ **Of the two jobs, neither** *holds* **much appeal.**

▶ **Each of the plays** ~~depict~~ *depicts* **a hero undone by a tragic flaw.**

Both, few, many, others, and *several* are plural.

▶ **Though many** *apply,* **few** *are* **chosen.**

All, any, enough, more, most, none, and *some* can be singular or plural, depending on the noun they refer to.

▶ **All of the cake** *was* **eaten.**

▶ **All of the candidates** *promise* **to improve the schools.**

8e *Who, which,* and *that* as subjects

When the **relative pronouns** *who, which,* and *that* are used as subjects, the verb agrees with the **antecedent** of the pronoun (11b).

▶ Fear is an ingredient that *goes* into creating stereotypes.

▶ Guilt and fear are ingredients that *go* into creating

stereotypes.

Problems often occur with the words *one of the.* In general, *one of the* takes a plural verb, while *the only one of the* takes a singular verb.

▶ Carla is one of the employees who always ~~works~~ *work*

overtime.

Some employees always work overtime. Carla is among them. Thus *who* refers to *employees,* and the verb is plural.

▶ Ming is the only one of the employees who always ~~work~~ *works*

overtime.

Only one employee always works overtime, and that employee is Ming. Thus *one,* and not *employees,* is the antecedent of *who,* and the verb form must be singular.

8f Linking verbs and complements

A **linking verb** should agree with its subject, which usually precedes the verb, not with the **subject complement**, which follows it.

▶ These three key treaties ~~is~~ *are* the topic of my talk.

The subject is *treaties,* not *topic.*

▶ Nero Wolfe's passion ~~were~~ *was* orchids.

The subject is *passion,* not *orchids.*

8g Subjects with plural forms but singular meanings

Some words that end in -s seem to be plural but are singular in meaning and thus take singular verb forms.

▶ **Measles still ~~strike~~ many Americans.**
  ^{strikes} ∧

Some nouns of this kind (such as *statistics* and *politics*) may be either singular or plural, depending on context.

SINGULAR   Statistics *is* a course I really dread.

PLURAL   The statistics in that study *are* questionable.

8h Subjects that follow the verb

In English, verbs usually follow subjects. When this order is reversed, make the verb agree with the subject, not with a noun that happens to precede it.

▶ **Beside the barn ~~stands~~ silos filled with grain.**
  ^{stand} ∧

  The subject, *silos,* is plural, so the verb must be *stand.*

In sentences beginning with *there is* or *there are* (or *there was* or *there were*), *there* serves only as an introductory word; the subject follows the verb.

▶ **There *are* five basic positions in classical ballet.**

  The subject, *positions,* is plural, so the verb must also be plural.

8i Titles and words used as words

Titles and words used as words always take singular verb forms, even if their own forms are plural.

▶ *One Writer's Beginnings* ~~describe~~ Eudora Welty's childhood.
  ^{describes} ∧

▶ *Steroids* ~~are~~ a little word that packs a big punch in the world of sports.
  ^{is} ∧

8j Agreement with spoken forms of *be*

Conventions for subject-verb agreement with *be* in spoken or vernacular varieties of English may differ from those of academic English. For instance, an Appalachian speaker might say "I been down" rather than "I have been down"; a speaker of African American vernacular might say "He be at work" rather than "He is at work." You may want to quote such spoken phrases in your writing, but for most academic and professional writing, follow the conventions of academic English. (For information on using varieties of English appropriately, see Chapter 31.)

9 Adjectives and Adverbs

Adjectives and **adverbs** often add indispensable differences in meaning to the words they modify (describe). In basketball, for example, there is an important difference between a *flagrant* foul and a *technical* foul, a layup and a *reverse* layup, and an *angry* coach and an *abusively angry* coach. In each instance, the **modifiers** are crucial to accurate communication.

Adjectives modify **nouns** and **pronouns**; they answer the questions *which? how many?* and *what kind?* Adverbs modify **verbs**, adjectives, and other adverbs; they answer the questions *how? when? where?* and *to what extent?* Many adverbs are formed by adding *-ly* to adjectives (*slight, slightly*), but some are formed in other ways (*outdoors*) or have forms of their own (*very*).

9a Adjectives versus adverbs

When adjectives come after **linking verbs** (such as *is*), they usually describe the **subject**: *I am <u>patient</u>*. Note that

---

bedfordstmartins.com/easywriter For exercises, go to **Exercise Central** and click on **Adjectives and Adverbs**.

in specific sentences, some verbs may or may not be linking verbs—*appear, become, feel, grow, look, make, prove, seem, smell, sound,* and *taste,* for instance. When a word following one of these verbs modifies the subject, use an adjective; when it modifies the verb, use an adverb.

ADJECTIVE   Fluffy looked *angry*.

ADVERB   Fluffy looked *angrily* at the poodle.

Linking verbs suggest a state of being, not an action. In the preceding examples, *looked angry* suggests the state of being angry; *looked angrily* suggests an angry action.

In everyday conversation, you will often hear (and perhaps use) adjectives in place of adverbs. For example, people often say *go quick* instead of *go quickly*. When you write in academic and professional English, however, use adverbs to modify verbs, adjectives, and other adverbs.

▶ **You can feel the song's meter if you listen** ~~careful.~~ *carefully.*

▶ **The audience was** ~~real~~ *really* **disappointed by the show.**

Good, well, bad, **and** *badly.*   The modifiers *good, well, bad,* and *badly* cause problems for many writers because the distinctions between *good* and *well* and between *bad* and *badly* are often not observed in conversation. Problems also arise because *well* can function as either an adjective or an adverb.

▶ **I look** ~~well~~ *good* **in blue.**

▶ **Now that the fever has broken, I feel** ~~good~~ *well* **again.**

▶ **He plays the trumpet** ~~good.~~ *well.*

▶ **I feel** ~~badly~~ *bad* **for the Toronto fans.**

▶ **Their team played** ~~bad.~~ *badly.*

9b Comparatives and superlatives

Most adjectives and adverbs have three forms: **positive**, **comparative**, and **superlative**. You usually form the

> ## FOR MULTILINGUAL WRITERS
>
> **Using Adjectives with Plural Nouns**
>
> In Spanish, Russian, and many other languages, adjectives agree in number with the nouns they modify. In English, adjectives do not change number in this way: *the kittens are cute* (not *cutes*).

comparative and superlative of one- or two-syllable adjectives by adding *-er* and *-est*: *short, shorter, shortest*. With some two-syllable adjectives, longer adjectives, and most adverbs, use *more* and *most* (or *less* and *least*): *scientific, more scientific, most scientific; elegantly, more elegantly, most elegantly*. Some short adjectives and adverbs have irregular comparative and superlative forms: *good, better, best; badly, worse, worst*.

Comparatives versus superlatives.   In academic writing, use the comparative to compare two things; use the superlative to compare three or more things.

▶ Rome is a much *older* city than New York.

▶ Damascus is one of the ~~older~~ *oldest* cities in the world.

Double comparatives and superlatives.   Double comparatives and superlatives are those that unnecessarily use both the *-er* or *-est* ending and *more* or *most*. Occasionally, these forms can add a special emphasis, as in the title of Spike Lee's movie *Mo' Better Blues*. In academic and professional writing, however, do not use *more* or *most* before adjectives or adverbs ending in *-er* or *-est*.

▶ Paris is the ~~most~~ loveliest city in the world.

Absolute concepts.   Some adjectives and adverbs—such as *perfect, final,* and *unique*—are absolute concepts (a thing is perfect or it isn't), so it is illogical to form comparatives or superlatives of these words.

▶ Anne has ~~the most~~ *a* unique sense of humor.

10 Modifier Placement

To be effective, **modifiers** should clearly refer to the words they modify and be positioned close to those words. Consider this command:

  DO NOT USE THE ELEVATORS IN CASE OF FIRE.

Should we avoid the elevators altogether, or only in case there is a fire? Repositioning the modifier *in case of fire* eliminates such confusion—and makes clear that we are to avoid the elevators only if there is a fire: IN CASE OF FIRE, DO NOT USE THE ELEVATORS.

10a Misplaced modifiers

Modifiers can cause confusion or ambiguity if they are not close enough to the words they modify or if they seem to modify more than one word in the sentence.

▸ She teaches a seminar this term ~~on voodoo~~ at Skyline College. *on voodoo*

  The voodoo is not at the college; the seminar is.

▸ ~~Billowing from the window,~~ *He* saw clouds of smoke *billowing from the window.*

  People cannot billow from windows.

▸ *After he lost the 1962 race,* Nixon told reporters that he planned to get out of politics ~~after he lost the 1962 race.~~

  The unedited sentence implies that Nixon planned to lose the race.

Limiting modifiers. Be especially careful with the placement of limiting modifiers such as *almost, even, just, merely,* and *only.* In general, these modifiers should be placed right before or after the words they modify. Putting them in other

positions may produce not just ambiguity but a completely different meaning.

AMBIGUOUS   The court *only* hears civil cases on Tuesdays.

CLEAR   The court hears *only* civil cases on Tuesdays.

CLEAR   The court hears civil cases on Tuesdays *only*.

Squinting modifiers.   If a modifier can refer either to the word before it or to the word after it, it is a **squinting modifier**. Put the modifier where it clearly relates to only a single word.

SQUINTING   Students who practice writing *often* will benefit.

REVISED   Students who *often* practice writing will benefit.

REVISED   Students who practice writing will *often* benefit.

10b Disruptive modifiers

Disruptive modifiers interrupt the connections between parts of a sentence, making it hard for readers to follow the progress of the thought.

▶   *If they are cooked too long, vegetables will*
~~Vegetables will, if they are cooked too long,~~ lose most
of their nutritional value.

Split infinitives.   In general, do not place a modifier between the *to* and the **verb** of an **infinitive** (*to often complain*). Doing so makes it hard for readers to recognize that the two go together.

▶   Hitler expected the British to fairly quickly. *surrender*
   ~~surrender.~~

In some sentences, however, a modifier sounds awkward if it does not split the infinitive. Most language experts consider split infinitives acceptable in such cases. Another option is to reword the sentence to eliminate the infinitive altogether.

SPLIT   I hope *to* almost *equal* my last year's income.

REVISED   I hope that I will earn almost as much as I did last year.

10c Dangling modifiers

Dangling modifiers are words or **phrases** that modify nothing in the rest of a sentence. They often *seem* to modify something that is implied but not actually present in the sentence. Dangling modifiers frequently appear at the beginnings or ends of sentences.

DANGLING   Driving nonstop, Salishan Lodge is two hours from Portland.

REVISED   Driving nonstop from Portland, you can reach Salishan Lodge in two hours.

To revise a dangling modifier, often you need to add a **subject** that the modifier clearly refers to; sometimes you have to turn the modifier into a phrase or a **clause**.

▸ Reluctantly, the hound ~~was given~~ to a neighbor.
our family gave

In the original sentence, was the dog reluctant, or was someone else who is not mentioned reluctant?

▸ ~~As~~ a young boy, his grandmother told stories of her years as a migrant worker.
When he was

His grandmother was never a young boy.

▸ ~~Thumbing through the magazine, my~~ eyes automatically noticed the perfume ads.
My ... *as I was thumbing through the magazine.*

Eyes cannot thumb through a magazine.

11 Pronouns

As words that stand in for **nouns, pronouns** carry a lot of weight in everyday discourse. These directions show why it's important for a pronoun to refer clearly to a specific noun or pronoun **antecedent**:

When you see a dirt road on the left side of Winston Lane, follow it for two more miles.

The word *it* could mean either the dirt road or Winston Lane.

11a Pronoun case

Most speakers of English know intuitively when to use *I, me,* and *my.* The choices reflect differences in **case,** the form a pronoun takes to indicate its function in a sentence. Pronouns functioning as **subjects** or **subject complements** are in the **subjective case** (*I*); those functioning as **objects** are in the **objective case** (*me*); those functioning as possessives are in the **possessive case** (*my*).

SUBJECTIVE	OBJECTIVE	POSSESSIVE
I	me	my/mine
we	us	our/ours
you	you	your/yours
he/she/it	him/her/it	his/her/hers/its
they	them	their/theirs
who/whoever	whom/whomever	whose

Case problems tend to occur in the following situations.

In subject complements. Many Americans routinely use the objective case for subject complements, especially in conversation: *Who's there? It's me.* If the subjective case for a subject complement sounds stilted or awkward (*It's I*), try rewriting the sentence using the pronoun as the subject (*I'm here*).

▶ *She was the*
~~The~~ first person to see Kishore after the awards ~~was~~
    ^   ^
~~she.~~

Before gerunds. Pronouns before a **gerund** should be in the possessive case.

▶ The doctor argued for ~~him~~ *his* writing a living will.
                           ^

✅ CHECKLIST

Editing Pronouns

- Make sure all pronouns in subject complements are in the subjective case. (11a)
- Check for correct use of *who, whom, whoever,* and *whomever.* (11a)
- In compound structures, check that pronouns are in the same case they would be in if used alone. (11a)
- When a pronoun follows *than* or *as,* complete the sentence mentally to determine whether the pronoun should be in the subjective or objective case. (11a)
- Check that pronouns agree with indefinite-pronoun antecedents, and revise sexist pronouns. (11b)
- Identify the antecedent that a pronoun refers to. Supply one if none appears in the sentence. If more than one possible antecedent is present, revise the sentence. (11c)

With *who, whoever, whom,* and *whomever.* Today's speakers tend not to use *whom* and *whomever,* which can create a very formal tone. But for academic and professional writing in which some formality is appropriate, remember that problems distinguishing between *who* and *whom* occur most often in two situations: when they begin a question, and when they introduce a **dependent clause** (13c). You can determine whether to use *who* or *whom* at the beginning of a question by answering the question using a **personal pronoun**. If the answer is in the subjective case, use *who*; if it is in the objective case, use *whom.*

>   *Whom*
> ► ~~Who~~ did you visit?
>   ∧

I visited *them. Them* is objective, so *whom* is correct.

>   *Who*
> ► ~~Whom~~ do you think wrote the story?
>   ∧

I think *she* wrote the story. *She* is subjective, so *who* is correct.

The case of a pronoun in a dependent clause is determined by its function in the clause, no matter how that clause functions in the sentence. If the pronoun acts as a subject or subject complement in the clause, use *who* or *whoever.*

If the pronoun acts as an object in the clause, use *whom* or *whomever.*

▶ Anyone can hypnotize a person ~~whom~~ wants to be
       ^{who}
   hypnotized.

    The verb of the clause is *wants,* and its subject is *who.*

▶ ~~Whoever~~ the party suspected of disloyalty was exe-
   ^{Whomever}
   cuted.

    Whomever is the object of *suspected* in the clause *whomever the party suspected of disloyalty.*

In compound structures. When a pronoun is part of a compound subject, complement, or object, put it in the same case you would use if the pronoun were alone.

▶ When ~~him~~ and Zelda were first married, they lived in
        ^{he}
   New York.

▶ The boss invited ~~she~~ and her family to dinner.
                    ^{her}

▶ This morning saw yet another conflict between my
   sister and ~~I.~~
              ^{me.}

In elliptical constructions. Elliptical constructions are sentences in which some words are understood but left out. When an elliptical construction ends in a pronoun, put the pronoun in the case it would be in if the construction were complete.

▶ His sister has always been more athletic than *he* [is].

In some elliptical constructions, the case of the pronoun depends on the meaning intended.

▶ Willie likes Lily more than *she* [likes Lily].

    She is the subject of the omitted verb *likes.*

▶ Willie likes Lily more than [he likes] *her.*

    Her is the object of the omitted verb *likes.*

With *we* and *us* before a noun. If you are unsure about whether to use *we* or *us* before a noun, use whichever pronoun would be correct if the noun were omitted.

>   We
>   ~~Us~~ fans never give up hope.
>   ^

Without *fans, we* would be the subject.

>   us
>   The Rangers depend on ~~we~~ fans.
>   ^

Without *fans, us* would be the object of the preposition *on*.

11b Pronoun-antecedent agreement

The **antecedent** of a pronoun is the word the pronoun refers to. Pronouns and antecedents are said to agree when they match up in **person**, **number**, and **gender**.

SINGULAR   The *choirmaster* raised *his* baton.

PLURAL   The *boys* picked up *their* music.

Compound antecedents. When a compound antecedent is joined by *or* or *nor*, the pronoun agrees with the nearer or nearest antecedent. If the parts of the antecedent are of different genders or persons, however, this kind of sentence can be awkward and may need to be revised.

AWKWARD   Neither Annie nor Henry got *his* work done.

REVISED   Annie didn't get *her* work done, and neither did
           Henry.

When a compound antecedent contains both singular and plural parts, the sentence may sound awkward unless the plural part comes last.

>   Neither the newspaper nor the radio stations would
>
>   reveal *their* sources.

Collective-noun antecedents. A **collective noun** such as *herd, team,* or *audience* may refer to a group as a single unit. If so, use a singular pronoun.

▶ The *committee* presented *its* findings to the board.

When a collective noun refers to the members of the group as individuals, however, you should use a plural pronoun.

▶ The *herd* stamped *their* hooves and snorted nervously.

Indefinite-pronoun antecedents. Indefinite pronouns do not refer to specific persons or things. Most indefinite pronouns are always singular; a few are always plural. Some can be singular or plural depending on the context.

▶ *One* of the ballerinas lost *her* balance.

▶ *Many* in the audience jumped to *their* feet.

SINGULAR *Some* of the furniture was showing *its* age.

PLURAL *Some* of the farmers abandoned *their* land.

Sexist pronouns. Pronouns often refer to antecedents that may be either male or female. Writers used to use a masculine pronoun, known as the "generic *he*," to refer to such antecedents: *Everyone should know <u>his</u> legal rights.* However, such wording ignores or even excludes females—and thus should be revised: *Everyone should know <u>his</u> or <u>her</u> legal rights,* for example, or *People should know <u>their</u> legal rights.*

11c Clear pronoun reference

If a pronoun does not refer clearly to a specific antecedent, readers will have trouble making the connection between the two.

Ambiguous antecedents. When a pronoun can refer to more than one antecedent, revise the sentence to make the meaning clear.

▶ The car went over the bridge just before ~~it~~ ^the bridge^ fell into the water.

What fell into the water—the car or the bridge? The revision makes it clear that the pronoun *it* refers to the antecedent *the bridge.*

> Kerry told Ellen̶ ̶t̶h̶a̶t̶ ̶s̶h̶e̶ should be ready soon."
>   *"I*
>   ^ ^   ^

Reporting Kerry's words directly, in quotation marks, eliminates the ambiguity.

Vague use of *it, this, that,* and *which*.   The words *it,
this, that,* and *which* often function as a shortcut for referring
to something mentioned earlier. Like other pronouns, each
must refer to a specific antecedent.

> When the senators realized the bill would be
>
> defeated, they tried to postpone the vote but failed.
>
> *The entire effort*
> I̶t̶ was a fiasco.
> ^

> *and her sudden wealth*
> Nancy just found out that she won the lottery, ̶w̶h̶i̶c̶h̶
>   ^
> explains her resignation.

Indefinite use of *you, it,* and *they*.   In conversation, we
frequently use *you, it,* and *they* in an indefinite sense in such
expressions as *you never know* and *on television, they said.* In
academic and professional writing, however, use *you* only
to mean "you, the reader," and *they* or *it* only to refer to a
clear antecedent.

> *people*
> Commercials try to make ̶y̶o̶u̶ buy without thinking.
>   ^

> *The*
> ̶O̶n̶ ̶t̶h̶e̶ Weather Channel ̶i̶t̶ reported a powerful
> ^
> earthquake in China.

> *Many restaurants in France*
> I̶n̶ ̶F̶r̶a̶n̶c̶e̶,̶ ̶t̶h̶e̶y̶ allow dogs ̶i̶n̶ ̶m̶a̶n̶y̶ ̶r̶e̶s̶t̶a̶u̶r̶a̶n̶t̶s̶.̶
> ^   ^

Implied antecedents.   A pronoun may suggest a noun
antecedent that is implied but not present in the sentence.

> Detention centers routinely blocked efforts by
>   *detainees.*
> ̶d̶e̶t̶a̶i̶n̶e̶e̶s̶'̶ families and lawyers to locate ̶t̶h̶e̶m̶.̶
>   ^

12 Comma Splices and Fused Sentences

A **comma splice** results from placing only a comma between **independent clauses**—groups of words that can stand alone as a sentence. We often see comma splices in advertising, where they can give slogans a catchy rhythm.

▶ **It's not just a job, it's an adventure.**

—U.S. NAVY RECRUITING SLOGAN

Another common error is a **fused**, or **run-on**, **sentence**, which results from joining two independent clauses with no punctuation or connecting word between them. The Navy slogan as a fused sentence would be "It's not just a job it's an adventure."

In academic and professional English, using comma splices or fused sentences will almost always be identified as an error.

12a Separating the clauses into two sentences

The simplest way to revise comma splices or fused sentences is to separate them into two sentences.

COMMA SPLICE   My mother spends long hours every

spring tilling the soil and moving manure. T

this part of gardening is nauseating.

If the two clauses are very short, making them two sentences may sound abrupt and terse, so some other method of revision is probably preferable.

12b Linking the clauses with a comma and a coordinating conjunction

If the two clauses are closely related and equally important, join them with a comma and a **coordinating conjunction** (*and, but, or, nor, for, so,* or *yet*).

> bedfordstmartins.com/easywriter For exercises, go to **Exercise Central** and click on **Comma Splices and Fused Sentences**.

FUSED
SENTENCE

Interest rates fell people began borrowing more
money.

(inserted: comma and "so" after "fell")

12c Linking the clauses with a semicolon

If the ideas in the two clauses are closely related and you want to give them equal emphasis, link them with a semicolon.

COMMA SPLICE

This photograph is not at all realistic it uses dreamlike images to convey its message.

(inserted: semicolon after "realistic")

Be careful when you link clauses with a **conjunctive adverb** like *however* or *therefore* or with a **transition** like *in fact*. In such sentences, the two clauses must be separated by a semicolon or by a comma and a coordinating conjunction.

COMMA SPLICE

Many Third World countries have high birthrates therefore most of their citizens are young.

(inserted: semicolon after "birthrates"; comma after "therefore")

12d Rewriting the two clauses as one independent clause

Sometimes you can reduce two spliced or fused independent clauses to a single independent clause.

FOR MULTILINGUAL WRITERS

Judging Sentence Length

If you speak a language that tends to use long sentences—Arabic, Farsi, or Chinese, for instance—be careful not to join English sentences in a way that results in comma-splice errors. Note that in standard academic and professional English, a sentence should contain only one independent clause *unless* the clauses are joined by a comma and a coordinating conjunction or by a semicolon.

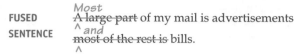
FUSED *Most*
SENTENCE ~~A large part~~ of my mail is advertisements
  ^ *and*
  ~~most of the rest is~~ bills.
  ^

12e Rewriting one independent clause as a dependent clause

When one independent clause is more important than the other, try converting the less important one to a **dependent clause** by adding an appropriate **subordinating conjunction**.

COMMA *Although*
SPLICE Zora Neale Hurston is regarded as one of
  ^ America's major novelists, she died in obscurity.

In the revision, the writer emphasizes the second clause and makes the first one into a dependent clause by adding the subordinating conjunction *although*.

FUSED *, which reacted against mass production,*
SENTENCE The arts and crafts movement called for hand-
  ^
  made objects.~~it reacted against mass production.~~
  ^

In the revision, the writer chooses to emphasize the first clause (the one describing what the movement advocated) and make the second clause into a dependent clause.

12f Linking the two clauses with a dash

In informal writing, you can use a dash to join the two clauses, especially when the second clause elaborates on the first clause.

COMMA Exercise trends come and go‚̄ this year yoga is hot.
SPLICE ^

13 Sentence Fragments

In advertisements, you will find **sentence fragments** in frequent use.

> *Taste or nutrition? Convenience or savings?* At Pop's, you don't have to choose. Get a healthy, mouth-watering breakfast for

less than you probably pay for a cup of coffee—24 hours a day. And we're right downtown, minutes from campus. *Ready when you are. Breakfast is served!*

As complete sentences, the information in the italicized fragments would be less informal and less memorable.

Sentence fragments are groups of words that are punctuated as sentences but lack some element necessary to an **independent clause**. Although you will often see and hear sentence fragments, you will seldom, if ever, want to use them in academic or professional writing, where many readers will regard them as errors.

13a   Phrase fragments

A **phrase** is a group of words that lacks a **subject**, a **verb**, or both. When a **verbal phrase**, a **prepositional phrase**, a **noun phrase**, or an **appositive phrase** is punctuated like a sentence, it becomes a fragment. To revise a phrase fragment, attach it to an independent clause, or make it a separate sentence.

▶ **NBC is broadcasting the debates. With discussions** *with*

 afterward.

> The second word group is a prepositional phrase, not a sentence. The editing combines the phrase with an independent clause.

▶ **The town's growth is controlled by zoning laws. A** *a*

 strict set of regulations for builders and corporations.

> *A strict set of regulations for builders and corporations* is an appositive phrase renaming the noun *zoning laws*. The editing attaches the fragment to the sentence containing that noun.

▶ **Kamika stayed out of school for three months after**
  She did so to
  Linda was born. ~~To~~ recuperate and to take care of her
  ^
  baby.

To recuperate and to take care of her baby includes verbals, not verbs. The revision—adding a subject (*she*) and a verb (*did*)—turns the fragment into a separate sentence.

Fragments beginning with transitions.   If you introduce an example or explanation with a transitional word or phrase like *also, for example, such as,* or *that,* be certain you write a sentence, not a fragment.

                                                      , such
▶ **Joan Didion has written on many subjects/~~Such~~ as the**
                                                       ^
  Hoover Dam and migraine headaches.

The second word group is a phrase, not a sentence. The editing combines it with an independent clause.

13b Compound-predicate fragments

A fragment occurs when one part of a **compound predicate** lacks a subject but is punctuated as a separate sentence. Such a fragment usually begins with *and, but,* or *or.* You can revise it by attaching it to the independent clause that contains the rest of the **predicate**.

                          and
▶ **They sold their house/~~And~~ moved into an apartment.**
                           ^

13c Clause fragments

A **dependent clause** contains both a subject and a verb, but it cannot stand alone as a sentence; it depends on an independent clause to complete its meaning. A dependent clause usually begins with a **subordinating conjunction**, such as *after, because, before, if, since, though, unless, until, when, where, while, who, which,* or *that.* You can usually combine dependent-clause fragments with a nearby independent clause.

▶ **When I decided to switch to part-time work/,I gave up**
                                              ^
  a lot of my earning potential.

If you cannot smoothly attach a clause to a nearby independent clause, try deleting the opening subordinating word and turning the dependent clause into a sentence.

▶ Most injuries in automobile accidents occur in two
　 　　　An
ways. ~~When an~~ occupant either is hurt by something
　 　　^
inside the car or is thrown from the car.

Sentence Style

Writing

Sentence
Grammar

Sentence
Style

Punctuation/
Mechanics

Language

Multilingual
Writers

Research

Documentation

14 Consistency and Completeness

If you listen carefully to the conversations around you, you will hear inconsistent and incomplete structures all the time. For instance, during an interview with journalist Bill Moyers, Jon Stewart discussed the supposed objectivity of news reporting:

> But news has never been objective. It's always . . . what does every newscast start with? "Our top stories tonight." That's a list. That's a subjective . . . some editor made a decision: "Here's our top stories. Number one: There's a fire in the Bronx."

Because Stewart is talking casually, some of his sentences begin one way but then move in another direction. The mixed structures pose no problem for the viewer, but sentences such as these can be confusing in writing.

14a Revising faulty sentence structure

Beginning a sentence with one grammatical pattern and then switching to another one confuses readers.

MIXED   The fact that I get up at 5:00 AM, a wake-up time that explains why I'm always tired in the evening.

The sentence starts out with a **subject** (*The fact*) followed by a **dependent clause** (*that I get up at 5:00 AM*). The sentence needs a **predicate** to complete the **independent clause**, but instead it moves to another **phrase** followed by a dependent clause (*a wake-up time that explains why I'm always tired in the evening*), and a **fragment** results.

REVISED   The fact that I get up at 5:00 AM explains why I'm always tired in the evening.

Deleting *a wake-up time that* changes the rest of the sentence into a predicate.

REVISED   I get up at 5:00 AM, a wake-up time that explains why I'm always tired in the evening.

Deleting *The fact that* turns the beginning of the sentence into an independent clause.

14b Matching subjects and predicates

Another kind of mixed structure, called faulty predication, occurs when a subject and predicate do not fit together grammatically or simply do not make sense together.

▶ A characteristic that I admire is ~~a person who is generous.~~ *generosity.*

A person is not a characteristic.

▶ The rules of the corporation ~~expect~~ employees ~~to~~ be on time. *require that*

Rules cannot expect anything.

Is when, is where, the reason . . . is because.   Although you will often hear these expressions in everyday use, such constructions are inappropriate in academic or professional writing.

▶ A stereotype is ~~when someone characterizes~~ a group~~unfairly.~~ *an unfair characterization of*

▶ Spamming is ~~where companies send~~ electronic junk mail. *the practice of sending*

▶ ~~The reason~~ I like to play soccer ~~is~~ because it provides aerobic exercise.

14c Consistent compound structures

Sometimes writers omit certain words in compound structures. If the omitted word does not fit grammatically with other parts of the compound, the omission can be inappropriate.

▶ His skills are weak, and his performance only average. *is*

The omitted verb *is* does not match the verb in the other part of the compound (*are*), so the writer needs to include it.

● bedfordstmartins.com/easywriter For exercises, go to **Exercise Central** and click on **Consistency and Completeness**.

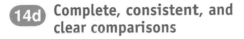
14d Complete, consistent, and clear comparisons

When you compare two or more things, the comparison must be complete and clear.

▶ I was embarrassed because my parents were so
  from my friends' parents.
  different,
              ∧

Adding *from my friends' parents* completes the comparison.

                                        the one by
▶ **Woodberry's biography is better than Fields.**
                                              ∧

The original sentence illogically compares a book with a person.

UNCLEAR	Aneil always felt more affection for his brother than his sister.
CLEAR	Aneil always felt more affection for his brother *than his sister did*.
CLEAR	Aneil always felt more affection for his brother *than he did for his sister*.

15 Coordination and Subordination

You may notice a difference between your spoken and your written language. In speech, people tend to use *and* and *so* as all-purpose connectors.

> He enjoys psychology, and he has to study hard.

The meaning of this sentence may be perfectly clear in speech, which provides clues with voice, facial expressions, and gestures. But in writing, the sentence could have more than one meaning.

> Although he enjoys psychology, he has to study hard.

> He enjoys psychology although he has to study hard.

⟹ bedfordstmartins.com/easywriter For exercises, go to **Exercise Central** and click on **Coordination and Subordination**.

The first sentence links two ideas with a **coordinating conjunction**, *and*; the other two sentences link ideas with a **subordinating conjunction**, *although*. A coordinating conjunction gives the ideas equal emphasis, and a subordinating conjunction emphasizes one idea more than another.

15a Relating equal ideas

When you want to give equal emphasis to different ideas in a sentence, link them with a coordinating conjunction (*and, but, for, nor, or, so, yet*) or a semicolon.

▶ **They acquired horses, *and* their ancient nomadic spirit was suddenly free of the ground.**

▶ **There is perfect freedom in the mountains, *but* it belongs to the eagle and the elk, the badger and the bear.** —N. SCOTT MOMADAY, *The Way to Rainy Mountain*

Coordination can help make explicit the relationship between two separate ideas.

▶ **My son watches *The Simpsons* religiously. ~~Forced~~** *forced* **to choose, he would probably take Homer Simpson over his sister.**

Connecting these two sentences with a semicolon strengthens the connection between two closely related ideas.

When you connect ideas in a sentence, make sure that the relationship between the ideas is clear.

▶ **Watching television is a common way to spend leisure time, ~~and~~** *but* **it makes viewers apathetic.**

What does being a common form of leisure have to do with making viewers apathetic? Changing *and* to *but* better relates the two ideas.

15b Distinguishing main ideas

Subordination allows you to distinguish major points from minor points or to bring in supporting details. If, for

instance, you put your main idea in an **independent clause**, you might then put any less significant ideas in **dependent clauses**, **phrases**, or even single words. The following sentence shows the subordinated point in italics:

▶ **Mrs. Viola Cullinan was a plump woman** *who lived in a three-bedroom house somewhere behind the post office.*

—MAYA ANGELOU, "My Name Is Margaret"

The dependent clause adds important information about Mrs. Cullinan, but it is subordinate to the independent clause.

Notice that the choice of what to subordinate rests with the writer and depends on the intended meaning. Angelou might have given the same basic information differently.

▶ **Mrs. Viola Cullinan,** *a plump woman,* **lived in a three-bedroom house somewhere behind the post office.**

Subordinating the information about Mrs. Cullinan's size to that about her house would suggest a slightly different meaning, of course. As a writer, you must think carefully about what you want to emphasize and must subordinate information accordingly.

Subordination also establishes logical relationships among ideas. These relationships are often specified by subordinating conjunctions.

SOME COMMON SUBORDINATING CONJUNCTIONS

after	if	though
although	in order that	unless
as	once	until
as if	since	when
because	so that	where
before	than	while
even though	that	

The following sentence is shown with the subordinate clause italicized and the subordinating word underlined.

▶ **She usually rested her smile until late afternoon** <u>*when*</u> *her women friends dropped in and Miss Glory, the cook, served them cold drinks on the closed-in porch.*

—MAYA ANGELOU, "My Name Is Margaret"

Using too many coordinate structures can be monotonous and can make it hard for readers to recognize the most important ideas. Subordinating lesser ideas can help high-light the main ideas.

▶ **Many people come home tired in the evening, so they**
  Though they
  turn on the TV to relax. ~~They~~ may intend to watch just
       ^
  the news, ~~but then~~ a game show comes on next,
  which   *Eventually,*
  ~~and~~ they decide to watch ~~it~~ for just a short while, ~~and~~
  ^   ^
  they get too comfortable to get up, and they end up

  spending the whole evening in front of the TV.

The editing uses subordination to make clear to the reader that some of the ideas are more important than others.

Determining what to subordinate

  Although our
▶ **~~Our~~ new boss can be difficult, ~~although~~ she has**
  ^
  revived and maybe even saved the division.

The editing puts the more important information—that the new boss has saved part of the company—in an indepen-dent clause and subordinates the rest.

Avoiding excessive subordination

When too many subordinate clauses are strung together, readers may have trouble keeping track of the main idea expressed in the independent clause.

TOO MUCH SUBORDINATION

▶ **Philip II sent the Spanish Armada to conquer England,**
  which was ruled by Elizabeth, who had executed Mary
  because she was plotting to overthrow Elizabeth,
  who was a Protestant, whereas Mary and Philip were
  Roman Catholics.

REVISED

▶ **Philip II sent the Spanish Armada to conquer England,**
  which was ruled by Elizabeth, a Protestant. She had

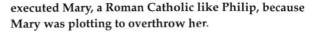

executed Mary, a Roman Catholic like Philip, because
Mary was plotting to overthrow her.

Putting the facts about Elizabeth executing Mary into an independent clause makes key information easier to recognize.

16 Conciseness

You can see the importance of concise writing in directions, particularly those on medicines. Consider the following directions found on one common prescription drug:

> Take one tablet daily. Some nonprescription drugs may aggravate your condition, so read all labels carefully. If any include a warning, check with your doctor.

Squeezing words onto a three-inch label is probably not your ordinary writing situation, but more often than not, you will want to write as concisely as you can.

16a Eliminating redundant words

Sometimes writers add words for emphasis, saying that something is large *in size* or red *in color* or that two ingredients should be combined *together*. The italicized words are redundant (unnecessary for meaning), as are the deleted words in the following examples.

▶ ~~Compulsory~~ $\overset{A}{\underset{\wedge}{}}$attendance at assemblies is required.

▶ The auction featured ~~contemporary~~ "antiques" made recently.

▶ Many different forms of hazing occur, such as physical ~~abuse~~ and mental abuse.

bedfordstmartins.com/easywriter For exercises, go to **Exercise Central** and click on **Conciseness**.

16b Eliminating empty words

Words that contribute little or no meaning to a sentence include vague **nouns** like *area, kind, situation,* and *thing* as well as vague **modifiers** like *definitely, major, really,* and *very.* Delete such words, or find a more specific way to say what you mean.

▸ ~~The~~ <u>H</u>ousing ~~situation~~ can have a really significant ^ ^ ^ *strongly influence*
~~impact on the social aspect of~~ a student's life. *social* ^

16c Replacing wordy phrases

Many common **phrases** can be reduced to a word or two with no loss in meaning.

WORDY	CONCISE
at all times	always
at that point in time	then
at the present time	now/today
due to the fact that	because
for the purpose of	for
in order to	to
in spite of the fact that	although
in the event that	if

16d Simplifying sentence structure

Using the simplest grammatical structures can tighten and strengthen your sentences considerably.

▸ Hurricane Katrina, ~~which was certainly~~ one of the

most powerful storms ever to hit the Gulf Coast,

caused damage ~~to a very wide area.~~ *widespread*
^ ^

Using strong verbs. *Be* **verbs** (*is, are, was, were, been*) often result in wordiness.

▸ A high-fat, high-cholesterol diet ~~is bad for~~ your heart. *harms* ^

Avoiding expletives. Sometimes **expletive** constructions such as *there is, there are,* and *it is* introduce a topic

effectively; often, however, your writing will be better without them.

▶ ~~There are~~ many people ~~who~~ fear success because they
    ^M
believe they do not deserve it.

▶ ~~It is necessary for~~ presidential candidates ^to perform
                         ^P   need
well on television.

Using active voice. Some writing situations call for the passive **voice**, but it is always wordier than the active—and often makes for dull or even difficult reading (7e).

▶ ~~In Gower's research, it was~~ found that pythons often
    ^Gower
dwell in trees.

17 Parallelism

If you look and listen, you will see parallel grammatical structures in everyday use. Bumper stickers often use parallelism to make their messages memorable (*Don't follow me; I'm lost too*), as do song lyrics and jump-rope rhymes. In addition to creating pleasing rhythmic effects, parallelism helps clarify meaning.

17a Items in a series or list

All items in a series should be in parallel form—all **nouns**, all **verbs**, all **prepositional phrases**, and so on. Parallelism makes a series both graceful and easy to follow.

▶ In the eighteenth century, armed forces could fight *in open fields* and *on the high seas.* Today, they can clash *on the ground anywhere, on the sea, under the sea,* and *in the air.*

—DONALD SNOW AND EUGENE BROWN, *The Contours of Power*

bedfordstmartins.com/easywriter For exercises, go to **Exercise Central** and click on **Parallelism**.

The parallel structure of the phrases, and of the sentences themselves, highlights the contrast between the eighteenth century and today.

▶ The quarter horse skipped, pranced, and ~~was sashaying~~ *sashayed* onto the track.

▶ The children ran down the hill, skipped over the lawn, and *jumped* into the swimming pool.

▶ The duties of the job include babysitting, housecleaning, and ~~preparation of~~ *preparing* meals.

Items in a list, in a formal outline, and in headings should be parallel.

▶ Kitchen rules: (1) Coffee to be made only by library staff. (2) Coffee service to be closed at 4:00 PM. (3) Doughnuts to be kept in cabinet. (4) ~~No faculty members should handle coffee materials.~~ *Coffee materials not to be handled by faculty.*

17b Paired ideas

Parallel structures can help you pair two ideas effectively. The more nearly parallel the two structures are, the stronger the connection between the ideas will be.

▶ I type in one place, but I write all over the house.

—TONI MORRISON

▶ Writers are often more interesting on the page than they are in ~~person.~~ *the flesh.*

In these examples, the parallel structures help readers see an important contrast between two ideas or acts.

With conjunctions. When you link ideas with *and, but, or, nor, for, so,* or *yet,* try to make the ideas parallel in structure. Always use the same structure after both parts of a **correlative conjunction**: *either . . . or, both . . . and,*

neither . . . nor, not . . . but, not only . . . but also, just as . . . so, and *whether . . . or.*

▸ Consult a friend ^who is^ in your class or who is good at math.

▸ The wise politician promises the possible and ^accepts^ ~~should accept~~ the inevitable.

▸ I wanted not only to go away to school but also to ^live in^ New England.

17c Words necessary for clarity

In addition to making parallel elements grammatically similar, be sure to include any words—**prepositions**, **articles**, verb forms, and so on—that are necessary for clarity.

▸ We'll move to a city in the Southwest or ^in^ Mexico.

   To a city in Mexico or to Mexico in general? The editing clarifies the meaning.

18 Shifts

A shift in writing is an abrupt change of some sort that results in inconsistency. Sometimes a writer will shift deliberately, as Dave Barry does in noting he "would have to say that the greatest single achievement of the American medical establishment is nasal spray." Barry's shift in tone from the serious (the American medical establishment) to the banal (nasal spray) makes us laugh, as Barry wishes us to. Unintentional shifts, however, can be jolting and confusing to readers.

18a Shifts in tense

If the **verbs** in a passage refer to actions occurring at different times, they may require different **tenses**. Be careful, however, not to change tenses without a good reason.

▸ A few countries produce almost all of the world's

   illegal drugs, but addiction ~~affected~~ *affects* many countries.
                                  ^

18b Shifts in voice

Do not shift between the **active voice** (she *sold* it) and the **passive voice** (it *was sold*) without a reason. Sometimes a shift in voice is justified, but often it only confuses readers.

▸ Two youths approached ~~me, and I was~~ asked for my
                                     me

   wallet.

The original sentence shifts from active to passive voice, so it is unclear who asked for the wallet.

18c Shifts in point of view

Unnecessary shifts in point of view between first **person** (*I* or *we*), second person (*you*), and third person (*he, she, it, one,* or *they*), or between **singular** and **plural subjects** can be very confusing to readers.

▸ ~~One~~ *You* can do well on this job if you budget your time.
   ^

Is the writer making a general statement or giving advice to someone? Revising the shift eliminates this confusion.

▸ Nurses receive much less pay than doctors, even
                   nurses have

   though ~~a nurse has~~ the primary responsibility for daily
               ^

   patient care.

The writer had no reason to shift from plural to singular.

18d Shifts between direct and indirect discourse

When you quote someone's exact words, you are using **direct discourse**: *She said, "I'm an editor."* When you report

---

⬤ bedfordstmartins.com/easywriter For exercises, go to **Exercise Central** and click on **Shifts**.

what someone says without repeating the exact words, you are using **indirect discourse**: *She said she was an editor.* Shifting between direct and indirect discourse in the same sentence can cause problems, especially with questions.

▹ Bob asked what ~~could~~ he do ~~to help?~~
    he

The editing eliminates an awkward shift by reporting Bob's question indirectly. It could also be edited to quote Bob directly: *Bob asked, "What can I do to help?"*

18e Shifts in tone and diction

Watch out for shifts in your **tone** (overall attitude toward a topic or audience) and **diction** (choice of words). These shifts can confuse readers and leave them wondering what your real attitude is.

INCONSISTENT TONE

The question of child care forces a society to make profound decisions about its values. If some conservatives had their way, June Cleaver would still be in the kitchen baking cookies for Wally and the Beaver and waiting for Ward to bring home the bacon, but with only one income, the Cleavers would be lucky to afford hot dogs.

REVISED

The question of child care forces a society to make profound decisions about its values. Some conservatives believe that women with young children should not work outside the home, but many mothers are forced to do so for financial reasons.

The shift in diction from formal to informal makes readers wonder whether the writer is presenting a serious analysis or a humorous satire. As revised, the passage makes more sense because the words are consistently formal.

Punctuation/
Mechanics

Writing

Sentence
Grammar

Sentence
Style

Punctuation/
Mechanics

Language

Multilingual
Writers

Research

Documentation

19 Commas

It's hard to go through a day without encountering directions of some kind, and commas often play a crucial role in how you interpret instructions. See how important the comma is in the following directions for making hot cereal:

> Add Cream of Wheat slowly, stirring constantly.

That sentence tells the cook to *add the cereal slowly.* If the comma came before the word *slowly,* however, the cook might add all of the cereal at once and *stir slowly.*

19a Setting off introductory elements

In general, use a comma after any word, **phrase**, or **clause** that precedes the **subject** of the sentence.

▶ In Fitzgerald's novel‸the color green takes on great symbolic qualities.

▶ Sporting a pair of specially made running shoes‸Julie prepared for the race.

▶ To win the game‸Connor needed skill and luck.

▶ Pen poised in anticipation‸Maya waited for the test to begin.

▶ Since my mind was not getting enough stimulation‸ I decided to read some good literature.

Some writers omit the comma after a short introductory element that does not seem to require a pause after it. However, you will never be wrong if you use a comma.

---

bedfordstmartins.com/easywriter For exercises, go to **Exercise Central** and click on **Commas**.

19b Separating clauses in compound sentences

A comma usually precedes a **coordinating conjunction** (*and, but, or, nor, for, so,* or *yet*) that joins two **independent clauses** in a **compound sentence**.

▶ **The climbers must reach the summit today, or they will have to turn back.**

With very short clauses, you can sometimes omit the comma (*she saw her chance and she took it*). But always use the comma if there is a chance the sentence will be misread without it.

✔ CHECKLIST

Editing for Commas

Research for this book shows that five of the most common errors in college writing involve commas.

- Check that a comma separates an introductory word, phrase, or clause from the main part of the sentence. (19a)

- Look at every sentence that contains a coordinating conjunction (*and, but, for, nor, or, so,* or *yet*). If the groups of words before and after this conjunction both function as complete sentences, use a comma before the conjunction. (19b)

- Look at each adjective clause beginning with *which, who, whom, whose, when,* or *where* and at each phrase and appositive. If the rest of the sentence would have a different meaning without the clause, phrase, or appositive, do not set off the element with commas. (19c)

- Make sure that adjective clauses beginning with *that* are not set off with commas. Do not use commas between subjects and verbs, verbs and objects or complements, or prepositions and objects; to separate parts of compound constructions other than compound sentences; to set off restrictive clauses; or before the first or after the last item in a series. (19i)

- Do not use a comma alone to separate sentences. (See Chapter 12.)

▶ **I opened the junk drawer, and the cabinet door
jammed.**
 ∧

Use a semicolon rather than a comma when the clauses are
long and complex or contain their own commas.

▶ **When these early migrations took place, the ice was
still confined to the lands in the far north; but eight
hundred thousand years ago, when man was already
established in the temperate latitudes, the ice moved
southward until it covered large parts of Europe and
Asia.** —Robert Jastrow, *Until the Sun Dies*

19c Setting off nonrestrictive elements

Nonrestrictive elements are clauses, phrases, and words
that do not limit, or restrict, the meaning of the words they
modify. Since such elements are not essential to the meaning of a sentence, they should be set off from the rest of the
sentence with commas. **Restrictive elements**, however, *do*
limit meaning; they should *not* be set off with commas.

RESTRICTIVE   Drivers *who have been convicted of drunken
               driving* should lose their licenses.

In the preceding sentence, the clause *who have been convicted
of drunken driving* is essential to the meaning because it limits the word it modifies, *Drivers*, to only those drivers who
have been convicted of drunken driving. Therefore, it is *not*
set off with commas.

NONRESTRICTIVE   The two drivers involved in the accident,
                  who have been convicted of drunken driving,
                  should lose their licenses.

In this sentence, however, the clause *who have been convicted
of drunken driving* is not essential to the meaning because it
does not limit what it modifies, *The two drivers involved in the
accident*, but merely provides additional information about
these drivers. Therefore, the clause *is* set off with commas.

To decide whether an element is restrictive or nonrestrictive, mentally delete the element, and see if the deletion

changes the meaning of the rest of the sentence or makes it unclear. If the deletion *does* change the meaning, you should probably not set the element off with commas. If it *does not* change the meaning, the element probably requires commas.

Adjective and adverb clauses. An **adjective clause** that begins with *that* is always restrictive; do not set it off with commas. An adjective clause beginning with *which* may be either restrictive or nonrestrictive; however, some writers prefer to use *which* only for nonrestrictive clauses, which they set off with commas. An **adverb clause** that follows a main clause does *not* usually require a comma to set it off unless the adverb clause expresses contrast.

NONRESTRICTIVE CLAUSES

▶ **I borrowed books from the rental library of Shake-speare and Company,** *which was the library and book-store of Sylvia Beach at 12 rue de l'Odeon.*

—ERNEST HEMINGWAY, *A Moveable Feast*

The adjective clause is not necessary to the meaning of the independent clause and therefore is set off with a comma.

▶ **The park became a popular gathering place,** **although nearby residents complained about the noise.**

The adverb clause expresses contrast; therefore, it is set off with a comma.

RESTRICTIVE CLAUSES

▶ **The claim** *that men like seriously to battle one another to some sort of finish* **is a myth.**

—JOHN MCMURTRY, "Kill 'Em! Crush 'Em! Eat 'Em Raw!"

The adjective clause is necessary to the meaning because it explains which claim is a myth; therefore, the clause is not set off with commas.

▶ **The man/who rescued Jana's puppy/won her eternal gratitude.**

The adjective clause is necessary to the meaning because it identifies the man, so it takes no commas.

Phrases. **Participial phrases** may be restrictive or nonrestrictive. **Prepositional phrases** are usually restrictive, but sometimes they are not essential to the meaning of a sentence and thus are set off with commas.

NONRESTRICTIVE PHRASES

▶ **The bus drivers, rejecting the management offer, remained on strike.**

Using commas around the participial phrase makes it nonrestrictive, telling us that all of the drivers remained on strike.

RESTRICTIVE PHRASES

▶ **The bus drivers/rejecting the management offer/ remained on strike.**

If the phrase *rejecting the management offer* limits the meaning of *The bus drivers*, the commas should be deleted. The revised sentence says that only some of the bus drivers, the ones who rejected the offer, remained on strike, implying that the other drivers went back to work.

Appositives. An **appositive** is a **noun** or **noun phrase** that renames a nearby noun. When an appositive is not essential to identify what it renames, it is set off with commas.

NONRESTRICTIVE APPOSITIVES

▶ **Savion Glover, the award-winning dancer, taps like poetry in motion.**

Savion Glover's name identifies him; the appositive *the award-winning dancer* provides extra information.

RESTRICTIVE APPOSITIVES

▶ **Mozart's opera/*The Marriage of Figaro*/was considered revolutionary.**

The phrase *The Marriage of Figaro* is essential to the meaning of the sentence because Mozart wrote more than one opera. Therefore, it is *not* set off with commas.

19d Separating items in a series

▶ **He has plundered our seas, ravaged our coasts, burnt our towns, and destroyed the lives of our people.**

—Declaration of Independence

You may see a series with no comma after the next-to-last item, particularly in newspaper writing. Occasionally, however, omitting the comma can cause confusion.

▶ **All the cafeteria's vegetables—broccoli, green beans, peas, and carrots—were cooked to a gray mush.**

Without the comma after *peas,* you wouldn't know if there were three choices (the third being a *mixture* of peas and carrots) or four.

Coordinate adjectives, those that relate equally to the noun they modify, should be separated by commas.

▶ **The long, twisting, muddy road led to a shack in the woods.**

In a sentence like *The cracked bathroom mirror reflected his face,* however, *cracked* and *bathroom* are not coordinate because *bathroom mirror* is the equivalent of a single word, which is modified by *cracked.* Hence they are *not* separated by commas.

You can usually determine whether adjectives are coordinate by inserting *and* between them. If the sentence makes sense with the *and,* the adjectives are coordinate and should be separated by commas.

▶ **They are sincere *and* talented *and* inquisitive researchers.**

The sentence makes sense with the *and*s, so the adjectives should be separated by commas: *They are sincere, talented, inquisitive researchers.*

▶ **Byron carried an elegant *and* pocket watch.**

The sentence does not make sense with *and,* so the adjectives *elegant* and *pocket* should not be separated by commas: *Byron carried an elegant pocket watch.*

19e Setting off parenthetical and transitional expressions

Parenthetical expressions add comments or information. Because they often interrupt the flow of a sentence, they are usually set off with commas.

▶ **Some studies, incidentally, have shown that chocolate, of all things, helps prevent tooth decay.**

Transitions (such as *as a result*), **conjunctive adverbs** (such as *however*), and other expressions used to connect parts of sentences are usually set off with commas.

▶ **Ozone is a by-product of dry cleaning, for example.**

19f Setting off contrasting elements, interjections, direct address, and tag questions

▶ **I asked you, *not your brother,* to sweep the porch.**
▶ *Holy cow,* **did you see that?**
▶ **Remember, *sir,* that you are under oath.**
▶ **The governor did not veto the bill, *did she*?**

19g Setting off parts of dates and addresses

Dates. Use a comma between the day of the week and the month, between the day of the month and the year, and between the year and the rest of the sentence, if any.

▶ **On Wednesday, November 26, 2008, gunmen arrived in Mumbai by boat.**

Do not use commas with dates in inverted order or with dates consisting of only the month and the year.

▶ **She dated the letter *5 August 2008.***
▶ **Thousands of Germans swarmed over the wall in *November 1989.***

Addresses and place names.   Use a comma after each part of an address or a place name, including the state if there is no ZIP code. Do not precede a ZIP code with a comma.

▸ **Forward my mail to the Department of English, The Ohio State University, Columbus, Ohio 43210.**

▸ **Portland, Oregon, is much larger than Portland, Maine.**

19h Setting off quotations

Commas set off a quotation from words used to introduce or identify the source of the quotation. A comma following a quotation goes *inside* the closing quotation mark.

▸ **A German proverb warns, "Go to law for a sheep, and lose your cow."**

▸ **"All I know about grammar," said Joan Didion, "is its infinite power."**

Do not use a comma after a question mark or an exclamation point.

▸ **"Out, damned spot!/" cries Lady Macbeth.**

Do not use a comma to introduce a quotation with *that* or when you do not quote a speaker's exact words.

▸ **The writer of Ecclesiastes concludes that/ "all is vanity."**

▸ **Patrick Henry declared/ that he wanted either liberty or death.**

19i Unnecessary commas

Excessive use of commas can spoil an otherwise fine sentence.

Around restrictive elements.   Do not use commas to set off restrictive elements—elements that limit, or define, the meaning of the words they modify or refer to (19c).

▶ I don't let my children watch TV shows/that are violent.

▶ The actor/Russell Crowe/might win the award.

Between subjects and verbs, verbs and objects or complements, and prepositions and objects. Do not use a comma between a subject and its **verb**, a verb and its **object** or **complement**, or a **preposition** and its object.

▶ Watching movies late at night/allows me to relax.

▶ Parents must decide/how much TV their children may watch.

▶ The winner of/the trophy for community service stepped forward.

In compound constructions. In compound constructions other than compound sentences, do not use a comma before or after a coordinating conjunction that joins the two parts (19b).

▶ Improved health care/and more free trade were two of the administration's goals.

The *and* joins parts of a compound subject, which should not be separated by a comma.

▶ Mark Twain trained as a printer/and worked as a steamboat pilot.

The *and* joins parts of a compound predicate, which should not be separated by a comma.

In a series. Do not use a comma before the first or after the last item in a series.

▶ The auction included/furniture, paintings, and china.

▶ The swimmer took slow, elegant, powerful/strokes.

20 Semicolons

The following public-service announcement, posted in New York City subway cars, reminded commuters what to do with a used newspaper at the end of the ride:

> Please put it in a trash can; that's good news for everyone.

The semicolon in the subway announcement separates two clauses that could have been written as separate sentences. Semicolons, which create a pause stronger than that of a comma but not as strong as the full pause of a period, show close connections between related ideas.

20a Linking independent clauses

Though a comma and a **coordinating conjunction** often join **independent clauses** (19b), semicolons provide writers with subtler ways of signaling closely related clauses. The clause following a semicolon often restates an idea expressed in the first clause; it sometimes expands on or presents a contrast to the first.

▶ **Immigration acts were passed; newcomers had to prove, besides moral correctness and financial solvency, their ability to read.**

> —MARY GORDON, "More Than Just a Shrine"

Gordon uses a semicolon to join the two clauses, giving the sentence an abrupt rhythm that suits the topic: laws that imposed strict requirements.

If two independent clauses joined by a coordinating conjunction contain commas, you may use a semicolon instead of a comma before the conjunction to make the sentence easier to read.

▶ **Every year, whether the Republican or the Democratic party is in office, more and more power drains away**

⊙ bedfordstmartins.com/easywriter For exercises, go to **Exercise Central** and click on **Semicolons**.

from the individual to feed vast reservoirs in far-off
places; and we have less and less say about the shape
of events which shape our future.

—WILLIAM F. BUCKLEY JR., "Why Don't We Complain?"

20b Linking independent clauses joined by conjunctive adverbs or transitions

A semicolon—not a comma—should link independent
clauses joined by a **conjunctive adverb** such as *however*
or *therefore* or a **transition** such as *as a result* or *for example*.
Using a comma in this construction creates a **comma splice**
(see Chapter 12).

▶ **The circus comes as close to being the world in micro-
cosm as anything I know; in a way, it puts all the rest of
show business in the shade.**

—E. B. WHITE, "The Ring of Time"

▶ **Every kid should have access to a computer/; further-
more, access to the Internet should be free.**

20c Separating items in a series containing other punctuation

Ordinarily, commas separate items in a series (19d). But
when the items themselves contain commas or other punctuation, semicolons make the sentence clearer.

▶ **Anthropology encompasses archaeology, the study of
ancient civilizations through artifacts/; linguistics, the
study of the structure and development of language/;
and cultural anthropology, the study of language, cus-
toms, and behavior.**

20d Misused semicolons

Use a comma, not a semicolon, to separate an independent
clause from a **dependent clause** or **phrase**.

▸ The police found fingerprints, which they used to identify the thief.

▸ The new system would encourage students to register for courses online, thus streamlining registration.

Use a colon, not a semicolon, to introduce a series or list.

▸ The reunion tour includes the following bands: Urban Waste, Murphy's Law, Rapid Deployment, and Ism.

21 End Punctuation

Periods, question marks, and exclamation points often appear in advertising to create special effects:

> You have a choice to make.
> Where can you turn for advice?
> Ask our experts today!

End punctuation tells us how to read each sentence—as a matter-of-fact statement, a question for the reader, or an enthusiastic exclamation.

21a Periods

Use a period to close sentences that make statements or give mild commands.

▸ **All books are either dreams or swords.**   —AMY LOWELL

▸ **Don't use a fancy word if a simpler word will do.**

> —GEORGE ORWELL, "Politics and the English Language"

A period also closes **indirect questions**, which report rather than ask questions.

▸ **I asked how old the child was.**

🔗 bedfordstmartins.com/easywriter For exercises, go to **Exercise Central** and click on **End Punctuation**.

In American English, periods are used with most abbreviations. However, more and more abbreviations are appearing without periods.

Mr.	MD	BCE *or* B.C.E.
Ms.	PhD	AD *or* A.D.
Sen.	Jr.	PM *or* p.m.

Some abbreviations rarely if ever appear with periods. These include the postal abbreviations of state names, such as *FL* and *TN*, and most groups of initials (*GE, CIA, AIDS, YMCA, UNICEF*). If you are not sure whether a particular abbreviation should include periods, check a dictionary or follow the style guidelines you are using for a research paper. (For more about abbreviations, see Chapter 26.)

Do not use an additional period when a sentence ends with an abbreviation that has its own period.

▶ **The social worker referred me to John Pintz Jr./**

21b Question marks

Use question marks to close sentences that ask direct questions.

▶ **How is the human mind like a computer, and how is it different?**
> —Kathleen Stassen Berger and Ross A. Thompson,
> *The Developing Person through Childhood and Adolescence*

Question marks do not close indirect questions, which report rather than ask questions.

▶ **She asked whether I opposed his nomination?.**

21c Exclamation points

Use an exclamation point to show surprise or strong emotion. Use these marks sparingly because they can distract your readers or suggest that you are exaggerating.

▶ **In those few moments of geologic time will be the story of all that has happened since we became a nation. And what a story it will be!**

—JAMES RETTIE, "But a Watch in the Night"

▶ **This university is so large, so varied, that attempting to tell someone everything about it would take three years!**
                                                                    ^

22 Apostrophes

The little apostrophe can make a big difference in meaning. The following sign at a neighborhood swimming pool, for instance, says something different from what the writer probably intended:

> Please deposit your garbage (and your guests) in the trash receptacles before leaving the pool area.

The sign indicates that guests, not their garbage, should be deposited in trash receptacles. Adding a single apostrophe would offer a more neighborly statement: *Please deposit your garbage (and your guests') in the trash receptacles before leaving the pool area.*

22a Signaling possessive case

The **possessive case** denotes ownership or possession. Add an apostrophe and -*s* to form the possessive of most **singular nouns**, including those that end in -*s*, and of **indefinite pronouns** (8d). The possessive forms of **personal pronouns** do not take apostrophes: *yours, his, hers, its, ours, theirs.*

▶ The *bus's* fumes overpowered her.

▶ George *Lucas's* movies have been wildly popular.

▶ *Anyone's* guess is as good as mine.

🔵 bedfordstmartins.com/easywriter For exercises, go to **Exercise Central** and click on **Apostrophes**.

Plural nouns. To form the possessive case of **plural** nouns not ending in -s, add an apostrophe and -s. For plural nouns ending in -s, add only the apostrophe.

▸ The *men's* department sells business attire.

▸ The *clowns'* costumes were bright green and orange.

Compound nouns. For **compound nouns**, make the last word in the group possessive.

▸ Both her *daughters-in-law's* birthdays fall in July.

Two or more nouns. To signal individual possession by two or more owners, make each noun possessive.

▸ **Great differences exist between *Jerry Bruckheimer's* and *Ridley Scott's* films.**

Bruckheimer and Scott produce different films.

To signal joint possession, make only the last noun possessive.

▸ *Wallace and Gromit's* **creator is Nick Park.**

Wallace and Gromit have the same creator.

22b Signaling contractions

Contractions are two-word combinations formed by leaving out certain letters, which are replaced by an apostrophe (*it is, it has/it's; will not/won't*).

Contractions are common in conversation and informal writing. Academic and professional work, however, often calls for greater formality.

Distinguishing *its* and *it's*. *Its* is a **possessive pronoun**—the possessive form of *it*. *It's* is a contraction for *it is* or *it has*.

▸ **This disease is unusual; *its* symptoms vary from person to person.**

▸ *It's* **a difficult disease to diagnose.**

22c With certain plurals

Many style guides now advise against using apostrophes for any plurals.

▶ **The gymnasts need marks of *8s* and *9s* to qualify for the finals.**

Other guidelines call for an apostrophe and *-s* to form the plural of numbers, letters, and words referred to as terms. Check your instructor's preference.

23 Quotation Marks

"Hilarious!" "A great family movie!" "A must see!" The quotation marks are a key component of statements like these from movie ads; they make the praise more believable by indicating that it comes from people other than the movie promoter. Quotation marks identify a speaker's exact words or the titles of short works.

23a Signaling direct quotation

▶ **The crowd chanted "Yes, we can" as they waited for the speech to begin.**

▶ **She smiled and said, "Son, this is one incident that I will never forget."**

Use quotation marks to enclose the words of each speaker within running dialogue. Mark each shift in speaker with a new paragraph.

"I want no proof of their affection," said Elinor; "but of their engagement I do."
   "I am perfectly satisfied of both."
   "Yet not a syllable has been said to you on the subject, by either of them."   —JANE AUSTEN, *Sense and Sensibility*

 bedfordstmartins.com/easywriter For exercises, go to **Exercise Central** and click on **Quotation Marks**.

Single quotation marks.   Single quotation marks enclose a quotation within a quotation. Open and close the quoted passage with double quotation marks, and change any quotation marks that appear *within* the quotation to single quotation marks.

▶ **Baldwin says, "The title 'The Uses of the Blues' does not refer to music; I don't know anything about music."**

Long quotations.   To quote a long passage, set the quotation off by starting it on a new line and indenting it from the left margin. This format, known as block quotation, does not require quotation marks.

MLA documentation style (see Chapter 42) requires you to format a prose passage of more than four typed lines as a block quotation. The block should be indented one inch, or ten spaces. In APA style (see Chapter 43), block quotation is used for a quotation of forty words or more, and the block is indented five spaces. *The Chicago Manual of Style* (see Chapter 44) recommends setting off quotations of eight lines or more, or more than one hundred words. *The CSE Manual* (see Chapter 45) endorses the use of block quotations but does not provide precise guidelines for when to use them. The following example illustrates MLA style.

> In "Suspended," Joy Harjo tells of her first awareness of jazz as a child:
>
>> My rite of passage into the world of humanity occurred then, via jazz. The music made a startling bridge between the familiar and strange lands, an appropriate vehicle, . . . for we were there when jazz was born. I recognized it, that humid afternoon in my formative years, as a way to speak beyond the confines of ordinary language. I still hear it. (84)

Quoting poetry.   When quoting poetry, if the quotation is brief (fewer than four lines), you should include it within your text if you are using MLA style. Separate the lines of the poem with slashes, each preceded and followed by a space, in order to tell the reader where one line of the poem ends and the next begins.

In one of his best-known poems, Robert Frost remarks, "Two roads
diverged in a yellow wood, and I — / I took the one less traveled
by / And that has made all the difference" (lines 18–20)

To quote more than three lines of poetry, indent the block
one inch (or ten spaces) from the left margin. Do not use
quotation marks. Take care to follow the spacing, capitalization, punctuation, and other features of the original
poem.

The duke in Robert Browning's poem "My Last Duchess" is clearly
a jealous, vain person, whose arrogance is illustrated through
this statement:

> She thanked men, — good! but thanked
> Somehow — I know not how — as if she ranked
> My gift of a nine-hundred-years-old name
> With anybody's gift. (lines 31–34)

23b For titles of short works and definitions

Use quotation marks to enclose the titles of short poems,
short stories, articles, essays, songs, sections of books,
and episodes of television and radio programs. Quotation
marks also enclose definitions.

▶ The essay "Big and Bad" analyzes some reasons for the
popularity of SUVs.

▶ In social science, the term *sample size* means "the number of individuals being studied in a research project."

—KATHLEEN STASSEN BERGER and ROSS A. THOMPSON,
The Developing Person through Childhood and Adolescence

23c With other punctuation

Periods and commas go *inside* closing quotation marks.

▶ "Don't compromise yourself," said Janis Joplin. "You
are all you've got."

Colons, semicolons, and footnote numbers go *outside* closing quotation marks.

▶ I felt one emotion after finishing "Eveline": sorrow.

▶ Tragedy is defined by Aristotle as "an imitation of an
action that is serious and of a certain magnitude."[1]

Question marks, exclamation points, and dashes go *inside* if
they are part of the quoted material, *outside* if they are not.

▶ The cashier asked, "Would you like to super-size that?"

▶ What is the theme of "The Birth-Mark"?

23d Misused quotation marks

Do not use quotation marks for **indirect quotations**—those
that do not use someone's exact words.

▶ Mother smiled and said that ⁄she was sure she would
never forget the incident.⁄

Do not use quotation marks just to add emphasis to particular words or phrases.

▶ The hikers were startled by the appearance of a
⁄gigantic⁄ grizzly bear.

Do not use quotation marks around slang or colloquial language; they create the impression that you are apologizing for using those words. If you have a good reason to use slang or a colloquial term, use it without quotation marks.

▶ **After our twenty-mile hike, we were completely**

exhausted and ready to /turn in./

24 Other Punctuation

Parentheses, brackets, dashes, colons, slashes, and ellipses are all around us. Pick up the television listings, for instance, and you will find these punctuation marks in abundance, helping viewers preview programs in a clear and efficient way.

⑦⑧ **College Football** *3:30* 501019/592361—Northwestern Wildcats at Ohio State Buckeyes. The Buckeyes are looking for their 20th straight win over Northwestern. (Live) [Time approximate.]

These marks of punctuation can signal relationships among sentence parts, create particular rhythms, and help readers follow your thoughts.

24a Parentheses

Use parentheses to enclose material that is of minor or secondary importance in a sentence—material that supplements, clarifies, comments on, or illustrates what precedes or follows it.

▶ **Inventors and men of genius have almost always been regarded as fools at the beginning (and very often at the end) of their careers.** —FYODOR DOSTOYEVSKY

▶ **My research indicated problems with the flat tax (a single-rate tax with no deductions).**

bedfordstmartins.com/easywriter For exercises, go to **Exercise Central** and click on **Other Punctuation**.

Parentheses are also used to enclose textual citations and numbers or letters in a list.

▶ **Freud and his followers have had a most significant impact on the ways abnormal functioning is understood and treated (Joseph, 1991).**

> —RONALD J. COMER, *Abnormal Psychology*

The in-text citation in this sentence shows the style of the American Psychological Association (APA).

▶ **Five distinct styles can be distinguished: (1) Old New England, (2) Deep South, (3) Middle American, (4) Wild West, and (5) Far West or Californian.**

> —ALISON LURIE, *The Language of Clothes*

With other punctuation.   A period may be placed either inside or outside a closing parenthesis, depending on whether the parenthetical text is part of a larger sentence. A comma, if needed, is always placed *outside* a closing parenthesis (and never before an opening one).

▶ **Gene Tunney's single defeat in an eleven-year career was to a flamboyant and dangerous fighter named Harry Greb ("The Human Windmill"), who seems to have been, judging from boxing literature, the dirtiest fighter in history.**   —JOYCE CAROL OATES, "On Boxing"

24b   Brackets

Use brackets to enclose parenthetical elements in material that is itself within parentheses. Also use brackets to enclose explanatory words or comments that you are inserting into a quotation.

▶ **Eventually, the investigation had to examine the major agencies (including the National Security Agency [NSA]) that were conducting covert operations.**

▶ **Massing notes that "on average, it [Fox News] attracts more than eight million people daily—more than double the number who watch CNN."**

The bracketed words clarify *it* in the original quotation.

In the quotation in the following sentence, the artist Gauguin's name is misspelled. The bracketed word *sic,* which means "so," tells readers that the person being quoted—not the writer who has picked up the quotation—made the mistake.

▶ **One admirer wrote, "She was the most striking woman I'd ever seen—a sort of wonderful combination of Mia Farrow and one of Gaugin's [*sic*] Polynesian nymphs."**

24c Dashes

Use dashes to insert a comment or to highlight material in a sentence.

▶ **The pleasures of reading itself—who doesn't remember?—were like those of Christmas cake, a sweet devouring.**
—EUDORA WELTY, "A Sweet Devouring"

A single dash can be used to emphasize material at the end of a sentence, to mark a sudden change in tone, to indicate hesitation in speech, or to introduce a summary or an explanation.

▶ **In the twentieth century it has become almost impossible to moralize about epidemics—except those which are transmitted sexually.**
—SUSAN SONTAG, *AIDS and Its Metaphors*

▶ **In walking, the average adult person employs a motor mechanism that weighs about eighty pounds—sixty pounds of muscle and twenty pounds of bone.**
—EDWIN WAY TEALE

Dashes give more emphasis than parentheses to the material they enclose or set off. Most word-processing software creates a dash when you type two hyphens (--) with no spaces before, between, or after. Many word-processing programs automatically convert two typed hyphens into a solid dash.

24d Colons

Use a colon to introduce an explanation, an example, an appositive, a series, a list, or a quotation.

▶ **At the baby's one-month birthday party, Ah Po gave him the Four Valuable Things: ink, inkslab, paper, and brush.** —MAXINE HONG KINGSTON, *China Men*

Use a colon rather than a comma to introduce a quotation when the lead-in is a complete sentence on its own.

▶ **The State of the Union address contained one surprising statement: "America is addicted to oil."**

Colons are also used after salutations in formal letters; with numbers indicating hours, minutes, and seconds; with ratios; with biblical chapters and verses; with titles and subtitles; and in bibliographic entries.

▶ **Dear Dr. Chapman:**

▶ **4:59 PM**

▶ **a ratio of 5:1**

▶ *The Joy of Insight: Passions of a Physicist*

▶ **Boston: Bedford/St. Martin's, 2010**

Misused colons. Do not put a colon between a **verb** and its **object** or **complement** (unless the object is a quotation), between a **preposition** and its object, or after such expressions as *such as*, *especially*, and *including*.

▶ **Some natural fibers are:/cotton, wool, silk, and linen.**

▶ **In poetry, additional power may come from devices such as:/simile, metaphor, and alliteration.**

24e Slashes

Use slashes to mark line divisions between two or three lines of poetry quoted within text. When using a slash to separate lines of poetry (23a), precede and follow it with a space.

▶ Shakespeare's Sonnet 29 states, "For thy sweet love rememb'red such wealth brings / That then I scorn to change my state with kings."

Use a slash to separate alternatives, parts of fractions, and Internet addresses.

▶ **Then there was Daryl, the cabdriver/bartender.**

—JOHN L'HEUREUX, *The Handmaid of Desire*

▶ **1/2**

▶ **bedfordstmartins.com/easywriter**

 **24f** Ellipses

Ellipses, or ellipsis points, are three equally spaced dots. Ellipses are usually used to indicate that something has been omitted from a quoted passage. Just as you should carefully use quotation marks around any material that you quote directly from a source, so you should carefully use ellipses to indicate that you have left out part of a quotation that otherwise appears to be a complete sentence. Ellipses have been used in the following example to indicate two omissions—one in the middle of the first sentence and one at the end of the second sentence.

ORIGINAL TEXT

▶ **The quasi-official division of the population into three economic classes called high-, middle-, and low-income groups rather misses the point, because as a class indicator the amount of money is not as important as the source.** —PAUL FUSSELL, "Notes on Class"

WITH ELLIPSES

▶ **As Paul Fussell argues, "The quasi-official division of the population into three economic classes . . . rather misses the point. . . ."**

When you omit the last part of a quoted sentence, add a period after the ellipses—for a total of four dots. Be sure a complete sentence comes before the four dots. If your

shortened quotation ends with a source citation (such as a page number, a name, or a title), place the documentation source in parentheses after the three ellipsis points and the closing quotation mark but before the period.

▶ **Packer argues, "The Administration is right to reconsider its strategy . . . " (34).**

You can also use ellipses to indicate a pause or a hesitation in speech in the same way that you can use a dash for that purpose.

▶ **Then the voice, husky and familiar, came to wash over us—"The winnah, and still heavyweight champeen of the world . . . Joe Louis."**

—MAYA ANGELOU, *I Know Why the Caged Bird Sings*

25 Capitalization

Capital letters are a key signal in everyday life. Look around any store to see their importance: you can shop for Levi's or *any* blue jeans, for Pepsi or *any* cola, for Kleenex or *any* tissue. In each of these instances, the capital letter indicates the name of a particular brand.

25a The first word of a sentence

With very few exceptions, capitalize the first word of a sentence. If you are quoting a full sentence, capitalize its first word.

▶ **Kennedy said, "Let us never negotiate out of fear."**

Capitalization of a nonquoted sentence following a colon is optional.

▶ **Gould cites the work of Darwin: The [*or* the] theory of natural selection incorporates the principle of evolutionary ties among all animals.**

---

bedfordstmartins.com/easywriter For exercises, go to **Exercise Central** and click on **Capitalization**.

Capitalize a sentence within parentheses unless the parenthetical sentence is inserted into another sentence.

▶ **Gould cites the work of Darwin. (Other researchers cite more recent evolutionary theorists.)**

▶ **Gould cites the work of Darwin (see p. 150).**

When citing poetry, follow the capitalization of the original poem. Though most poets capitalize the first word of each line in a poem, some do not.

▶ **Morning sun heats up the young beech tree**
  leaves and almost lights them into fireflies

                                        —JUNE JORDAN, "Aftermath"

25b Proper nouns and proper adjectives

Capitalize **proper nouns** (those naming specific persons, places, and things) and most **adjectives** formed from proper nouns. All other nouns are **common nouns** and are not capitalized unless they are used as part of a proper noun: *a street,* but *Elm Street.*

Capitalized nouns and adjectives include personal names; nations, nationalities, and languages; months, days of the week, and holidays (but not seasons of the year); geographical names; structures and monuments; ships, trains, aircraft, and spacecraft; organizations, businesses, and government institutions; academic institutions and courses; historical events and eras; and religions, their deities, followers, and sacred writings. For trade names, follow the capitalization you see in company advertising or on the product itself.

PROPER	COMMON
Alfred Hitchcock, Hitchcockian	a director
Brazil, Brazilian	a nation, a language
Pacific Ocean	an ocean
Challenger	a spaceship
Library of Congress	a federal agency
Political Science 102	a political science course
the Qur'an	a holy book
Catholicism, Catholics	a religion
Cheerios, eBay	cereal, an auction site

25c Titles before proper names

When used alone or following a proper name, most titles are not capitalized. One common exception is the word *president*, which many writers capitalize whenever it refers to the President of the United States.

Professor Lisa Ede   my history professor
Dr. Teresa Ramirez   Teresa Ramirez, our doctor

25d Titles of works

Capitalize most words in titles of books, articles, speeches, stories, essays, plays, poems, documents, films, paintings, and musical compositions. Do not capitalize **articles** (*a, an, the*), **prepositions**, **conjunctions**, and the *to* in an **infinitive** unless they are the first or last words in a title or subtitle.

Walt Whitman: A Life   Declaration of Independence
"As Time Goes By"   *The Producers*
"Crazy in Love"   *Harry Potter and the Sorcerer's Stone*

25e Compass directions

Capitalize compass directions only if the word designates a specific geographical region.

▶ **John Muir headed west, motivated by the desire to explore.**

▶ **Water rights are an increasingly contentious issue in the West.**

FOR MULTILINGUAL WRITERS

Learning English Capitalization

Capitalization systems vary considerably. Arabic, Chinese, Hebrew, and Hindi, for example, do not use capital letters at all. English may be the only language to capitalize the first-person singular pronoun (*I*), but Dutch and German capitalize some forms of the second-person pronoun (*you*)—and German also capitalizes all nouns.

25f Family relationships

Capitalize family relationships only if the word is used as part of a name or as a substitute for the name.

▶ **When she was a child, my mother shared a room with my aunt.**

▶ **I could always tell when Mother was annoyed with Aunt Rose.**

26 Abbreviations and Numbers

Anytime you open up a telephone book, you see an abundance of abbreviations and numbers, as in the following movie theater listing from the Berkeley, California, telephone book:

Oaks Theater   1875 Solano Av   Brk

Abbreviations and numbers allow writers to present detailed information in a small amount of space.

26a Abbreviations

Certain titles, including those indicating academic degrees, are normally abbreviated when used before or after a person's name.

Ms. Susanna Moller   Henry Louis Gates Jr.
Mr. Mark Otuteye   Karen Lancry, MD

Religious, academic, and government titles should be spelled out in academic writing but can be abbreviated in other writing when they appear before a full name.

Rev. Fleming Rutledge   Reverend Rutledge
Prof. Jaime Mejía   Professor Mejía
Sen. Christopher Dodd   Senator Dodd

---

bedfordstmartins.com/easywriter For exercises, go to **Exercise Central** and click on **Abbreviations and Numbers**.

Business, government, and science terms. As long as you can be sure your readers will understand them, use common abbreviations such as *PBS, NASA,* and *DNA.* If an abbreviation may be unfamiliar, spell out the full term the first time you use it, and give the abbreviation in parentheses; after that, you can use the abbreviation by itself. Use abbreviations such as *Co., Inc., Corp.,* and *&* only if they are part of a company's official name.

▶ **The Comprehensive Test Ban (CTB) Treaty was first proposed in the 1950s. For those nations signing it, the CTB would bring to a halt all nuclear weapons testing.**

▶ **Sears, Roebuck & Co. was the only large ~~corp.~~ in town.**
  corporation

With numbers. The following abbreviations are acceptable with specific years and times.

399 BC ("before Christ") or 399 BCE ("before the common era")
AD 49 (*anno Domini,* Latin for "year of our Lord") or 49 CE
  ("common era")
11:15 AM (*or* a.m.)
9:00 PM (*or* p.m.)

Symbols such as % and $ are acceptable with figures (*$11*) but not with words (*eleven dollars*). Units of measurement can be abbreviated in charts and graphs (*4 in.*) but not in the body of a paper (*four inches*).

In notes and source citations. Some abbreviations required in notes and in source citations are not appropriate in the body of a paper.

cf.	compare (*confer*)
e.g.	for example (*exempli gratia*)
et al.	and others (*et alia*)
etc.	and so forth (*et cetera*)
i.e.	that is (*id est*)
N.B.	note well (*nota bene*)

In addition, except in notes and source citations, do not abbreviate such terms as *chapter, page,* and *volume* or the names of months, states, cities, or countries. Two exceptions are *Washington, D.C.,* and *U.S.,* which is acceptable as an **adjective** but not as a **noun**: *U.S. borders* but *in the United States.*

26b Numbers

If you can write out a number in one or two words, do so.
Use figures for longer numbers.

▶ Her screams were ignored by ~~38~~ people.
   ^thirty-eight^

▶ A baseball is held together by ~~two hundred sixteen~~ red
   ^216^
   stitches.

If one of several numbers *of the same kind* in the same sentence requires a figure, you should use figures for all the numbers in that sentence.

▶ An audio system can range in cost from ~~one hundred~~
   ^$100^
   ~~dollars~~ to $2,599.

When a sentence begins with a number, either spell out the number or rewrite the sentence.

▶ ~~119~~ years of CIA labor cost taxpayers sixteen million
   ^One hundred nineteen^
   dollars.

Most readers find it easier to read figures than three-word numbers; thus, the best solution may be to rewrite this sentence: *Taxpayers spent sixteen million dollars for 119 years of CIA labor.*

In general, use figures for the following:

ADDRESSES	23 Main Street; 175 Fifth Avenue
DATES	September 17, 1951; 6 June 1983; 4 BCE; the 1860s
DECIMALS AND FRACTIONS	65.34; 8½
EXACT AMOUNTS OF MONEY	$7,348; $1.46 trillion; $2.50; thirty-five (*or* 35) cents
PERCENTAGES	77 percent (*or* 77%)

| SCORES AND STATISTICS | an 8–3 Red Sox victory; an average age of 22 |
| TIME OF DAY | 6:00 AM (*or* a.m.) |

27 Italics

The slanted type known as *italics* is more than just a pretty typeface. Indeed, italics give words special meaning or emphasis. In the sentence "Many people read *People* on the subway every day," the italics (and the capital letter) tell us that *People* is a publication. You may use your computer to produce italic type; if not, underline words that you would otherwise italicize.

27a For titles

In general, use italics for titles and subtitles of long works; use quotation marks for shorter works (23b).

BOOKS	*Fun Home: A Family Tragicomic*
CHOREOGRAPHIC WORKS	Agnes de Mille's *Rodeo*
FILMS AND VIDEOS	*Slumdog Millionaire*
LONG MUSICAL WORKS	*Brandenburg Concertos*
LONG POEMS	*Bhagavad Gita*
MAGAZINES AND JOURNALS	*Ebony;* the *New England Journal of Medicine*
NEWSPAPERS	the Cleveland *Plain Dealer*
PAINTINGS AND SCULPTURE	Georgia O'Keeffe's *Black Iris*
PAMPHLETS	Thomas Paine's *Common Sense*
PLAYS	*Sweeney Todd*

⏵ bedfordstmartins.com/easywriter For exercises, go to **Exercise Central** and click on **Italics**.

RADIO SERIES	*All Things Considered*
RECORDINGS	*The Ramones Leave Home*
SOFTWARE	*Quicken*
TELEVISION SERIES	*The Wire*
WEB SITES	*Salon*

Do not italicize titles of sacred books, such as the Bible and the Qur'an; public documents, such as the Constitution and the Magna Carta; or your own papers.

27b For words, letters, and numbers used as terms

▶ On the back of his jersey was the famous 24.

▶ One characteristic of some New York speech is the absence of postvocalic *r*—for example, pronouncing the word *four* as "fouh."

27c For non-English words

Italicize words from other languages unless they have become part of English—like the French "bourgeois" or the Italian "pasta," for example. If a word is in an English dictionary, it does not need italics.

▶ At last one of the phantom sleighs gliding along the street would come to a stop, and with gawky haste Mr. Burness in his fox-furred *shapka* would make for our door.   —VLADIMIR NABOKOV, *Speak, Memory*

27d For aircraft, ships, and trains

Spirit of St. Louis   Amtrak's *Silver Star*   U.S.S. *Iowa*

27e For emphasis

Italics can help create emphasis in writing, but use them sparingly for this purpose. It is usually better to create emphasis with sentence structure and word choice.

▶ Great literature and a class of literate readers are noth-
ing new in India. What is new is the emergence of a
gifted generation of Indian writers *working in English.*

—SALMAN RUSHDIE

28 Hyphens

Hyphens are undoubtedly confusing to many people—
hyphen problems are now one of the twenty most common
surface errors in student writing (see pp. 9–10). The confusion is understandable. Over time, the conventions for
hyphen use in a given word can change (*tomorrow* was once
spelled *to-morrow*). New words, even compounds such as
firewall, generally don't use hyphens, but controversy continues to rage over whether to hyphenate *email* (or is it
e-mail?). And some words are hyphenated when they serve
one kind of purpose in a sentence and not when they serve
another.

28a With compound words

Compound nouns. Some are one word (*rowboat*), some
are separate words (*hard drive*), and some require hyphens
(*sister-in-law*). You should consult a dictionary to be sure.

Compound adjectives. Hyphenate most **compound adjectives** that precede a noun, but not those that follow a
noun.

a *well-liked* boss   My boss is *well liked.*
a *six-foot* plank   The plank is *six feet long.*

In general, the reason for hyphenating compound adjectives is to facilitate reading.

▶ Designers often use potted plants as living-room dividers.
                                               ^

Without the hyphen, *living* may seem to modify *room dividers.*

Never hyphenate an *-ly* adverb and an adjective.

▶ They used a widely⁄distributed mailing list.

Fractions and compound numbers. Use a hyphen to write out fractions and to spell out compound numbers from twenty-one to ninety-nine.

one-seventh	thirty-seven
two and seven-sixteenths	three hundred fifty-four thousand

28b With prefixes and suffixes

Most words containing prefixes or suffixes are written without hyphens: *antiwar, Romanesque.* Here are some exceptions:

BEFORE CAPITALIZED BASE WORDS	un-American, non-Catholic
WITH FIGURES	pre-1960, post-1945
WITH CERTAIN PREFIXES AND SUFFIXES	all-state, ex-partner, self-possessed, quasi-legislative, mayor-elect, fifty-odd
WITH COMPOUND BASE WORDS	pre-high school, post-cold war
FOR CLARITY OR EASE OF READING	re-cover, anti-inflation, troll-like

Re-cover means "cover again"; the hyphen distinguishes it from *recover,* meaning "get well." In *anti-inflation* and *troll-like,* the hyphens separate confusing clusters of vowels and consonants.

28c Unnecessary hyphens

Unnecessary hyphens are at least as common a problem as omitted ones. Do not hyphenate the parts of a two-word verb such as *depend on, turn off,* or *tune out* (37b).

▶ Each player must pick⁄up a medical form before football tryouts.

The words *pick up* act as a verb and should not be hyphenated.

However, be careful to check that two words do indeed function as a verb in the sentence; if they function as an adjective, a hyphen may be needed.

▶ **Let's sign up for the early class.**

The verb *sign up* should not have a hyphen.

▶ **Where is the sign-up sheet?**

The compound adjective *sign-up,* which modifies the noun *sheet,* needs a hyphen.

Do not hyphenate a subject complement—a word group that follows a linking verb (such as a form of *be* or *seem*) and describes the subject.

▶ **Audrey is almost three̸years̸old.**

✅ CHECKLIST

Editing for Hyphens

- Double-check compound words to be sure they are properly closed up, separated, or hyphenated. If in doubt, consult a dictionary. (28a)
- Check all terms that have prefixes or suffixes to see whether you need hyphens. (28b)
- Do not hyphenate two-word verbs or word groups that serve as subject complements. (28c)

Language

Writing

Sentence
Grammar

Sentence
Style

Punctuation/
Mechanics

Language

Multilingual
Writers

Research

Documentation

29 Writing to the World

People today often communicate instantaneously across vast distances and cultures. Businesspeople complete multinational transactions, students take online classes at distant universities, and grandparents check in with family members across multiple time zones. You may already find yourself writing to (or with) people from other cultures, language groups, and countries. In this era of rapid global communication, you must know how to write effectively to the world.

29a What you consider "normal"

More than likely, your judgments about what is "normal" are based on assumptions that you are not aware of. Most of us tend to see our own way as the "normal" or right way to do things. If your ways seem inherently right, then perhaps you assume that other ways are somehow less than right. To communicate effectively with people across cultures, recognize the norms that guide your own behavior and how those norms differ from those of other people.

- Know that most ways of communicating are influenced by cultural contexts and differ from one culture to the next.
- Notice the ways that people from cultures other than your own communicate, and be flexible.
- Respect the differences among individuals within a culture. Don't assume that all members of a community behave in the same way or value the same things.

29b Meaning

All writers face challenges in trying to communicate across space, languages, and cultures. You can address these challenges by working to be sure that you understand what others say—and that they understand you. In such situations, take care to be explicit about the meanings of the words you use. In addition, don't hesitate to ask people to explain a point if you're not absolutely sure you understand, and invite responses by asking whether you're making yourself clear.

29c Your authority as a writer

Writers communicating across cultures often encounter audiences who have differing attitudes about authority and about the relationship between the writer and the people being addressed. In the United States, students are often asked to establish authority in their writing—by drawing on personal experience, by reporting on research, or by taking a position for which they can offer strong evidence and support. But some cultures position student writers as novices, whose job is to learn from others who have greater authority. When you write, think carefully about your audience's expectations and attitudes toward authority.

- Whom are you addressing, and what is your relationship to him or her?
- What knowledge are you expected to have? Is it appropriate for you to demonstrate that knowledge—and if so, how?
- What is your goal—to answer a question? to make a point? to agree? something else?
- What tone is appropriate? If in doubt, show respect: politeness is rarely if ever inappropriate.

29d Your responsibility to your audience

In the United States, Canada, and Great Britain, many audiences expect a writer to get to the point as directly as possible and to articulate that point efficiently and unambiguously. But audiences in some other cultures find such writing blunt and ineffective, preferring a more subtle or indirect style. Thus you must think carefully about whether audience members expect the writer to make the meaning of a text explicitly clear or whether the audience will take more responsibility for figuring out what is being said. You should consider what your audience members already know about the subject and look for cues about what they expect or need you to provide.

29e Evidence

Every writer should think carefully about how to use evidence in writing and pay attention to what counts as evidence to members of particular cultures. Are facts,

concrete examples, or firsthand experience convincing to the intended audience? Is the testimony of experts weighed heavily as evidence? What people are considered trustworthy experts, and why? Will the audience value citations from religious or philosophical texts, proverbs, or everyday wisdom? Are there other sources that would be considered strong evidence? If analogies are used as support, which kinds are most powerful?

Once you determine what counts as evidence in your own thinking and writing, think about where you learned to use and value this kind of evidence. You can ask these same questions about the use of evidence by members of other cultures.

29f Organization

The organizational patterns that you find pleasing are likely to be deeply embedded in your own culture. Many U.S. readers expect a well-organized piece of writing to use the following structure: introduction and thesis, necessary background, overview of the parts, systematic presentation of evidence, consideration of other viewpoints, and conclusion.

However, in cultures that value indirection, subtlety, or repetition, writers tend to prefer different organizational patterns. When writing for world audiences, think about how you can organize material to get your message across effectively. Consider where to state your thesis or main point (at the beginning, at the end, somewhere else, or not at all) and whether to use a straightforward organization or to employ digressions to good effect.

29g Style

Effective style varies broadly across cultures and depends on the rhetorical situation—purpose, audience, and so on. Even so, there is one important style question to consider when writing across cultures: what level of formality is most appropriate? In most writing to a general audience in the United States, a fairly informal style is often acceptable, even appreciated. Many cultures, however, tend to value a more formal approach. When in doubt, err on the side of formality in writing to people from other cultures, especially to your elders or to those in authority. Use

appropriate titles (*Dr. Moss, Professor Mejía*); avoid slang and informal structures, such as **sentence fragments**; use complete words and sentences (even in email); and use first names only if invited to do so.

30 Language That Builds Common Ground

The supervisor who refers to her staff as "team members" (rather than as "my staff" or as "subordinates") has chosen language intended to establish common ground with people who are important to her. Your own language can work to build common ground if you carefully consider the sensitivities and preferences of others and if you watch for words that betray your assumptions, even though you have not directly stated them.

30a Stereotypes and unstated assumptions

To some extent, we all think in terms of stereotypes, and sometimes they can be helpful in making generalizations. Stereotyping any individual on the basis of generalizations about a group, however, can lead to inaccurate and even hurtful conclusions. Careful writers want to make sure that language doesn't stereotype any group or individual.

Other unstated assumptions that enter into thinking and writing can destroy common ground by ignoring the differences between others and ourselves. For example, a student in a religion seminar who uses *we* to refer to Christians and *they* to refer to members of other religions had better be sure that everyone in the class is Christian, or some may feel left out of the discussion.

Sometimes assumptions even lead writers to call special attention to a group affiliation when it is not relevant to the point, as in *a woman bus driver, a Jewish doctor, a lesbian politician,* or *an elderly but still active homeowner.*

---

bedfordstmartins.com/easywriter For exercises, go to **Exercise Central** and click on **Language That Builds Common Ground**.

30b   Assumptions about gender

Powerful and often invisible gender-related words affect our thinking and our behavior. Consider the traditional use of *man* and *mankind* to refer to people of both sexes and the use of *he, him, his,* and *himself* to refer to people of unknown sex. Because such usage ignores half the human race, it hardly helps a writer build common ground. Sexist language—words and **phrases** that stereotype or ignore members of either sex or that unnecessarily call attention to gender—can usually be revised fairly easily. There are several alternatives to using masculine **pronouns** to refer to persons of unknown sex:

▶   *Lawyers*   *they*
  A ~~lawyer~~ must pass the bar exam before ~~he~~ can practice.

▶   *or she*
  A lawyer must pass the bar exam before he can practice.

▶   *practicing.*
  A lawyer must pass the bar exam before ~~he can practice.~~

Try to eliminate common sexist **nouns** from your writing.

INSTEAD OF	TRY USING
anchorman, anchorwoman	anchor
businessman	businessperson, business executive
congressman	member of Congress, representative
fireman	firefighter
male nurse	nurse
man, mankind	humans, human beings, humanity, the human race, humankind
policeman, policewoman	police officer
woman engineer	engineer

30c   Assumptions about race and ethnicity

In building common ground, writers must watch for any words that ignore differences not only among individual members of a race or ethnic group but also among subgroups. Writers must be aware, for instance, of the many nations to which American Indians belong and of the diverse places from which Americans of Spanish-speaking ancestry come.

Preferred terms. Identifying preferred terms is some-times not an easy task, for they can change often and vary widely.

- The word *colored* was once widely used in the United States to refer to Americans of African ancestry. By the 1950s, the preferred term had become *Negro*; in the 1960s, *black* came to be preferred by most, though certainly not all, members of that community. Then, in the late 1980s, some leaders of the community urged that *black* be replaced by *African American*.

- The word *Oriental,* once used to refer to people of East Asian descent, is now considered offensive.

- Once widely preferred, the term *Native American* is chal-lenged by those who argue that the most appropriate way to refer to indigenous peoples is by the specific name such as *Chippewa, Tlinget,* or *Hopi.* It has also become common for tribal groups to refer to themselves as *Indians* or *Indian tribes.*

- Among Americans of Spanish-speaking descent, the preferred terms of reference are many: *Chicano/Chicana, Hispanic, Latin American, Latino/Latina, Mexican American, Dominican,* and *Puerto Rican,* to name but a few.

Clearly, then, ethnic terminology changes often enough to challenge even the most careful writers—including writ-ers who belong to the groups they are writing about. The best advice may be to consider your words carefully, to lis-ten for the way members of groups refer to themselves (or ask about preferences), and to check in a current dictionary for any term you're unsure of.

30d Other kinds of difference

Remember that your audiences may include people from many areas of the United States as well as from other countries, of many different ages and socioeconomic back-grounds, of many different abilities, of differing religious views, and of different sexual orientations. In short, you can almost never assume that audiences are just like you or that they share your background and experiences. Keeping this range of differences in mind can help you avoid over-generalizing or stereotyping audiences—and thus help you to build common ground.

31 Varieties of Language

Comedian Dave Chappelle has said, "Every black American is bilingual. We speak street vernacular, and we speak job interview." As Chappelle understands, English comes in many varieties that differ from one another in pronunciation, vocabulary, usage, and grammar. You probably already adjust the variety of language you use depending on how well—and how formally—you know the audience you are addressing. Language variety can improve your communication with your audience if you think carefully about the effect you want to achieve.

31a Standard varieties of English

The variety of English often referred to as "standard" or "standard academic" is taught prescriptively in schools, represented in this and all other textbooks, used in the national media, and written and spoken widely by those wielding social and economic power. As the language used in business and most public institutions, standard English is a variety you will want to be completely familiar with. Standard English, however, is only one of many effective varieties of English and itself varies according to purpose and audience, from the more formal style used in academic writing to the informal style characteristic of casual conversation.

31b Ethnic varieties of English

Whether you are an American Indian or trace your ancestry to Europe, Asia, Africa, Latin America, or elsewhere, you have an ethnic heritage that probably lives on in the English language. See how one Hawaiian writer uses an ethnic variety of English to paint a picture of young teens hearing a scary "chicken skin" story about sharks from their grandmother.

> "—So, rather dan being rid of da shark, da people were stuck with many little ones, for dere mistake."
>   Then Grandma Wong wen' pause, for dramatic effect, I guess, and she wen' add, "Dis is one of dose times. . . . Da time of da sharks."

Those words ended another of Grandma's chicken skin stories. The stories she told us had been passed on to her by her grandmother, who had heard them from her grandmother. Always skipping a generation.

—RODNEY MORALES, "When the Shark Bites"

Notice how the narrator uses both standard and ethnic varieties of English—presenting information necessary to the story line mostly in standard English and using a local, ethnic variety to represent spoken language, which helps us hear the characters talk. Another important reason for the shift from standard English is to demonstrate that the writer is a member of the community whose language he is representing and thus to build his credibility with others in the community. Take care, however, in using the language of communities other than your own. When used inappropriately, such language can have an opposite effect, perhaps destroying credibility and alienating your audience.

31c Regional varieties of English

Using regional language is an effective way to evoke a character or place. See how a linguistic anthropologist weaves together regional and standard academic English in writing about one Carolina community when she lets a resident of Roadville speak her mind—and in her own words.

For Roadville, schooling is something most folks have not gotten enough of, but everybody believes will do something toward helping an individual "get on." In the words of one oldtime resident, "Folks that ain't got no schooling don't get to be nobody nowadays."

—SHIRLEY BRICE HEATH, *Ways with Words*

FOR MULTILINGUAL WRITERS

Recognizing Global Varieties of English

English is used in many countries around the world, resulting in many global varieties. For example, British English differs somewhat from U.S. English in certain vocabulary (*bonnet* for *hood* of a car), syntax (*to hospital* rather than *to the hospital*), spelling (*centre* rather than *center*), and, of course, pronunciation. If you have learned a British variety of English, you will want to recognize the ways in which it differs from the U.S. standard.

32 Word Choice

Deciding which word is the right word can be a challenge. It's not unusual to find many words that have similar but subtly different meanings, and each makes a different impression on your audience. For instance, the "pasta with marinara sauce" presented in a restaurant may look and taste much like the "macaroni and gravy" served at an Italian family dinner, but the choice of one label rather than the other tells us not only about the food but also about the people serving it and the people they expect to serve it to.

32a Appropriate formality

In an email or letter to a friend or close associate, informal language is often appropriate. For most academic and professional writing, however, more formal language is appropriate, since you are addressing people you do not know well.

EMAIL TO SOMEONE YOU KNOW WELL

▶ Myisha is great—hire her if you can!

LETTER OF RECOMMENDATION TO SOMEONE YOU DO NOT KNOW

▶ I am pleased to recommend Myisha Fisher. She will bring good ideas and extraordinary energy to your organization.

Slang and colloquial language. Slang, or extremely informal language, is often confined to a relatively small group and changes very quickly, though some slang gains wide use (*yuppie, zine*). Colloquial language, such as *a lot, in a bind,* or *snooze,* is less informal, more widely used, and longer lasting than most slang.

Writers who use slang and colloquial language run the risk of not being understood or of not being taken seriously.

---

bedfordstmartins.com/easywriter For exercises, go to **Exercise Central** and click on **Word Choice**.

If you are writing for a general audience about gun-control legislation and you use the term *gat,* some readers may not know what you mean, and others may be irritated by what they see as a frivolous reference to a deadly serious subject.

Jargon. Jargon is the special vocabulary of a trade or profession that enables members to speak and write concisely to one another. Jargon should usually be reserved for an audience that will understand the terms.

JARGON

▶ The VDTs in composition were down last week, so we had to lay out on dummies and crop and size the art with a wheel.

REVISED FOR A GENERAL AUDIENCE

▶ The video display terminals were not working last week in the composing room, where models of the newspaper pages are made up for printing, so we had to arrange the contents of each page on a large sheet and use a wheel, a kind of circular slide rule, to figure out the size and shape of the illustrations.

Pompous language, euphemisms, and doublespeak. Stuffy or pompous language is unnecessarily formal for the purpose, audience, or topic. It often gives writing an insincere or unintentionally humorous tone, making a writer's ideas seem insignificant or even unbelievable.

POMPOUS

▶ Pursuant to the August 9 memorandum regarding unit costs of automotive fuels, it is incumbent upon us to endeavor to make maximal utilization of telephonic communication in lieu of personal visitation.

REVISED

▶ As of August 9, gas prices require us to use the telephone whenever possible rather than make personal visits.

FOR MULTILINGUAL WRITERS

Avoiding Fancy Language

In writing standard academic English, which is fairly formal, students are often tempted to use many "big words" instead of simple language. Although learning impressive words can be a good way to expand your vocabulary, it is usually best to avoid flowery or fancy language in college writing. Academic writing at U.S. universities tends to value clear, concise prose.

Euphemisms are words and **phrases** that make unpleasant ideas seem less harsh. *Your position is being eliminated* seeks to soften the blow of being fired or laid off. Although euphemisms can sometimes appeal to an audience by showing that you are considerate of people's feelings, they can also sound insincere or evasive.

Doublespeak is language used to hide or distort the truth. During massive layoffs in the business world, companies may describe a job-cutting policy as *employee repositioning*, *deverticalization*, or *rightsizing*. The public—and particularly those who lose their jobs—recognize such terms as doublespeak.

32b Denotation and connotation

The words *enthusiasm, passion,* and *obsession* all carry roughly the same denotation, or dictionary meaning. But the connotations, or associations, are quite different: an *enthusiasm* is a pleasurable and absorbing interest; a *passion* has a strong emotional component and may affect someone positively or negatively; an *obsession* is an unhealthy attachment that excludes other interests.

Note the differences in connotation among the following three statements:

▶ **Students Against Racism (SAR) erected a temporary barrier on the campus oval, saying the structure symbolized "the many barriers to those discriminated against by university policies."**

▶ **Left-wing agitators threw up an eyesore right on the oval to try to stampede the university into giving in to their demands.**

▶ **Supporters of human rights for all students challenged
the university's investment in racism by erecting a
protest barrier on campus.**

The first statement is the most neutral, merely stating facts
(and quoting the assertion about university policy to represent it as someone's opinion); the second, by using words
with negative connotations (*agitators, eyesore, stampede*), is
strongly critical; the third, by using words with positive
connotations (*supporters of human rights*) and presenting
assertions as facts (*the university's investment in racism*),
gives a favorable slant to the protest.

32c General and specific language

Effective writers balance general words (those that name
groups or classes) with specific words (those that identify
individual and particular things). Abstractions, which are
types of general words, refer to things we cannot perceive
through our five senses. Specific words are often concrete,
naming things we can see, hear, touch, taste, or smell.

GENERAL	LESS GENERAL	SPECIFIC	MORE SPECIFIC
book	dictionary	abridged dictionary	my 2004 edition of the *American Heritage College Dictionary*

ABSTRACT	LESS ABSTRACT	CONCRETE	MORE CONCRETE
culture	visual art	painting	van Gogh's *Starry Night*

32d Figurative language

Figurative language, or figures of speech, paints pictures
in readers' minds, allowing readers to "see" a point readily
and clearly. Far from being a frill, such language is crucial
to understanding.

Similes, metaphors, and analogies.   Similes use *like, as,
as if,* or *as though* to make explicit the comparison between
two seemingly different things.

▶ **The comb felt as if it was raking my skin off.**

—MALCOLM X, "My First Conk"

Metaphors are implicit comparisons, omitting the *like, as, as if,* or *as though* of similes.

▶ **The Internet is the new town square.**

—REP. JEB HENSARLING

Analogies compare similar features of two dissimilar things; they explain something unfamiliar by relating it to something familiar.

▶ **The mouse genome . . . [is] the Rosetta Stone for understanding the language of life.** —TOM FRIEND

Clichés and mixed metaphors. A cliché is an overused figure of speech, such as *busy as a bee.* By definition, we use clichés all the time, especially in speech, and many serve usefully as shorthand for familiar ideas. But if you use clichés to excess in your writing, readers may conclude that what you are saying is not very new or is even insincere.

Mixed metaphors make comparisons that are inconsistent.

▶ **The lectures were like brilliant comets streaking**
   dazzling
   through the night sky, showering listeners with
   flashes ^
   a torrential rain of insight.
   ^

The images of streaking light and heavy precipitation are inconsistent; in the revised sentence, all of the images relate to light.

32e Spell checkers

Research conducted for this book shows that spelling errors have changed dramatically in the past twenty years, thanks to spell checkers. Although these programs have weeded out many once-common misspellings, they are not fool-proof. Look out for these typical errors allowed by spell checkers:

- HOMONYMS. Spell checkers cannot distinguish between words such as *affect* and *effect* that sound alike but are spelled differently.

- PROPER NOUNS. A spell checker cannot tell you when you misspell a name.

- COMPOUND WORDS WRITTEN AS TWO WORDS. Spell checkers will not see a problem if you write *nowhere* incorrectly as *no where*.

- TYPOS. The spell checker will not flag *heat* even if you meant to write *heart*.

Spell checkers and wrong words. Wrong-word errors are the most common surface error in college writing today (see p. 2), and spell checkers are partly to blame. Spell checkers may suggest bizarre substitutions for proper names and specialized terms, and if you accept the suggestions automatically, you may introduce wrong-word errors. A student who typed *fantic* instead of *frantic* found that the spell checker had substituted *fanatic,* a replacement that made no sense. Be careful not to take a spell checker's recommendation without paying careful attention to the replacement word.

Adapting spell checkers to your needs. Always proofread carefully, even after running the spell checker. The following tips can help:

- Check a dictionary if a spell checker highlights or suggests a word you are not sure of.

- If you can enter new words in your spell checker's dictionary, include names, non-English terms, and other specialized words that you use regularly. Double-check that you enter the correct spelling!

- After you run the spell checker, look again for homonyms that you mix up regularly.

- Remember that spell checkers are not sensitive to capitalization.

Multilingual
Writers

Writing

Sentence
Grammar

Sentence
Style

Punctuation/
Mechanics

Language

Multilingual
Writers

Research

Documentation

Xiaoming Li, now a college English teacher, says that before she came to the United States as a graduate student, she had been a "good writer" in China—in both English and Chinese. Once in the United States, however, she struggled to grasp what her teachers expected of her college writing. While she could easily use grammar books and dictionaries, her instructors' unstated expectations seemed to call for her to write in a way that was new to her.

Of course, writing for college presents many challenges. If you grew up speaking and writing in other languages, however, the transition to producing effective college writing can be even more complicated. Not only will you have to learn new information and new ways of thinking and arguing, but you also have to do it in a language that may not come naturally to you—especially in unfamiliar rhetorical situations.

33a U.S. academic writing

There is no single "correct" style of communication in any country, including the United States. Effective oral styles differ from effective written styles, and what is considered good writing in one field of study may not be appropriate in another. Even the variety of English often referred to as "standard" covers a wide range of styles (31a). Most students can benefit from some instruction in how new contexts require the use of different sets of conventions, strategies, and resources. This is especially the case for multilingual writers.

Early in your writing process, you should consider the **genre** or kind of text the instructor expects you to write. If you are not sure what kind of text you are supposed to write, ask your instructor for clarification. (Examples may also be available at your school's writing center.) You may want to find multiple examples so that you can develop a sense of how different writers approach the same writing task.

33b Adapting structures and phrases

If English is not your strongest language, you may find it useful to borrow and adapt transitional devices and pieces

> ✔ CHECKLIST
>
> **Features of Genres**
>
> Study the features of the kind of text you need to write.
>
> - What does the **genre** look like? How is the text laid out? How are any visual features incorporated?
> - How long is the whole text, each section, and each paragraph?
> - How does the text introduce the topic? Is the main point stated explicitly or implicitly?
> - What are the major divisions of the text? How are they marked?
> - How does each section contribute to the main point? How is the main point of each section supported?
> - How are the key terms defined? What kind of background information is provided?
> - What is the level of formality? Does the text use technical terms or contractions? Does the text take a personal stance (*I, we*), address the audience directly (*you*), or talk about the subject without explicitly referring to the writer or the reader?
> - How many sources are used in the text? How are they introduced?

of sentence structure from other writing in the genre you are working in. You should not copy the whole structure, however, or your borrowed sentences may seem plagiarized (Chapter 40). Find sample sentence structures from similar genres but on different topics so that you borrow a typical structure (which does not belong to anyone) rather than the idea or the particular phrasing. Write your own sentences first, and look at other people's sentences only to guide your revision.

ABSTRACT FROM A SOCIAL SCIENCE PAPER

Using the interpersonal communications research of J. K. Brilhart and G. J. Galanes, along with T. Hartman's personality assessment, I observed and analyzed the group dynamics of my project collaborators in a communications course. Based on results of the Hartman personality assessment, I predicted that a

single leader would emerge. However, complementary individual strengths and gender differences encouraged a distributed leadership style.

EFFECTIVE BORROWING OF STRUCTURES

Drawing on the research of Deborah Tannen on conversational styles, I analyzed the conversational styles of six first-year students at DePaul University. Based on Tannen's research, I expected that the three men I observed would use features typical of male conversational style and the three women would use features typical of female conversational style. In general, these predictions were accurate; however, some exceptions were also apparent.

33c Checking usage with search engines

To multilingual writers, search engines such as Google can provide a useful way of checking sentence structure and word usage. For example, if you are not sure whether you should use an **infinitive** form (*to* + verb) or a **gerund** (*-ing*) for the verb *confirm* after the main verb *expect* (36b), you can search for both *"expected confirming"* and *"expected to confirm"* to see which search term yields more results. A search for *"expected to confirm"* yields many more hits than a search for *"expected confirming."* These results indicate that *expected to confirm* is the more commonly used expression. Be sure to click through a few pages of the search engine's results to make sure that most results come from ordinary sentences rather than from headlines or phrases that may be constructed differently from standard English.

34   Sentence Structure

Short phrases, or sound bites, are everywhere—from the Dairy Council's "Got Milk?" to Volkswagen's "Drivers Wanted." These short, simple slogans may be memorable, but they don't say very much. In writing, you usually need more complex **sentences** to convey meaning. English sen-

tences are put together in ways that may differ from sentence patterns in other languages.

34a Explicit subjects and objects

English sentences consist of a **subject** and a **predicate**. While many languages can omit a sentence subject, English very rarely allows this. Though you might write *Responsible for analyzing data* on a résumé, in most varieties of spoken and written English you must explicitly state the subject.

▶ They took the Acela Express to Boston because ~~was~~ *it* fast.

English even requires a kind of "dummy" subject to fill the subject position in certain kinds of sentences.

▶ *It* is raining.
▶ *There* is a strong wind.

Transitive verbs typically require that **objects**—and sometimes other information—also be explicitly stated. For example, it is not enough to tell someone *Give!* even if it is clear what is to be given to whom. You must say, for example, *Give it to me* or *Give her the passport.*

34b Word order

In general, subjects, **verbs**, and objects must be placed in specific positions within a sentence.

SUBJECT VERB OBJECT ADVERB
▶ **Mario left Venice reluctantly.**

The only word in this sentence that can be moved to different locations is the **adverb** *reluctantly* (*Mario reluctantly left Venice* or *Reluctantly, Mario left Venice*). The three key elements of subject, verb, and object are moved out of their normal order only to create special effects.

 bedfordstmartins.com/easywriter For exercises, go to **Exercise Central** and click on **Sentence Structure**.

35 Nouns and Noun Phrases

Everyday life is filled with **nouns**: orange *juice*, the morning *news*, a *bus* to *work*, *meetings*, *pizza*, *email*, *Diet Coke*, *errands*, *dinner* with *friends*, a *chapter* in a good *book*. No matter what your first language is, it includes nouns. In English, **articles** (*a* book, *an* email, *the* news) often accompany nouns.

35a Count and noncount nouns

Nouns in English can be either **count nouns** or **noncount nouns**. Count nouns refer to distinct individuals or things that can be directly counted: *a doctor, an egg, a child; doctors, eggs, children*. Noncount nouns refer to masses, collections, or ideas without distinct parts: *milk, rice, courage*. You cannot count noncount nouns except with a preceding **phrase**: *a glass of* milk, *three grains of* rice, *a little* courage.

Count nouns usually have **singular** and **plural** forms: *tree, trees*. Noncount nouns usually have only a singular form: *grass*.

COUNT	NONCOUNT
people (plural of *person*)	humanity
tables, chairs, beds	furniture
letters	mail
pebbles	gravel
suggestions	advice

Some nouns can be either count or noncount, depending on meaning.

COUNT   Before video games, children played with *marbles*.

NONCOUNT   The palace floor was made of *marble*.

When you learn a noun in English, you need to learn whether it is count, noncount, or both. Many dictionaries provide this information.

🔗 bedfordstmartins.com/easywriter For exercises, go to **Exercise Central** and click on **Nouns and Noun Phrases**.

35b Determiners

Determiners are words that identify or quantify a noun, such as <u>*this*</u> *study*, <u>*all*</u> *people*, <u>*his*</u> *suggestions*.

COMMON DETERMINERS

- the articles *a, an, the*
- *this, these, that, those*
- *my, our, your, his, her, its, their*
- possessive nouns and noun phrases (*Sheila's* <u>*paper*</u>, *my friend's* <u>*book*</u>)
- *whose, which, what*
- *all, both, each, every, some, any, either, no, neither, many, much, (a) few, (a) little, several, enough*
- the numerals *one, two*, etc.

These determiners . . .	. . . can precede these noun types	Examples
a, an, every, each	singular count nouns	*a* book *an* American *each* word *every* Buddhist
this, that	singular count nouns noncount nouns	*this* book *that* milk
(a) little, much	noncount nouns	*a little* milk *much* affection
some, enough	noncount nouns plural count nouns	*some* milk *enough* trouble *some* books *enough* problems
the	singular count nouns plural count nouns noncount nouns	*the* doctor *the* doctors *the* information
these, those, *(a) few, many,* *both, several*	plural count nouns	*these* books *those* plans *a few* ideas *many* students *both* hands *several* trees

Determiners with singular count nouns. Every singular count noun must be preceded by a determiner. Place any adjectives between the determiner and the noun.

▶ *my*
   sister
   ^

▶ *the*
   growing population
   ^

▶ *that*
   old neighborhood
   ^

Determiners with plural nouns or noncount nouns. Noncount and plural nouns sometimes have determiners and sometimes do not. For example, *This research is important* and *Research is important* are both acceptable but have different meanings.

35c Articles

Articles (*a*, *an*, and *the*) are a type of determiner. In English, choosing which article to use—or whether to use an article at all—can be challenging. Although there are exceptions, the following general guidelines can help.

Using *a* or *an*. Use *a* and *an*, **indefinite articles**, with singular count nouns. Use *a* before a consonant sound (*a car*) and *an* before a vowel sound (*an uncle*). Consider sound rather than spelling: *a house, an hour*.

A or *an* tells readers they do not have enough information to identify specifically what the noun refers to. Compare these sentences:

▶ I need *a* new coat for the winter.

▶ I saw *a coat* that I liked at Dayton's, but it wasn't heavy enough.

The coat in the first sentence is hypothetical rather than actual. Since it is indefinite to the writer and the reader, it is used with *a*, not *the*. The second sentence refers to an actual coat, but since the writer cannot expect the reader to know which one, it is used with *a* rather than *the*.

If you want to speak of an indefinite quantity rather than just one indefinite thing, use *some* or *any* with a noncount noun or a plural count noun. Use *any* in negative sentences.

▶ This stew needs *some* more *salt*.

▶ I saw *some plates* that I liked at Gump's.

▶ This stew doesn't need *any* more salt.

Using *the*. Use the **definite article** *the* with both count and noncount nouns whose identity is known or is about to be made known to readers. The necessary information for identification can come from the **noun phrase** itself, from elsewhere in the text, from context, from general knowledge, or from a **superlative**.

▶ Let's meet at *the*̬ fountain in front of Dwinelle Hall.

The phrase *in front of Dwinelle Hall* identifies the specific fountain.

▶ Last Saturday, a fire that started in a restaurant spread to a nearby clothing store. ~~Store~~ *The store*̬ was saved, although it suffered water damage.

The word *store* is preceded by *the*, which directs our attention to the information in the previous sentence, where the store is first identified.

▶ She asked him to shut *the*̬ door when he left her office.

The context shows that she is referring to her office door.

▶ ~~Pope~~ *The pope*̬ is expected to visit Africa in October.

There is only one living pope.

▶ Bill is now *the*̬ best singer in the choir.

The superlative *best* identifies the noun *singer*.

No article. Noncount and plural count nouns can be used without an article to make generalizations:

▶ In this world nothing is certain but *death* and *taxes*.

—BENJAMIN FRANKLIN

Franklin refers not to a particular death or specific taxes but to death and taxes in general, so no article is used with *death* or with *taxes*.

English differs from many other languages that use the definite article to make generalizations. In English, a sentence like *The ants live in colonies* can refer only to particular, identifiable ants, not to ants in general.

36 Verbs and Verb Phrases

When we must act, **verbs** tell us what to do—from the street signs that say *stop* or *yield* to email commands such as *send* or *delete*. With a few stylistic exceptions, all written English sentences must include a verb.

36a Verb phrases

Verb phrases can be built up out of a **main verb** and one or more **auxiliary verbs**.

▶ **Immigration figures** *are rising* **every year.**

▶ **Immigration figures** *have risen* **every year.**

Verb phrases have strict rules of order. If you try to rearrange the words in either of these sentences, you will find that most alternatives are impossible. You cannot say *Immigration figures <u>rising are</u> every year.*

Putting auxiliary verbs in order. In the sentence *Immigration figures <u>may have been rising</u>,* the main verb *rising* follows three auxiliaries: *may, have,* and *been.* Together these auxiliaries and main verb make up a verb phrase.

- *May* is a modal that indicates possibility; it is followed by the base form of a verb.
- *Have* is an auxiliary verb that in this case indicates the perfect tense; it must be followed by a past participle (*been*).
- Any form of *be,* when it is followed by a present participle ending in *-ing* (such as *rising*), indicates the progressive tense.

🔗 bedfordstmartins.com/easywriter For exercises, go to **Exercise Central** and click on **Verbs and Verb Phrases**.

- *Be* followed by a past participle, as in *New immigration policies have <u>been passed</u> in recent years,* indicates the passive voice (7e).

As shown in the chart below, when two or more auxiliaries appear in a verb phrase, they must follow a particular order based on the type of auxiliary: (1) modal, (2) a form of *have* used to indicate a perfect tense, (3) a form of *be* used to indicate a progressive tense, and (4) a form of *be* used to indicate the passive voice. (Very few sentences include all four kinds of auxiliaries.)

Only one modal is permitted in a verb phrase.

▶ She will ~~can~~ speak Czech much better soon.

　　　　be able to

Forming auxiliary verbs. Whenever you use an auxiliary, check the form of the word that follows.

MODAL + BASE FORM. Use the base form of a verb after *can, could, will, would, shall, should, may, might,* and *must: Alice <u>can read</u> Latin.* In many other languages, modals like *can* or *must* are followed by the **infinitive** (*to* + base form). Do not substitute an infinitive for the base form in English.

▶ Alice can ~~to~~ read Latin.

	Modal	Perfect *Have*	Progressive *Be*	Passive *Be*	Main Verb	
Sonia	—	has	—	been	invited	to visit a family in Prague.
She	should	—	—	be	finished	with school soon.
The invitation	must	have	—	been	sent	in the spring.
She	—	has	been	—	studying	Czech.
She	may	—	be	—	feeling	nervous.
She	might	have	been	—	expecting	to travel elsewhere.
The trip	will	have	been	—	planned	for a month by the time she leaves.

PERFECT *HAVE, HAS,* OR *HAD* + PAST PARTICIPLE. To form the perfect tenses, use *have, has,* or *had* with a past participle: *Everyone <u>has gone</u> home. They <u>have been</u> working all day.*

PROGRESSIVE *BE* + PRESENT PARTICIPLE. A progressive form of the verb is signaled by two elements, a form of the auxiliary *be* (*am, is, are, was, were, be,* or *been*) and the *-ing* form of the next word: *The children are studying.* Be sure to include both elements.

▶   The children _∧ studying science.   *(are)*

▶   The children are <s>study</s> science.   *(studying)*

Some verbs are rarely used in progressive forms. These are verbs that express unchanging conditions or mental states rather than deliberate actions: *believe, belong, hate, know, like, love, need, own, resemble, understand.*

PASSIVE *BE* + PAST PARTICIPLE. Use *am, is, are, was, were, being, be,* or *been* with a past participle to form the passive voice.

▶   **Tagalog *is spoken* in the Philippines.**

Notice that the word following the progressive *be* (the present participle) ends in *-ing,* but the word following the passive *be* (the past participle) never ends in *-ing.*

PROGRESSIVE	Meredith *is* <u>studying</u> music.
PASSIVE	Natasha *was* <u>taught</u> by a famous violinist.

If the first auxiliary in a verb phrase is a form of *be* or *have,* it must show either present or past tense and must agree with the subject: *Meredith has played in an orchestra.*

36b   Infinitives and gerunds

Knowing whether to use an infinitive (*to read*) or a **gerund** (*reading*) in a sentence may be a challenge.

INFINITIVE

▶   **My adviser urged me *to apply* to several colleges.**

GERUND

▶ *Applying* took a great deal of time.

In general, infinitives tend to represent intentions, desires, or expectations, while gerunds tend to represent facts. The infinitive in the first sentence conveys the message that the act of applying was desired but not yet accomplished, while the gerund in the second sentence calls attention to the fact that the application process was actually carried out.

The association of intention with infinitives and facts with gerunds can often help you decide whether to use an infinitive or a gerund when another verb immediately precedes it.

INFINITIVES

▶ Kumar *expected to get* a good job after graduation.

▶ Last year, Fatima *decided to become* a math major.

▶ The strikers have *agreed to go* back to work.

GERUNDS

▶ Jerzy *enjoys going* to the theater.

▶ We *resumed working* after our coffee break.

▶ Kim *appreciated getting* candy from Sean.

A few verbs can be followed by either an infinitive or a gerund. With some, such as *begin* and *continue,* the choice makes little difference in meaning. With others, however, the difference in meaning is striking.

▶ Carlos was working as a medical technician, but he *stopped to study* English.

The infinitive indicates that Carlos left his job because he intended to study English.

▶ Carlos *stopped studying* English when he left the United States.

The gerund indicates that Carlos actually studied English but then stopped.

The distinction between fact and intention is a tendency, not a rule, and other rules may override it. Always use a gerund—not an infinitive—directly following a **preposition**.

▶ This fruit is safe for ~~to eat~~. *eating.*

You can also remove the preposition and keep the infinitive.

▶ This fruit is safe ~~for~~ to eat.

36c Conditional sentences

English distinguishes among many different types of conditional sentences—sentences that focus on questions of truth or likelihood and that are introduced by *if* or its equivalent. Each of the following examples makes different assumptions about the likelihood that what is stated in the *if* **clause** is true; each then draws the corresponding conclusion in the **main clause**.

▶ **If you *practice* (or *have practiced*) writing often, you *learn* (or *have learned*) what your main problems are.**

This sentence assumes that what is stated in the *if* clause may be true; the alternatives in parentheses indicate that any tense that is appropriate in a simple sentence may be used in both the *if* clause and the main clause.

▶ **If you *practice* writing for the rest of this term, you *will* (or *may*) understand the process better.**

This sentence makes a prediction and again assumes that what is stated may well turn out to be true. Only the main clause uses the future tense (*will understand*) or a modal that can indicate future time (*may understand*). The *if* clause must use the present tense.

▶ **If you *practiced* (or *were to practice*) writing every day, it *would* eventually *seem* easier.**

This sentence indicates doubt that what is stated will be put into effect. In the *if* clause, the verb is either past—actually, past subjunctive (7f)—or *were to* + the base form, though it refers to future time. The main clause contains *would* + the base form of the main verb.

▶ If you *practiced* writing on Mars, *you would find* no one to read your work.

This sentence imagines a situation that is impossible now. Again, the past subjunctive is used in the *if* clause, although past time is not being referred to, and *would* + the base form is used in the main clause.

▶ If you *had practiced* writing in ancient Egypt, you *would have used* hieroglyphics.

This sentence shifts the impossibility back to the past; obviously you will never find yourself in ancient Egypt. But a past impossibility demands a form that is "more past": the past perfect in the *if* clause and *would* + the present perfect form of the main verb in the main clause.

37 Prepositions and Prepositional Phrases

If you were traveling by rail and asked for directions, it would not be helpful to be told to "take the Chicago train." You would need to know whether to take the train *to* Chicago or the one *from* Chicago. Words such as *to* and *from*, which show the relations between other words, are **prepositions**.

37a The right preposition

Even if you usually know where to use prepositions, you may have difficulty knowing which preposition to use. Each of the most common prepositions has a wide range of different applications, and this range never coincides exactly from one language to another. See, for example, how *in* and *on* are used in English.

▶ The peaches are *in* the refrigerator.

▶ The peaches are *on* the table.

▶ Is that a diamond ring *on* your finger?

🔵 bedfordstmartins.com/easywriter For exercises, go to **Exercise Central** and click on **Prepositions and Prepositional Phrases**.

The Spanish translations of these sentences all use the same preposition (*en*), a fact that might lead you astray in English.

There is no easy solution to the challenge of using English prepositions idiomatically, but a few strategies can make it less troublesome.

Know typical examples. The **object** of the preposition *in* is often a container that encloses something; the object of the preposition *on* is often a horizontal surface that supports something touching it.

IN   The peaches are *in* the refrigerator.

        There are still some pickles *in* the jar.

ON   The peaches are *on* the table.

Learn related examples. Prepositions that are not used in typical ways may still show some similarities to typical examples.

IN   You shouldn't drive *in* a snowstorm.

        Like a container, the falling snow surrounds and seems to enclose the driver. The preposition *in* is used for many weather-related expressions.

ON   Is that a diamond ring *on* your finger?

        A finger is not a horizontal surface, but it supports a ring that touches it. The preposition *on* is used to describe things you wear.

Use your imagination. Create mental images that can help you remember figurative uses of prepositions.

IN   Michael is *in* love.

        Imagine a warm bath—or a raging torrent—in which Michael is immersed.

ON   I've just read a book *on* computer science.

        Imagine the book sitting on a shelf labeled "Computer Science."

Learn prepositions as part of a system. In identifying the location of a place or an event, the three prepositions

in, on, and *at* can be used. *At* specifies the exact point in space or time; *in* is required for expanses of space or time within which a place is located or an event takes place; and *on* must be used with the names of streets (but not exact addresses) and with days of the week or month.

AT There will be a meeting tomorrow *at* 9:30 AM *at* 160 Main Street.

IN I arrived *in* the United States *in* January.

ON The airline's office is *on* Fifth Avenue.

   I'll be moving to my new apartment *on* September 30.

37b Two-word verbs

Some words that look like prepositions do not always function as prepositions. Consider the following sentences:

▸ **The balloon rose *off* the ground.**

▸ **The plane took *off* without difficulty.**

In the first sentence, *off* is a preposition that introduces the **prepositional phrase** *off the ground.* In the second sentence, *off* neither functions as a preposition nor introduces a prepositional phrase. Instead, it combines with *took* to form a two-word **verb** with its own meaning. Such a verb is called a **phrasal verb**, and the word *off*, when used in this way, is called an **adverbial particle**. Many prepositions can function as particles to form phrasal verbs.

  The verb + particle combination that makes up a phrasal verb is a tightly knit entity that cannot usually be torn apart.

▸ **The plane took ~~off~~ without difficulty~~.~~**
     ^*off*^   ^

Exceptions include some phrasal verbs that are **transitive**, meaning that they take a **direct object**. Some of these verbs have particles that may be separated from the verb by the object.

▸ I *picked up my baggage* at the terminal.

▸ I *picked my baggage up* at the terminal.

If a **personal pronoun** is used as the direct object, it *must* separate the verb from its particle.

▶ **I picked** it **up ~~it~~ at the terminal.**

In some idiomatic two-word verbs, the second word is a preposition. With such verbs, the preposition can never be separated from the verb.

▶ **We *ran into* our neighbor on the train. [not *ran our neighbor into*]**

The combination *run* + *into* has a special meaning (find by chance). Therefore, *run into* is a two-word verb and *ran our neighbor into* is unacceptable.

Research

Writing

Sentence
Grammar

Sentence
Style

Punctuation/
Mechanics

Language

Multilingual
Writers

Research

Documentation

38 Conducting Research

Your employer asks you to recommend the best software for a project. You need to plan a week's stay in Montreal. Your instructor assigns a term project about a musician. Each of these situations calls for research, for examining various kinds of sources—and each calls for you to assess the data you collect, synthesize your findings, and come up with an original recommendation or conclusion. Many tasks that call for research require that your work culminate in a written document that refers to and lists the sources you used.

38a Beginning the research process

For academic research assignments, once you have a topic you need to move as efficiently as possible to analyze the research assignment, articulate a research question to answer, and form a hypothesis. Then, after preliminary research, you can refine your hypothesis into a working thesis and begin your research in earnest.

Considering the context for a research project. Ask yourself what the *purpose* of the project is—perhaps to describe, survey, analyze, persuade, explain, classify, compare, or contrast. Then consider your *audience.* Who will be most interested, and what will they need to know? What assumptions might they hold? What response do you want from them?

You should also examine your own *stance* or *attitude* toward your topic. Do you feel curious, critical, confused, or some other way about it? What influences have shaped your stance?

For a research project, consider how many and what *kinds of sources* you need to find. What kinds of evidence will convince your audience? What visuals—charts, photographs, and so on—might you need? Would it help to do field research, such as interviews, surveys, or observations?

Finally, consider practical matters, such as how long your project will be, how much time it will take, and when it is due.

Formulating a research question and hypothesis. After analyzing your project's context, work from your general topic to a research question and a hypothesis.

TOPIC	Farming
NARROWED TOPIC	Small family farms in the United States
ISSUE	Making a living from a small family farm
RESEARCH QUESTION	How can small family farms in the United States successfully compete with big agriculture?
HYPOTHESIS	Small family farmers can succeed by growing specialty products that consumers want and by participating in farmers' markets and community-supported agriculture programs that forge relationships with customers.

After you have explored sources to test your hypothesis and sharpened it by reading, writing, and talking with others, you can refine it into a working thesis (2b).

WORKING THESIS	Although recent data show that small family farms are more endangered than ever, some enterprising farmers have reversed the trend by growing specialized products and connecting with consumers through farmers' markets and community-supported agriculture programs.

Planning research. Once you have formulated a hypothesis, determine what you already know about your topic and try to remember where you got your information. Consider the kinds of sources you expect to consult and the number you think you will need, how current they should be, and where you might find them.

bedfordstmartins.com/easywriter For information and tips, click on **Research Resources**.

38b Kinds of sources

Keep in mind some important differences among types of sources.

Primary and secondary sources. Primary sources provide firsthand knowledge, while secondary sources report on or analyze the research of others. Primary sources are basic sources of raw information, including your own field research; films, works of art, or other objects you examine; literary works you read; and eyewitness accounts, photographs, news reports, and historical documents. Secondary sources are descriptions or interpretations of primary sources, such as researchers' reports, reviews, biographies, and encyclopedia articles. What constitutes a primary or secondary source depends on the purpose of your research. A film review, for instance, serves as a secondary source if you are writing about the film but as a primary source if you are studying the critic's writing.

Scholarly and popular sources. Nonacademic sources like magazines can help you get started on a research project, but you will usually want to depend more on authorities in a field, whose work generally appears in scholarly journals in print or online. The following list will help you distinguish scholarly and popular sources:

SCHOLARLY	POPULAR
Title often contains the word *Journal*	*Journal* usually does not appear in title
Source is available mainly through libraries and library databases	Source is generally available outside of libraries (at newsstands or from a home Internet connection)
Few or no commercial advertisements	Many advertisements
Authors are identified with academic credentials	Authors are usually journalists or reporters hired by the publication, not academics or experts
Summary or abstract appears on first page of article; articles are fairly long	No summary or abstract; articles are fairly short

SCHOLARLY

POPULAR

Articles cite sources and provide bibliographies

Articles may include quotations but do not cite sources or provide bibliographies

Older and more current sources. Most projects can benefit from both older, historical sources and more current ones. Some older sources are classics; others are simply dated.

38c Library resources

Almost any research project should begin with resources in your college library.

Reference librarians. Your library's staff—especially reference librarians—can be a valuable resource. You can talk with a librarian about your research project and get specific recommendations about databases and other helpful places to begin your research. Many libraries also have online tours and chat rooms where students can ask questions.

Catalogs. Library catalogs can tell you whether a book is housed in the library and, if so, offer a call number that

✓ C H E C K L I S T

Keyword Searches

When you search online catalogs, databases, and Web sites, use carefully chosen keywords to limit the scope of your search. Many search engines offer advanced-search pages for narrowing searches. Many catalogs, databases, and engines also allow you to refine your search using the **Boolean operators** AND, NOT, and OR as well as parentheses and quotation marks.

- **AND LIMITS YOUR SEARCH.** If you enter the terms *movie AND hero,* the search engine will return only items that contain both those terms.

- **NOT ALSO LIMITS YOUR SEARCH.** If you enter the terms *movie NOT hero,* the search tool will retrieve all items that contain *movie* unless they also include the term *hero.*

- **OR EXPANDS YOUR SEARCH.** If you enter the terms *movie OR hero,* the search term will retrieve every item that contains either term.

- **PARENTHESES CUSTOMIZE YOUR SEARCH.** Entering *Oscar AND (Sidney Poitier or Jodie Foster)* will locate items that mention either actor in connection with the Oscars.

- **QUOTATION MARKS NARROW YOUR SEARCH.** Quotation marks indicate that all the words in the phrase must appear together in that order.

    Catalogs and databases may also index their contents by subject headings. Try a keyword search on your topic to identify the exact subject heading (most libraries use the Library of Congress Subject Headings, or LCSH). Then search using the subject term to find all entries under that heading, whether or not the precise subject term is included in the title or description of an entry.

enables you to find the book on the shelf. Browsing through other books near the one you've found in the catalog can help you locate other works related to your topic. Catalogs also indicate whether you can find a particular periodical, either in print or in an online database, at the library.

Indexes and databases.   Most college libraries subscribe to a large number of indexes and databases that students can access for free. Some databases include the full text of articles

from newspapers, magazines, journals, and other works; some offer only short abstracts (summaries), which give an overview so you can decide whether to spend time finding and reading the whole text. Indexes of reviews provide information about a potential source's critical reception.

Check with a librarian for discipline-specific indexes and databases related to your topic.

Reference works. General reference works, such as encyclopedias, biographical resources, almanacs, digests, and atlases, can help you get an overview of a topic, identify subtopics, find more specialized sources, and identify keywords for searches.

Bibliographies. Bibliographies—lists of sources—in books or articles related to your topic can lead you to other valuable resources. Ask a librarian whether your library has more extensive bibliographies related to your research topic.

Other resources. Your library can help you borrow materials from other libraries (this can take time, so plan ahead). Check with reference librarians, too, about audio, video, multimedia, and art collections; government documents; and other special collections or archives that student researchers may be able to use.

38d Internet research

For many college students, the Internet is a favorite way of accessing information. It's true that much information—including authoritative sources identical to those your library provides—can be found online. Remember that library databases come from identifiable and professionally edited resources; you need to take special care to find out which information online is reliable and which is not (39a).

Internet searches. Research using a search tool such as Google usually begins with a keyword search (see p. 180). Many keyword searches bring up thousands of hits; you may find what you need on the first page or two of results, but if not, choose new keywords that lead to more specific sources.

Bookmarking tools. Today's powerful bookmarking tools can help you browse, sort, and track resources online. Social bookmarking sites, such as del.icio.us and Digg, allow users to tag information and share it with others. Users' tags are visible to all other users. If you find a helpful site, you can check how others have tagged it and browse similar tags for related information. You can also sort and group information with tags. Fellow users whose tags you trust can become part of your network so you can follow their sites of interest.

Web browsers can also help you bookmark online resources. However, unlike bookmarking tools in a browser, which are tied to one machine, you can use social bookmarking tools wherever you have an Internet connection.

Authoritative sources online. Many sources online are authoritative and reliable. You can browse collections in online virtual libraries, for example, or collections housed in government sites such as the Library of Congress, the National Institutes of Health, and the U.S. Census Bureau. For current national news, consult online versions of reputable newspapers such as the *Washington Post*, or electronic sites for news services such as C-SPAN. Google Scholar can help you limit searches to scholarly works.

Some journals (such as those from Berkeley Electronic Press) and general-interest magazines (such as *Salon*) are published only online; many other print publications make at least some of their content available free on the Web.

38e   Field research

For many research projects, you will need to collect field data. Consider *where* you can find relevant information, *how* to gather it, and *who* might be your best providers of information.

Interviews. Some information is best obtained by asking direct questions of other people. If you can talk with an expert—in person, on the telephone, or online—you may get information you cannot obtain through any other kind of research.

   1. Determine your exact purpose, and be sure it relates to your research question and your hypothesis.

2. Set up the interview well in advance. Specify how long it will take, and if you wish to tape-record the session, ask permission to do so.
3. Prepare a written list of factual and open-ended questions. If the interview proceeds in a direction that seems fruitful, do not feel that you have to ask all of your prepared questions.
4. Record the subject, date, time, and place of the interview.
5. Thank those you interview, either in person or in a letter or email.

Observation. Trained observers report that making a faithful record of an observation requires intense concentration and mental agility.

1. Determine the purpose of the observation, and be sure it relates to your research question and hypothesis.
2. Brainstorm about what you are looking for, but don't be rigidly bound to your expectations.
3. Develop an appropriate system for recording data. Consider using a split notebook or page: on one side, record your observations directly; on the other, record your thoughts or interpretations.
4. Record the date, time, and place of observation.

Opinion surveys. Surveys usually depend on questionnaires. On any questionnaire, the questions should be clear and easy to understand and designed so that you can analyze the answers easily. Questions that ask respondents to say *yes* or *no* or to rank items on a scale are particularly easy to tabulate.

1. Write out your purpose, and determine the kinds of questions to ask.
2. Figure out how to reach respondents.
3. Draft questions that call for short, specific answers.
4. Test the questions on several people, and revise questions that seem unfair, ambiguous, or too hard or time consuming.
5. For a questionnaire that will be mailed, draft a cover letter. Provide an addressed, stamped return envelope, and be sure to state a deadline.
6. On the final version of the questionnaire, leave adequate space for answers.
7. Proofread the questionnaire carefully.

39 Evaluating Sources and Taking Notes

All research builds on the careful and sometimes inspired use of sources—that is, on research done by others. Since you want the information you glean from sources to be reliable and persuasive, you must evaluate each potential source carefully.

39a Evaluating the usefulness and credibility of potential sources

Use these guidelines to assess the usefulness of a source:

- **YOUR PURPOSE.** What will this source add to your research project? Does it help you support a major point, demonstrate that you have thoroughly researched your topic, or help establish your own credibility through its authority?

- **RELEVANCE.** Is the source closely related to your research question? You may need to read beyond the title and opening paragraph to check for relevance.

- **PUBLISHER'S CREDENTIALS.** What do you know about the publisher of the source you are using? For example, is it a major newspaper known for integrity in reporting, or is it a tabloid? Is the publisher a popular source, or is it sponsored by a professional or scholarly organization?

- **AUTHOR'S CREDENTIALS.** Is the author an expert on the topic? An author's credentials may be presented in the article, book, or Web site, or you can search the Internet for information on the author.

- **DATE OF PUBLICATION.** Recent sources are often more useful than older ones, particularly in fields that change rapidly. However, the most authoritative works may be older ones. The publication dates of Internet sites can often be difficult to pin down. And even for sites that include the dates of posting, remember that the material posted may have been composed some time earlier.

- **ACCURACY OF SOURCE.** How accurate and complete is the information in the source? How thorough is the bibliography or list of works cited that accompanies the source? Can you find other sources that corroborate what your source is saying?

- **STANCE OF SOURCE.** Identify the source's point of view or rhetorical stance, and scrutinize it carefully. Does the

source present facts, or does it interpret or evaluate them? If it presents facts, what is included and what is omitted, and why? If it interprets or evaluates information that is not disputed, the source's stance may be obvious, but at other times you will need to think carefully about the source's goals. What does the author or sponsoring group want—to convince you of an idea? sell you something? call you to action in some way?

- CROSS-REFERENCING. Is the source cited in other works? If you see your source cited by others, looking at how they cite it and what they say about it can provide additional clues to its credibility.

- LEVEL OF SPECIALIZATION. General sources can be helpful as you begin your research, but you may then need the authority or currency of more specialized sources. On the other hand, extremely specialized works may be very hard to understand.

- AUDIENCE OF SOURCE. Was the source written for the general public? specialists? advocates or opponents?

For more on evaluating sources, see the source maps on pp. 186–91.

39b Reading and interpreting sources

After you have decided that a source is potentially useful, read it carefully and critically, asking yourself the following questions about how this research fits your writing project:

- How relevant is this material to your research question and hypothesis?

- Does the source include counterarguments that you should address?

- How persuasive is the evidence? Does it represent opposing viewpoints fairly? Will the source be convincing to your audience?

- Will you need to change your thesis to account for this information?

- What quotations or paraphrases from this source might you want to use?

As you read and take notes on your sources, keep in mind that you will need to present data and sources to other readers so that they can understand your point.

Source Map: Evaluating Articles

Determine the relevance of the source.

1 Look for an **abstract**, which provides a summary of the entire article. Is this source directly related to your research? Does it provide useful information and insights? Will your readers consider it persuasive support for your thesis?

Determine the credibility of the publication.

2 Consider the publication's **title**. Words in the title such as *Journal, Review,* and *Quarterly* may indicate that the periodical is a scholarly source. Most research projects rely on authorities in a particular field, whose work usually appears in scholarly journals. For more on distinguishing between scholarly and popular sources, see 38b.

3 Try to determine the **publisher or sponsor**. This journal is published by Johns Hopkins University Press. Academic presses such as this one generally review articles carefully before publishing them and bear the authority of their academic sponsors.

Determine the credibility of the author.

4 Evaluate the **author's credentials**. In this case, they are given in a note, which indicates that the author is a college professor and has written at least two books on related topics.

Determine the currency of the article.

5 Look at the **publication date**, and think about whether your topic and your credibility depend on your use of very current sources.

Determine the accuracy of the article.

6 Look at the **sources cited** by the author of the article. Here, they are documented in footnotes. Ask yourself whether the works the author has cited seem credible and current. Are any of these works cited in other articles you've considered?

In addition, consider the following questions:

- What is the article's stance or point of view? What are the author's goals? What does the author want you to know or believe?

- How does this source fit in with your other sources? Does any of the information it provides contradict or challenge other sources?

HUMAN RIGHTS QUARTERLY

2 Title of Publication

Prisons and Politics in Contemporary Latin America

Mark Ungar*

1 Abstract

915

ABSTRACT

Despite democratization throughout Latin America, massive human rights abuses continue in the region's prisons. Conditions have become so bad that most governments have begun to enact improvements, including new criminal codes and facility decongestion. However, once in place, these reforms are undermined by chaotic criminal justice systems, poor policy administration, and rising crime rates leading to greater detention powers for the police. After describing current prison conditions in Latin America and the principal reforms to address them, this article explains how political and administrative limitations hinder the range of agencies and officials responsible for implementing those changes.

I. INTRODUCTION

4 Author's Credentials

Prison conditions not only constitute some of the worst human rights violations in contemporary Latin American democracies, but also reveal fundamental weaknesses in those democracies. Unlike most other human rights problems, those in the penitentiary system cannot be easily explained with authoritarian legacies or renegade officials. The systemic killing, overcrowding, disease, torture, rape, corruption, and due process abuses all occur under the state's twenty-four hour watch. Since the mid-1990s,

* Mark Ungar is Associate Professor of Political Science at Brooklyn College, City University of New York. Recent publications include the books *Elusive Reform: Democracy and the Rule of Law in Latin America* (Lynne Rienner, 2002) and *Violence and Politics: Globalization's Paradox* (Routledge, 2001) as well as articles and book chapters on democratization, policing, and judicial access. He works with Amnesty International USA and local rights groups in Latin America.

Human Rights Quarterly 25 (2003) 909–934 © 2003 by The Johns Hopkins University Press

5 Publication Date **3** Publisher

10. INSPECTOR GENERAL DE CÁRCELES, INFORME ANNUAL (Caracas: Ministerio de Justicia 1994).
11. *Overcrowding Main Cause of Riots in Latin American Prisons*, AFP, 30 Dec. 1997.
12. Interviews with inmates, speaking on condition of anonymity in San Pedro prison (19 July 2000); Interviews with inmates, speaking on condition of anonymity in La Paz FELCN Prison (20 July 2000).
13. Typhus, cholera, tuberculosis, and scabies run rampant and the HIV rate may be as high as 25 percent. The warden of Retén de la Planta, where cells built for one inmate house three or four, says the prisons "are collapsing" because of insufficient budgets to train personnel. "Things fall apart and stay that way." Interview, Luis A. Lara Roche, Warden of Retén de la Planta, Caracas, Venezuela, 19 May 1995. At El Dorado prison in Bolívar state, there is one bed for every four inmates, cells are infested with vermin, and inmates lack clean bathing water and eating utensils.
14. *La Crisis Penitenciaria*, EL NACIONAL (Caracas), 2 Sept. 1988, at D2. On file with author.

6 Sources Cited

Source Map: Evaluating Web Sources

Is the sponsor credible?

1 Who is the **sponsor or publisher** of the source? See what information you can get from the URL. The domain names for government sites may end in *.gov* or *.mil* and for educational sites in *.edu*. The ending *.org* may—but does not always—indicate a nonprofit organization. If you see a tilde (~) or percent sign (%) followed by a name, or if you see a word such as *users* or *members,* the page's creator may be an individual, not an institution. In addition, check the header and footer, where the sponsor may be identified. The page shown here, from the domain **niemanwatchdog.org**, is from a site sponsored by the nonprofit Nieman Foundation for Journalism at Harvard University.

2 Look for an *About* **page** or a link to a home page for background information on the sponsor. Is a mission statement included? What are the sponsoring organization's purpose and point of view? Does the mission statement seem balanced? What is the purpose of the site (to inform, to persuade, to advocate for a cause, to advertise, or something else)? Does the information on the site come directly from the sponsor, or is the material reprinted from another source? If it is reprinted, check the original.

Is the author credible?

3 What are the **author's credentials**? Look for information accompanying the material on the page. You can also run a search on the author to find out more. Does the author seem qualified to write about this topic?

Is the information credible and current?

4 When was the information **posted or last updated**? Is it recent enough to be useful?

5 Does the page document sources with **footnotes or links**? If so, do the sources seem credible and current? Does the author include any additional resources for further information? Look for ways to corroborate the information the author provides.

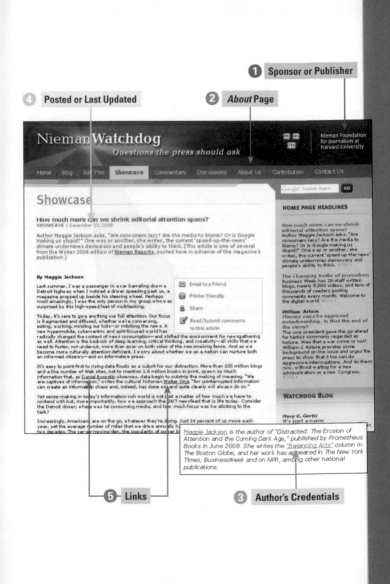

Source Map: Using Sources Effectively

 1 **How appropriate is the source for the argument you are making?** Read carefully, and be sure you understand exactly how the material in the source relates to your point. Student Amanda Rinder, in doing research for a paper about Chicago architecture, discovered a debate between preservationists and developers. This *Chicago Tribune* article by Paul Gapp documents the debate.

2 **What purpose does each source serve in your argument?** Identifying the purpose of each source can help keep your research relevant and ensure that you fill in gaps (and avoid repetition). Amanda used paraphrases (highlighted) and quotations (underlined) from the Gapp article to present an overview of the issues of architectural preservation and to offer support for the preservationists. She used images, including this one of the McCarthy Building, as examples of the architectural style that preservationists wanted to save. She also did background research on Paul Gapp and learned, from his obituary in the *New York Times*, that he had won a Pulitzer Prize for his architecture criticism. She did not ultimately use the obituary in her paper, but it helped her be certain of Gapp's credibility.

3 **Do your sources include fair representations of opposing views?** Consider what else you need to include to present a complete picture of the argument. Amanda paraphrased Gapp's balanced discussion of the pros and cons of protecting the McCarthy Building. She also found additional sources on both sides of the issue.

4 **How credible will your sources be to your audience?** Make sure that the evidence you choose will seem convincing. Amanda identified Gapp as "a *Chicago Tribune* architecture critic" to show him as an authority on her topic. Her other sources included books by architects and historians and other articles on architecture from major newspapers in Chicago and elsewhere.

To read Amanda Rinder's essay, go to bedfordstmartins.com/ easywriter and click on **Student Writing**. An excerpt appears in 44d.

MCCARTHY BUILDING PUTS LANDMARK LAW
ON A COLLISION COURSE WITH DEVELOPERS ◄── **1** Appropriate Source

[FINAL EDITION, C]
Chicago Tribune (pre-1997 Fulltext) - Chicago, Ill. ◄── **4** Credible Source
Author: Paul Gapp, Architecture critic
Date: Apr 20, 1986
Section: ARTS
Text Word Count: 1142
Document Text

Chicago's commitment to saving municipally designated landmarks is undergoing one of
its most crucial tests. If a little gem of a structure called the McCarthy Building is torn
down, the city's landmarks protection ordinance will be devalued almost to the vanish
point.

forgotten t   The McCarthy stands at the northeast corner of Dearborn and Washington Stre
anchor of   across from Daley Civic Center. Its dignified facades are defaced by so man
               that most pedestrians see the building only as a rude smear on the streetsc
Municipal   McCarthy's esthetic and historical value is undeniable, which is why the
by making   gave the building landmark status in the first place.

-- The Mc   Now, however, a real estate development group wants to demolish

-- The Chi   room for an office tower. Because the building stands on munic
               renewal land, the city has both the leverage to save it and a re
1921.   destruction. This landmark scenario is unprecedented and c

-- The Pag   The McCarthy and several other important old building
building c   early 1970s when the city began drafting the North L
only surviv   the private Landmarks Preservation Council (LPC)
               buildings, but the city brushed aside
-- The ham
1922 on d   Under an early version of the Nor
               more than 50 buildings--includin
-- The Oli   destroyed in a seven-block area.
structure c
               Among structures marked for d
-- The Def   listed on the federal National R
Thomas. I   Washington warned that their
McCarthy   and City Hall began reshufflin

When the   The tangle of events that fol
previous   mind about what should an
guarantee
$12.6 t   While this was going on,
building a   hotel, which fell to make
now well -
connect

Late la
group   And so we consider the present McCarthy Building situation, which might
group   as an impasse on its way to becoming a brouhaha.
place.
               The city council gave the McCarthy landmark status because it is a rare and distinguished
To ma   example of work by Van Osdel, who was Chicago's first professional architect. Created in
the city   an Italianate style just a year after the Great Chicago Fire of 1871, the McCarthy's
theatric   carefully detailed masonry and iron facades reflect the same look Van Osdel selected
               when he designed the third Palmer House hotel a few years later.   **2** Sources Serve
When   Purpose
Chicago   If the garish signs that degrade the McCarthy were simply removed, that alone would
tantam   reveal the building as a stunningly appealing relic from Chicago's 19th Century
directo   renaissance era. Replacing the little five-story building's lost cornice and restoring its
               base would present no technical problems.

Today, City Hall is trapped and squirming in the middle.

If it stands fast in favor of the McCarthy, it risks queering the land sale in an important
urban renewal area whose upgrading has already been plagued by political, legal, tax
assessment and other problems.

If it rescinds the McCarthy's landmark status and allows demolition, the city will have   **3** Fair Representation of
gone on record as favoring the allure of the dollar over Chicago's architectural heritage.   Opposing Views
(Moving the McCarthy to another site, which has also been suggested, would amount to
the same kind of surrender and set a dangerous precedent).

It's a tough decision, and the politicians will be faulted in either case. Yet anyone who
cares for the irreplaceable historical and cultural fabric of the city can hardly take
anything but the long view:

The McCarthy and most of Chicago's other official architecture landmarks were in place
long before any of today's politicians and real estate developers (or you and I) were born.
Is it too much to hope that they will continue to grace our ravaged but still great city long
after all of us are gone?

The New York Times
nytimes.com
August 11, 1992

Paul Gapp, 64, Journalist, Dies; Architecture Critic Won Pulitzer

By HERBERT MUSCHAMP

Paul Gapp, the Pulitzer Prizewinning architecture critic for The Chicago Tribune, died
July 30 at Northwest Memorial Hospital in Chicago. He was 64 years old and lived in
Chicago.

He died of lung cancer complicated by emphysema, his office said.

Mr. Gapp was born in Cleveland in
Columbia (Ohio) Dispatch after gradua
later he joined The Chicago
and features editor In 1972
editor for urban affairs
Prize for Crit

                                                in journalism with The
                                          ly in 1950. Six years
                                      me as assistant city
                                  74 and won the Pulitzer

                              which he once
                           pace and great
                        ildings in

39c Synthesizing sources

Throughout the research process, you are *synthesizing*—grouping similar pieces of data together, looking for patterns, and identifying the main points. Doing so enables you to use your sources effectively to pursue your research goals.

Using sources effectively can pose challenges. A national study of first-year college writing found that student writers trying to incorporate research sometimes used sources that were not directly relevant to their point, too specific to support the larger claim being made, or otherwise ineffective. Even after you have evaluated a source, then, take time to look at how well the source works in your specific situation. (If you change the focus of your work after you have begun doing research, be especially careful to check whether your sources still fit.)

39d Taking notes

While note-taking methods vary from one researcher to another, for each note you should (1) record enough information to help you recall the major points of the source; (2) put the information in the form in which you are most likely to incorporate it into your research project; and (3) note all the information you will need to cite the source accurately, including a subject heading and a label saying what type of note it is—paraphrase, summary, or quotation. Keep a running list that includes citation information for each source in an electronic file or on note cards that you can rearrange and alter as your project takes shape. This working bibliography will simplify the process of documenting sources for your final project.

Quoting. Quoting involves bringing a source's exact words into your text. Use an author's exact words when the wording is so memorable or expresses a point so well that you cannot improve or shorten it without weakening it, when the author is a respected authority whose opinion supports your own ideas, or when an author challenges or disagrees profoundly with others in the field. Here are guidelines for quoting:

- Copy quotations carefully, with punctuation, capitalization, and spelling exactly as in the original (23a).

- Enclose the quotation in quotation marks (23a).
- Use brackets if you introduce words of your own into the quotation or make changes in it (24b).
- Use ellipses if you omit words from the quotation (24f).
- If you later incorporate the quotation into your research project, copy it from the note precisely, including brackets and ellipses.
- Record the author's name, shortened title, and page number(s) on which the quotation appeared.
- Make sure you have a corresponding working-bibliography entry with complete source information.
- Label the note with a subject heading, and identify it as a quotation.

QUOTATION-STYLE NOTE

Comments from educators ◄——————— Subject heading

Lee, "I Think," *NY Times* (Web site) ◄——— Author and
                                            short title of
                                            source (no page
Melanie Weaver was stunned by some of   number for elec-
the term papers she received from a 10th-   tronic source)
grade class she recently taught as part of
an internship. "They would be trying to
make a point in a paper, [so] they would
put a smiley face in the end," said Ms.
Weaver, who teaches at Alvernia College in
Reading, Pa. "If they were presenting an
argument and they needed to present an
opposite view, they would put a frown."   Indication that
                                            note is direct
(Quotation) ◄——————————————————— quotation

Paraphrasing. When you paraphrase, you put brief material from an author (including major and minor points, usually in the order they are presented) into *your own words and sentence structures*. If you wish to cite some of the author's words within the paraphrase, enclose them in quotation marks. Here are guidelines for paraphrasing:

- Include all main points and any important details from the original source in the same order in which the author presents them.
- State the meaning in your own words and sentence structures. If you want to include any language from the original, enclose it in quotation marks.
- Save for another note your own comments, elaborations, or reactions.
- Record the author, shortened title, and page number(s), if the source has them, on which the original material appeared.
- Make sure you have a corresponding working-bibliography entry.
- Label the note with a subject heading, and identify it as a paraphrase to avoid confusion with a summary.
- Recheck to be sure that the words and sentence structures are your own and that they express the author's meaning accurately.

The following examples of paraphrases resemble the original either too little or too much.

ORIGINAL

> Language play, the arguments suggest, will help the development of pronunciation ability through its focus on the properties of sounds and sound contrasts, such as rhyming. Playing with word endings and decoding the syntax of riddles will help the acquisition of grammar. Readiness to play with words and names, to exchange puns and to engage in nonsense talk, promotes links with semantic development. The kinds of dialogue interaction illustrated above are likely to have consequences for the development of conversational skills. And language play, by its nature, also contributes greatly to what in recent years has been called *metalinguistic awareness*, which is turning out to be of critical importance in the development of language skills in general and of literacy skills in particular. —DAVID CRYSTAL, *Language Play* (180)

UNACCEPTABLE PARAPHRASE: STRAYING FROM THE AUTHOR'S IDEAS

> Crystal argues that playing with language—creating rhymes, figuring out how riddles work, making puns, playing with names, using invented words, and so on—helps children figure out a great deal about language, from the basics of pronunciation and grammar to how to carry on a conversation. Increasing their understanding of how language works in turn helps them become more interested in learning new languages and in pursuing education (180).

This paraphrase starts off well enough, but it moves away from paraphrasing the original to inserting the writer's ideas; Crystal says nothing about learning new languages or pursuing education.

UNACCEPTABLE PARAPHRASE: USING THE AUTHOR'S WORDS

Crystal suggests that language play, including rhyme, helps children improve <u>pronunciation ability</u>, that looking at <u>word endings and decoding the syntax of riddles</u> allows them to understand grammar, and that other <u>kinds of dialogue interaction</u> teach conversation. Overall, language play may <u>be of critical importance in the development of language and literacy skills</u> (180).

Because the underlined phrases are either borrowed from the original without quotation marks or changed only superficially, this paraphrase plagiarizes.

UNACCEPTABLE PARAPHRASE: USING THE AUTHOR'S SENTENCE STRUCTURES

Language play, Crystal <u>suggests</u>, <u>will improve</u> pronunciation by zeroing in on sounds <u>such as</u> rhymes. <u>Having fun with</u> word endings <u>and analyzing</u> riddle structure <u>will help</u> a person acquire grammar. <u>Being prepared to play with</u> language, <u>to use</u> puns and <u>talk</u> nonsense, <u>improves</u> the ability to use semantics. <u>These</u> playful methods of communication <u>are likely to</u> influence a person's ability to talk to others. <u>And language play</u> inherently <u>adds enormously to what has</u> recently <u>been</u> known as <u>*metalinguistic awareness*</u>, a concept <u>of great magnitude in developing</u> speech abilities <u>generally</u> and literacy abilities <u>particularly</u> (180).

Here is a paraphrase of the same passage that expresses the author's ideas accurately and acceptably:

ACCEPTABLE PARAPHRASE: IN THE STUDENT WRITER'S OWN WORDS

Crystal argues that playing with language—creating rhymes, figuring out riddles, making puns, playing with names, using invented words, and so on—helps children figure out a great deal, from the basics of pronunciation and grammar to how to carry on a conversation. This kind of play allows children to understand the overall concept of how language works, a concept that is key to learning to use—and read—language effectively (180).

Summarizing. A summary is a significantly shortened version of a passage or even a whole chapter, article, film,

or other work that captures main ideas *in your own words.*
Unlike a paraphrase, a summary uses just enough information to record the points you wish to emphasize. Here are
some guidelines for summarizing accurately:

- Include just enough information to recount the main
  points you want to cite. A summary is usually far shorter
  than the original.

- Use your own words. If you include any language from
  the original, enclose it in quotation marks.

- Record the author, shortened title, and page number(s)
  on which the original material appeared. For online or
  multimedia sources without page numbers, record any
  information that will help readers find the material.

- Make sure you have a corresponding working-
  bibliography entry.

- Label the note with a subject heading, and identify it as a
  summary to avoid confusion with a paraphrase.

- Recheck to be sure you have captured the author's meaning and that the words are entirely your own.

SUMMARY NOTE

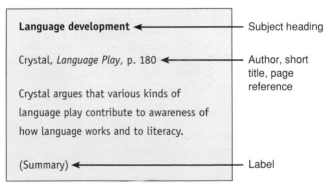

Annotating sources. Sometimes you may photocopy or
print out a source you intend to use. In such cases, you can
annotate the photocopies or printouts with your thoughts
and questions and highlight interesting quotations and key
terms.

You can copy online sources electronically, paste them
into a file, and annotate them there. Try not to rely too
heavily on copying or printing out whole pieces, however;
you still need to read the material very carefully. And resist
the temptation to treat copied material as notes, an action

FOR MULTILINGUAL WRITERS

Identifying Sources

While some language communities and cultures expect audiences to recognize the sources of important documents and texts, thereby eliminating the need to cite them directly, conventions for writing in North America call for careful attribution of any quoted, paraphrased, or summarized material. When in doubt, explicitly identify your sources.

that could lead to inadvertent plagiarizing. (In a computer file, using a different color for text pasted from a source will help prevent this problem.)

40 Integrating Sources and Avoiding Plagiarism

In some ways, there is really nothing new under the sun, in writing and research as well as in life. Whatever writing you do has been influenced by what you have already read and experienced. As you work on your research project, you will need to know how to integrate and acknowledge the work of others. And all writers need to understand current definitions of plagiarism (which have changed over time and differ from culture to culture) as well as the concept of intellectual property—those works protected by copyright and other laws—so that they can give credit where credit is due.

40a Integrating quotations, paraphrases, and summaries

Integrate source materials into your writing with care to ensure that the integrated materials make grammatical and logical sense.

---

bedfordstmartins.com/easywriter For tips on using sources and considering your own intellectual property, click on **Research Resources**.

Integrating quotations. Because your research project is primarily your own work, limit your use of quotations to those necessary to your thesis or memorable for your readers.

Short quotations should run in with your text, enclosed by quotation marks. Longer quotations should be set off from the text (23a). Integrate all quotations into the text so that they flow smoothly and clearly into the surrounding sentences. Be sure that the sentence containing the quotation is grammatically complete, especially if you incorporate a quotation into your own words.

SIGNAL PHRASES

Introduce the quotation with a signal phrase or signal **verb**, such as those underlined in these examples.

▶ <u>As Eudora Welty notes</u>, "learning stamps you with its moments. Childhood's learning," <u>she continues</u>, "is made up of moments. It isn't steady. It's a pulse" (9).

▶ In her essay, <u>Haraway strongly opposes</u> those who condemn technology outright, <u>arguing</u> that we must not indulge in a "demonology of technology" (181).

Choose a signal verb that is appropriate to the idea you are expressing and that accurately characterizes the author's viewpoint. Other signal verbs include words such as *acknowledges, agrees, asserts, believes, claims, concludes, describes, disagrees, lists, objects, offers, remarks, reports, reveals, says, suggests,* and *writes.*

When you write about literary and artistic works, generally follow the Modern Language Association (MLA) style, used in the examples in this chapter, and put verbs in signal phrases in the **present tense**. For papers on history and some other areas of the humanities that use *Chicago* style, use the present tense. The **past tense** is acceptable in *Chicago* style if you wish to emphasize that an author's point was made in the past.

If you are writing for the social sciences using the style of the American Psychological Association (APA) to describe research results, use verbs in the past tense or the **present perfect tense** (*the study <u>showed</u>, the study <u>has shown</u>*) in your signal phrase. When explaining the implications of research, use the present tense (*for future research, these findings <u>suggest</u>*).

When you write in the natural sciences using the Council of Science Editors (CSE) style, in general use the present tense for research reports and the past tense to describe specific experimental methods or observations, or to cite research published in the past.

BRACKETS AND ELLIPSES
In direct quotations, enclose in brackets any words you change or add, and indicate any deletions with ellipsis points.

▶ **"There is something wrong in the [Three Mile Island] area," one farmer told the Nuclear Regulatory Commission after the plant accident ("Legacy" 33).**

▶ **Economist John Kenneth Galbraith pointed out that "large corporations cannot afford to compete with one another. . . . In a truly competitive market someone loses" (Key 17).**

Be careful that any changes you make in a quotation do not alter its meaning. Use brackets and ellipses sparingly; too many make for difficult reading and might suggest that you have removed some of the context for the quotation.

Integrating paraphrases and summaries.   Introduce paraphrases and summaries clearly, usually with a signal phrase that includes the author of the source, as the underlined words in this example indicate.

▶ <u>**Professor of linguistics Deborah Tannen illustrates**</u> **how communication between women and men breaks down** <u>**and then suggests**</u> **that a full awareness of "genderlects" can improve relationships (297).**

40b Integrating visuals

If you are using visuals (such as graphs, cartoons, maps, photographs, charts, tables, or time lines), integrate them smoothly into your text.

- Make sure the graphic conveys information more efficiently than words alone could do.
- Position the visual immediately after the text it illustrates or refers to—or as close to it as possible.

- Refer to the visual by number in the text *before* it appears: *As Figure 3 demonstrates.*
- Explain or comment on the relevance of the visual. This can be done *after* the visual.
- Label each visual clearly and consistently: *Fig. 1. Photograph of the New York Skyline.*
- Check the documentation system you are using to make sure you label visuals appropriately; MLA, for instance, asks that you number and title tables and figures (*Table 1: Average Amount of Rainfall by Region*).
- If you are posting your work on a Web site, make sure you have permission to use any copyrighted visuals.

40c Knowing which sources to acknowledge

As you carry out research, it is important to understand the distinction between materials that require acknowledgment (in in-text citations, footnotes, or endnotes; and in the list of works cited or bibliography) and those that do not.

Materials that do not require acknowledgment.   You do not usually need to cite a source for the following:

- Common knowledge—facts that most readers already know.
- Facts available in a wide variety of sources, such as encyclopedias, almanacs, or textbooks.
- Your own findings from field research. You should, however, acknowledge people you interview as individuals rather than as part of a survey.

Materials that require acknowledgment.   You should cite all of your other sources to be certain to avoid plagiarism. Follow the documentation style required (see Chapters 42–45), and list the source in a bibliography or list of works cited. Be especially careful to cite the following:

- Sources for quotations, paraphrases, and summaries that you include.
- Facts not widely known or arguable assertions.
- All visuals from any source, including your own artwork, photographs you have taken, and graphs or tables you create from data found in a source.
- Any help provided by a friend, an instructor, or another person.

40d Avoiding plagiarism

Academic integrity enables us to trust those sources we use and to demonstrate that our own work is equally trustworthy. Plagiarism is especially damaging to academic integrity, whether it involves inaccurate or incomplete acknowledgment of sources in citations—sometimes called unintentional plagiarism—or deliberate plagiarism that is intended to pass off one writer's work as another's.

Whether it is intentional or not, plagiarism can have serious consequences. Students caught plagiarizing may fail the course or be expelled. Others who have plagiarized, even inadvertently, have had degrees revoked or have been stripped of positions or awards.

Unintentional plagiarism.   If your paraphrase is too close to the wording or sentence structure of a source (even if you identify the source); if after a quotation you do not identify the source (even if you include the quotation marks); or if you fail to indicate clearly the source of an idea that you did not come up with on your own, you may be accused of plagiarism even if your intent was not to plagiarize. This inaccurate or incomplete acknowledgment of sources often results either from carelessness or from not learning how to borrow material properly.

Take responsibility for your research and for acknowledging all sources accurately. To guard against unintentional plagiarism, photocopy or print out sources and identify the needed quotations right on the copy. You can also insert footnotes or endnotes into the text as you write.

Deliberate plagiarism.   Deliberate plagiarism—handing in an essay written by a friend or purchased or downloaded from an essay-writing company; cutting and pasting passages directly from source materials without marking them with quotation marks and acknowledging their sources; failing to credit the source of an idea or concept in your text—is what most people think of when they hear the word *plagiarism*. This form of plagiarism is particularly troubling because it represents dishonesty and deception: those who intentionally plagiarize present someone else's hard work as their own and claim knowledge they really don't have, thus deceiving their readers.

Deliberate plagiarism is also fairly simple to spot: your instructor will be well acquainted with your writing and

---

FOR MULTILINGUAL WRITERS

Thinking about Plagiarism as a Cultural Concept

Many cultures do not recognize Western notions of plagiarism, which rest on a belief that writers can own their language and ideas. Indeed, in many cultures and communities, using the words and ideas of others without attribution is considered a sign of deep respect as well as an indication of knowledge. In academic writing in the United States, however, you should credit all materials except those that are common knowledge, that are available in a wide variety of sources, or that are your own creations or your own findings from field research.

---

likely to notice any sudden shifts in the style or quality of your work. In addition, by typing a few words from a project into a search engine, your instructor can identify "matches" very easily.

41 Writing a Research Project

When you are working on a research project, there comes a time to draw the strands of your research together and articulate your conclusions in writing.

41a Drafting your text

To group the information you have collected, try arranging your notes and visuals to identify connections, main ideas, and possible organization. You may also want to develop a working outline, a storyboard, or an idea map, or you can plot out a more detailed organization in a formal outline.

For almost all research writing, drafting should begin well before the deadline in case you need to gather more information or do more drafting. Begin drafting wherever you feel most confident. If you have an idea for an introduction, begin there. If you are not sure how you want to introduce the project but do know how you want to approach one point, begin with that, and return to the introduction later.

Working title and introduction. The title and introduction set the stage for what is to come. Ideally, the title announces the subject in an intriguing or memorable way. The introduction should draw readers in and provide any background they will need to understand your discussion. You may want to open with a question, explain how you will answer it, and end with your explicit thesis statement.

Conclusion. A good conclusion helps readers know what they have learned. One effective strategy is to begin with a reference to your thesis and then expand to a more general conclusion that reminds readers why your discussion is significant. Or you may want to remind readers of your main points. Try to conclude with something that will have an impact—but guard against sounding preachy.

41b Reviewing and revising a research project

Once you've completed your draft, reread it slowly. As you do so, reconsider the project's purpose and audience, your stance and thesis, and the evidence you have gathered. Next, ask others to read and respond to your draft. Asking specific questions of your readers will result in the most helpful advice.

Once you get feedback, reread your draft very carefully, making notes for necessary changes and additions. Look closely at your support for your thesis, and gather additional information if necessary. Pay particular attention to how you have used both print and visual sources, and make sure you have full documentation for them. (For more on revising, see 2g.)

41c Preparing a list of sources

Once you have a final draft with your source materials in place, you are ready to prepare your list of sources. Create an entry for each source used in your final draft, consulting your notes and working bibliography. Then double-check your draft against your list of sources cited; be sure that you have listed every source mentioned in the in-text citations or notes and that you have not listed any sources not cited in your project. (For guidelines on documentation styles, see Chapters 42–45.)

41d Editing and proofreading

When you have revised your draft, check grammar, usage, spelling, punctuation, and mechanics. Consider the advice of spell checkers and grammar checkers carefully before accepting it. (For more information on editing, see 2h.) Proofread the final version of your project carefully. Work with a hard copy, since reading onscreen often leads to inaccuracies. Proofread once for typographical and grammatical errors and once again to make sure you haven't introduced new errors. You may find that reading the final draft backwards helps you focus on details.

FOR MULTILINGUAL WRITERS

Asking a Native Speaker to Review Your Draft

You may find it helpful to ask a native speaker to read over your draft and point out any words or patterns that are unclear or not idiomatic.

Documentation

Writing

Sentence
Grammar

Sentence
Style

Punctuation/
Mechanics

Language

Multilingual
Writers

Research

Documentation

42 MLA Style

Many fields in the humanities ask students to follow Modern Language Association (MLA) style to format manuscripts and to document various kinds of sources. This chapter introduces MLA guidelines. For further reference, consult the *MLA Handbook for Writers of Research Papers,* Seventh Edition, 2009.

42a MLA manuscript format

The MLA recommends the following format for the manuscript of a research paper. However, check with your instructor before preparing your final draft.

First page and title. The MLA does not require a title page. Type each of the following items on a separate line on the first page, beginning one inch from the top and flush with the left margin: your name, the instructor's name, the course name and number, and the date. Double-space between each item; then double-space again and center the title. Double-space between the title and the beginning of the text.

Margins and spacing. Leave one-inch margins at the top and bottom and on both sides of each page. Double-space the entire text, including set-off quotations, notes, and the list of works cited. Indent the first line of a paragraph one-half inch, or five spaces. Indent set-off quotations one inch, or ten spaces.

Page numbers. Include your last name and the page number on each page, one-half inch below the top and flush with the right margin.

Long quotations. To quote a long passage (more than four typed lines), set the quotation off by starting it on a new line and indenting each line one inch, or ten spaces, from the left margin. Do not enclose the passage in quotation marks (23a).

---

bedfordstmartins.com/easywriter To access the advice in this chapter online, click on **Documenting Sources**.

Headings. MLA style allows, but does not require, headings. Many students and instructors find them helpful. (See 6c for guidelines on using headings and subheadings.)

Visuals. Visuals (photographs, drawings, charts, graphs, and tables) should be placed as near as possible to the relevant text. (See 40b for guidelines on incorporating visuals into your text.) Tables should have a label and number (*Table 1*) and a clear caption. The label and caption should be aligned on the left, on separate lines. Give the source information below the table. All other visuals should be labeled *Figure* (abbreviated *Fig.*), numbered, and captioned. The label and caption should appear on the same line, followed by source information. Remember to refer to each visual in your text, indicating how it contributes to the point(s) you are making.

42b In-text citations

MLA style requires proper citation in the text of an essay for every quotation, paraphrase, summary, or other material requiring documentation. In-text citations document material from other sources with both signal phrases and parenthetical references. Parenthetical references should include the information your readers need to locate the full reference in the list of works cited at the end of the text. An in-text citation in MLA style gives the reader two kinds of information: (1) it indicates *which source* on the works-cited page the writer is referring to, and (2) it explains *where in the source* the material quoted, paraphrased, or summarized can be found.

The basic MLA in-text citation includes the author's last name either in a signal phrase introducing the source material or in parentheses at the end of the sentence. It also includes the page number in parentheses at the end of the sentence.

DIRECTORY OF MLA STYLE FOR IN-TEXT CITATIONS

1. Citation using a signal phrase *208*
2. Parenthetical citation *208*
3. Author named in a signal phrase *208*
4. Author named in a parenthetical reference *209*

continued

continued

5. Two or three authors *209*
6. Four or more authors *209*
7. Organization as author *209*
8. Unknown author *209*
9. Author of two or more works cited in the same project *209*
10. Two or more authors with the same last name *210*
11. Multivolume work *210*
12. Literary work *210*
13. Work in an anthology or a collection *211*
14. Sacred text *211*
15. Indirect source (author quoting someone else) *211*
16. Two or more sources in one parenthetical reference *211*
17. Encyclopedia or dictionary entry *211*
18. Electronic or nonprint source *212*
19. Entire work *212*
20. Visuals included in the text *212*

1. CITATION USING A SIGNAL PHRASE

In his discussion of Monty Python routines, Crystal notes that
the group relished "breaking the normal rules" of language (107).

2. PARENTHETICAL CITATION

A noted linguist explains that Monty Python humor often relied
on "bizarre linguistic interactions" (Crystal 108).

Note in the following examples where punctuation is
placed in relation to the parentheses.

3. AUTHOR NAMED IN A SIGNAL PHRASE. The MLA recommends
using the author's name in a signal phrase to introduce the
material and citing the page number(s) in parentheses.

Lee claims that his comic-book creation, Thor, was "the first
regularly published superhero to speak in a consistently archaic
manner" (199).

4. AUTHOR NAMED IN A PARENTHETICAL REFERENCE. When you do not mention the author in a signal phrase, include the author's last name before the page number(s) in the parentheses. Use no punctuation between the author's name and the page number(s).

> The word *Bollywood* is sometimes considered an insult because it implies that Indian movies are merely "a derivative of the American film industry" (Chopra 9).

5. TWO OR THREE AUTHORS. Use all the authors' last names in a signal phrase or in parentheses.

> Gortner, Hebrun, and Nicolson maintain that "opinion leaders" influence other people in an organization because they are respected, not because they hold high positions (175).

6. FOUR OR MORE AUTHORS. Use the first author's name and *et al.* ("and others"), or name all the authors in a signal phrase or in parentheses. Follow the same form for the entry in the list of works cited.

> As Belenky, Clinchy, Goldberger, and Tarule assert, examining the lives of women expands our understanding of human development (7).

7. ORGANIZATION AS AUTHOR. Give the organization's full name or a shortened form of it in a signal phrase or parenthetical reference.

> Any study of social welfare involves a close analysis of "the impacts, the benefits, and the costs" of its policies (Social Research Corporation iii).

8. UNKNOWN AUTHOR. Use the full title of the work or a shortened version in a signal phrase or parenthetical reference.

> "Hype," by one analysis, is "an artificially engendered atmosphere of hysteria" ("Today's Marketplace" 51).

9. AUTHOR OF TWO OR MORE WORKS CITED IN THE SAME PROJECT. If your list of works cited has more than one work by the same author, give the title of the work you are citing or a shortened version in a signal phrase or parenthetical reference.

Gardner shows readers their own silliness in his description of a "pointless, ridiculous monster, crouched in the shadows, stinking of dead men, murdered children, and martyred cows" (*Grendel* 2).

10. TWO OR MORE AUTHORS WITH THE SAME LAST NAME. Include the author's first *and* last names in a signal phrase or first initial and last name in a parenthetical reference.

Children will learn to write if they are allowed to choose their own subjects, James Britton asserts, citing the Schools Council study of the 1960s (37-42).

11. MULTIVOLUME WORK. In a parenthetical reference, note the volume number first and then the page number(s), with a colon and one space between them.

Modernist writers prized experimentation and gradually even sought to blur the line between poetry and prose, according to Forster (3: 150).

If you name only one volume of the work in your list of works cited, include only the page number in the parentheses.

12. LITERARY WORK. Literary works are often available in many different editions. For a prose work, cite the page number(s) from the edition you used followed by a semicolon, and then give other identifying information that will lead readers to the passage in any edition. Indicate the act or scene in a play, or both (*37; sc. 1*). For a novel, indicate the part or chapter (*175; ch. 4*).

Dostoyevsky's character Mitya wonders aloud about the "terrible tragedies realism inflicts on people" (376; bk. 8, ch. 2).

For a poem, instead of page numbers cite the part (if there is one) and line(s), separated by a period. If you are citing only line numbers, use the word *line*(*s*) in the first reference (*lines 33-34*).

Whitman speculates, "All goes onward and outward, nothing collapses, / And to die is different from what any one supposed, and luckier" (6.129-30).

For a verse play, give the act, scene, and line numbers, separated by periods.

> As *Macbeth* begins, the witches greet Banquo as "Lesser than
> Macbeth, and greater" (1.3.65).

13. WORK IN AN ANTHOLOGY OR A COLLECTION. For an essay, a short story, or another piece of prose reprinted in an anthology, use the name of the author of the work, not the editor of the anthology, but use the page number(s) from the anthology.

> Narratives of captivity play a major role in early writing by
> women in the United States, as Silko demonstrates (219).

14. SACRED TEXT. To cite a sacred text such as the Qur'an or the Bible, give the title of the edition you used, followed by location information, such as the book, chapter, and verse, separated by a period. In your text, spell out the names of books. In parenthetical references, use abbreviations for books with names of five or more letters (*Gen.* for *Genesis*).

> He ignored the admonition "Pride goes before destruction, and
> a haughty spirit before a fall" (*New Oxford Annotated Bible,*
> Prov. 16.18).

15. INDIRECT SOURCE (AUTHOR QUOTING SOMEONE ELSE). Use the abbreviation *qtd. in* to indicate that you are quoting from someone else's report of a conversation, interview, letter, or the like.

> Arthur Miller says, "When somebody is destroyed everybody finally
> contributes to it, but in Willy's case, the end product would be
> virtually the same" (qtd. in Martin and Meyer 375).

16. TWO OR MORE SOURCES IN ONE PARENTHETICAL REFERENCE. Separate the information with semicolons.

> Some economists recommend that *employment* be redefined to
> include unpaid domestic labor (Clark 148; Nevins 39).

17. ENCYCLOPEDIA OR DICTIONARY ENTRY. An entry from a reference work—such as an encyclopedia or a dictionary—without an author will appear on the works-cited list under

the entry's title. Enclose the title in quotation marks, and place it in parentheses. Omit the page number if the reference work arranges entries alphabetically.

> The term *prion* was coined by Stanley B. Prusiner from the
> words *proteinaceous* and *infectious* and a suffix meaning *particle*
> ("Prion").

18. ELECTRONIC OR NONPRINT SOURCE. Give enough information in a signal phrase or in parentheses for readers to locate the source in your list of works cited. Many works found online or in electronic databases lack stable page numbers; you will have to omit the page number from the parenthetical citation in such cases. However, if you are citing a work with stable pagination, such as an article as a PDF file, include the page number in parentheses.

> As a *Slate* analysis has noted, "Prominent sports psychologists
> get praised for their successes and don't get grief for their
> failures" (Engber).

The source, an article on a Web site, does not have stable pagination.

> According to Whitmarsh, the British military had experimented
> with using balloons for observation as far back as 1879 (328).

The source, an online PDF of a print article, includes stable page numbers.

If the source includes numbered sections, paragraphs, or screens, include the abbreviation (*sec.*), paragraph (*par.*), or screen (*scr.*) number in parentheses.

> Sherman notes that the "immediate, interactive, and on-the-
> spot" nature of Internet information can make nondigital media
> seem outdated (sec. 32).

19. ENTIRE WORK. Include the reference in the text without any page numbers.

> Jon Krakauer's *Into the Wild* both criticizes and admires the
> solitary impulses of its young hero, which end up killing him.

20. VISUALS INCLUDED IN THE TEXT. When you include an image in your text, number it and include a parenthetical reference

in your text (*see Fig. 2*). Number figures (photos, drawings, cartoons, maps, graphs, and charts) and tables separately. Each visual should include a caption with the figure or table number and information that allows the reader to find the source on the works-cited page.

> This trend is illustrated in a chart distributed by the College
> Board as part of its 2002 analysis of aggregate SAT data (see
> Fig. 1).

Soon after this sentence, readers find the figure and caption:

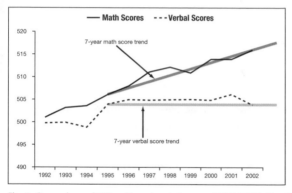

Fig. 1. Comparison of SAT math and verbal scores (1992-2002). Trend lines added. Source: Kristin Carnahan and Chiara Coletti, *Ten-Year Trend in SAT Scores Indicates Increased Emphasis on Math Is Yielding Results: Reading and Writing Are Causes for Concern.* New York: College Board, 2002; 9; print.

If you include complete source information in the figure caption and do not use the source elsewhere in your writing project, adding the source to your list of works cited is optional.

You can also choose to use just a short descriptive caption that directs readers to the works-cited page for complete citation information about the figure. In such cases, be sure that the caption begins with the words under which the source is alphabetized on the works-cited page. An image that you have personally created might appear with a caption like the following:

> Fig. 4. Young woman reading a magazine. Personal photograph by
> author.

42c Explanatory and bibliographic notes

MLA style recommends explanatory notes for information or commentary that does not readily fit into your text but is needed for clarification or further explanation. In addition, MLA style permits bibliographic notes for information about a source. Use superscript numbers (^{1}) in the text to refer readers to the notes, which may appear as endnotes (typed under the heading *Notes* on a separate page after the text but before the list of works cited) or as footnotes at the bottom of the page.

1. SUPERSCRIPT NUMBER IN TEXT

Stewart emphasizes the existence of social contacts in Hawthorne's life so that the audience will accept a different Hawthorne, one more attuned to modern times than the figure in Woodberry.^{3}

2. NOTE

^{3}Woodberry does, however, show that Hawthorne was often an unsociable individual. He emphasizes the seclusion of Hawthorne's mother, who separated herself from her family after the death of her husband, often even taking meals alone (28).

42d List of works cited

A list of works cited is an alphabetical list of the sources you have referred to in your essay. (If your instructor asks you to list everything you have read as background, call the list *Works Consulted*.)

DIRECTORY TO MLA STYLE FOR A LIST OF WORKS CITED

Guidelines for Author Listings

1. One author *217*
2. Multiple authors *217*
3. Organization or group author *218*
4. Unknown author *218*
5. Two or more works by the same author *219*

Books

6. Basic format for a book *219*
   SOURCE MAP *220–21*
7. Author and editor both named *222*
8. Editor, no author named *222*
9. Anthology *222*
10. Work in an anthology or chapter in a book with an editor *222*
11. Two or more items from the same anthology *222*
12. Graphic narrative *223*
13. Translation *223*
14. Book with both translator and editor *223*
15. Translation of a section of a book *223*
16. Translation of a book by an unknown author *223*
17. Book in a language other than English *223*
18. Edition other than the first *224*
19. One volume of a multivolume work *224*
20. Two or more volumes of a multivolume work *224*
21. Preface, foreword, introduction, or afterword *224*
22. Entry in a reference book *224*
23. Book that is part of a series *224*
24. Republication (modern edition of an older book) *224*
25. Publisher's imprint *225*
26. Book with a title within the title *225*
27. Sacred text *225*

Print Periodicals

28. Article in a journal *228*
   SOURCE MAP *226–27*
29. Article in a magazine *228*
30. Article in a newspaper *228*
31. Article that skips pages *228*
32. Editorial or letter to the editor *228*
33. Review *228*
34. Unsigned article *229*

Electronic Sources

35. Work from an online database *229*
   SOURCE MAP *230–31*
36. Article in an online journal *232*
37. Article in an online magazine or newspaper *232*
38. Online editorial or letter to the editor *233*
39. Online review *233*

continued

continued

40. Online book *233*
41. Online poem *233*
42. Entry in an online reference work *234*
43. Work from a Web site *234*
   SOURCE MAP *236–37*
44. Article downloaded from the Web *234*
45. Entire Web site *234*
46. Web log (blog) *235*
47. Post or comment on a Web log (blog) *235*
48. Entry in a wiki *235*
49. Posting to a discussion group *238*
50. Email *238*
51. Posting to a social networking site *238*
52. CD-ROM *238*

Multimedia Sources (including online versions)

53. Film, video, or DVD *238*
54. Television or radio program *239*
55. Broadcast interview *239*
56. Unpublished or personal interview *240*
57. Sound recording *240*
58. Musical composition *241*
59. Lecture or speech *241*
60. Live performance *241*
61. Podcast *241*
62. Work of art or photograph *242*
63. Map or chart *242*
64. Cartoon or comic strip *242*
65. Advertisement *243*
66. Video or computer game *243*

Other Sources (including online versions)

67. Report or pamphlet *243*
68. Government publication *243*
69. Published proceedings of a conference *244*
70. Dissertation *244*
71. Dissertation abstract *244*
72. Published interview *244*
73. Unpublished letter *245*
74. Manuscript or other unpublished work *245*
75. Legal source *245*

Guidelines for author listings. The list of works cited is arranged alphabetically. The in-text citations in your writing point readers toward particular sources on the list (42b).

NAME CITED IN SIGNAL PHRASE IN TEXT

Crystal explains . . .

NAME IN PARENTHETICAL CITATION IN TEXT

. . . (Crystal 107).

BEGINNING OF ENTRY ON LIST OF WORKS CITED

Crystal, David.

Models 1–5 below explain how to arrange author names. The information that follows the name of the author depends on the type of work you are citing—a book (models 6–27); a print periodical (models 28–34); a written text from an electronic source, such as an article from a Web site or database (models 35–52): sources from art, film, radio, or other media, including online versions (models 53–66); and other kinds of sources (models 67–75). Consult the model that most closely resembles the kind of source you are using.

1. ONE AUTHOR. Put the last name first, followed by a comma, the first name (and initial, if any), and a period.

Crystal, David.

2. MULTIPLE AUTHORS. List the first author with the last name first (see model 1). Give the names of any other authors with the first name first. Separate authors' names with commas, and include the word *and* before the last person's name.

Martineau, Jane, Desmond Shawe-Taylor, and Jonathan Bate.

For four or more authors, either list all the names, or list the first author followed by a comma and *et al.* ("and others").

Lupton, Ellen, Jennifer Tobias, Alicia Imperiale, Grace Jeffers, and
Randi Mates.

Lupton, Ellen, et al.

✓ CHECKLIST

Formatting a List of Works Cited

- Start your list on a separate page after the text of your essay and any notes.

- Continue the consecutive numbering of pages.

- Center the heading *Works Cited* (not italicized or in quotation marks) one inch from the top of the page.

- Start each entry flush with the left margin; indent subsequent lines one-half inch or five spaces. Double-space the entire list.

- List sources alphabetically by the first word. Start with the author's name, if available, or the editor's name. If no author or editor is given, start with the title.

- List the author's last name first, followed by a comma and the first name. If a source has multiple authors, subsequent authors' names appear first name first (see model 2).

- Capitalize every important word in titles and subtitles. Italicize titles of books, periodicals, databases, and other longer works; enclose titles of shorter works in quotation marks.

- In general, use a period and a space after each element of the entry; look at the models in this chapter for information on punctuating particular kinds of entries.

- List the city of publication without a state or country. Follow it with a colon and a shortened form of the publisher's name—omit *Co.* or *Inc.,* shorten names such as *HarperCollins* to *Harper* or *Simon & Schuster* to *Simon,* and abbreviate *University Press* to *UP*.

- List inclusive page numbers for a part of a larger work.

- List the medium of the work (such as *Print* or *Web*).

3. ORGANIZATION OR GROUP AUTHOR. Give the name of the organization listed as the author.

Getty Trust.

United States. Government Accountability Office.

4. UNKNOWN AUTHOR. When the author is not identified, begin the entry with the title. Italicize titles of books and long works, but put titles of articles and other short works in quotation marks.

"California Sues EPA over Emissions."

New Concise World Atlas.

5. TWO OR MORE WORKS BY THE SAME AUTHOR. Arrange the entries alphabetically by title. Include the author's name in the first entry; but in subsequent entries, use three hyphens followed by a period. (For the basic format for citing a book, see model 6. For the basic format for citing an article from an online newspaper, see model 37.)

> Chopra, Anupama. "Bollywood Princess, Hollywood Hopeful."
>
> > *New York Times*. New York Times, 10 Feb. 2008. Web.
> >
> > 13 Feb. 2008.
>
> ---. *King of Bollywood: Shah Rukh Khan and the Seductive World of*
> > *Indian Cinema*. New York: Warner, 2007. Print.

NOTE: Use three hyphens only when the work is by *exactly* the same author(s) as the previous entry.

✔️ CHECKLIST

Combining Parts of Models

What should you do if your source doesn't match the model exactly? Suppose, for instance, that your source is a translated essay that appears in the fifth edition of an anthology.

- Identify a basic model to follow. If you decide that your source looks most like an essay in an anthology, you would start with a citation that looks like model 10.

- Look for models that show the additional elements in your source. For the example above, you would need to add elements of model 14 (for the translation) and model 18 (for an edition other than the first).

- Add new elements from other models to your basic model in the order indicated.

- If you still aren't sure how to arrange the pieces to create a combination model, check the *MLA Handbook* or ask your instructor.

Books

6. BASIC FORMAT FOR A BOOK. Begin with the author name(s). (See models 1–5.) Then include the title and subtitle, the city of publication, the publisher, the publication date, and the medium of publication (*Print*). The source map on pp. 220–21 shows where to find this information in a typical book.

> Crystal, David. *Language Play*. Chicago: U of Chicago P, 1998.
> > Print.

Source Map: Books, MLA Style

Take information from the book's title page and copyright page (on the reverse side of the title page), not from the cover or a library catalog. A citation for the book on p. 221 would include these elements:

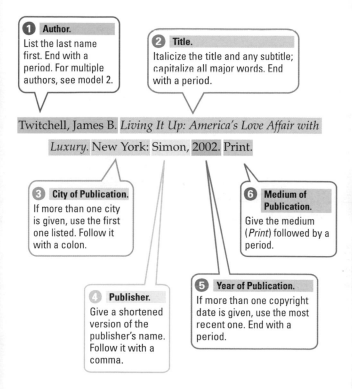

1 Author.
List the last name first. End with a period. For multiple authors, see model 2.

2 Title.
Italicize the title and any subtitle; capitalize all major words. End with a period.

Twitchell, James B. *Living It Up: America's Love Affair with Luxury.* New York: Simon, 2002. Print.

3 City of Publication.
If more than one city is given, use the first one listed. Follow it with a colon.

6 Medium of Publication.
Give the medium (*Print*) followed by a period.

4 Publisher.
Give a shortened version of the publisher's name. Follow it with a comma.

5 Year of Publication.
If more than one copyright date is given, use the most recent one. End with a period.

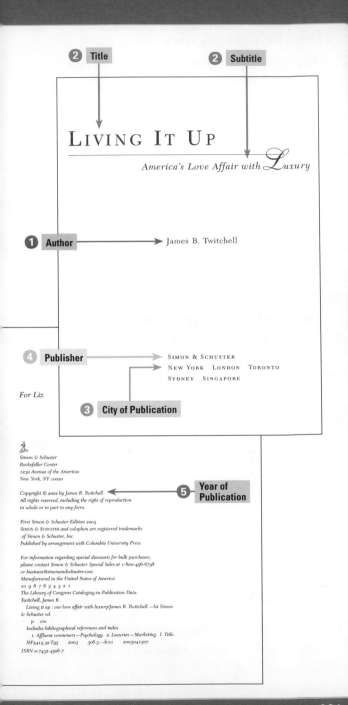

2 Title

2 Subtitle

LIVING IT UP

America's Love Affair with Luxury

1 Author → James B. Twitchell

4 Publisher →

SIMON & SCHUSTER
NEW YORK   LONDON   TORONTO
SYDNEY   SINGAPORE

3 City of Publication

For Liz

Simon & Schuster
Rockefeller Center
1230 Avenue of the Americas
New York, NY 10020

5 Year of Publication

First Simon & Schuster Edition 2003
SIMON & SCHUSTER and colophon are registered trademarks
of Simon & Schuster, Inc.
Published by arrangement with Columbia University Press

For information regarding special discounts for bulk purchases,
please contact Simon & Schuster Special Sales at 1-800-456-6798
or business@simonandschuster.com
Manufactured in the United States of America
10 9 8 7 6 5 4 3 2 1
The Library of Congress Cataloging-in-Publication Data
Twitchell, James B.
   Living it up : our love affair with luxury/James B. Twitchell.—1st Simon
& Schuster ed.
     p. cm.
   Includes bibliographical references and index.
   1. Affluent consumers—Psychology. 2. Luxuries—Marketing. I. Title.
   HF5415.32.T95   2003   306.3—dc21   2003041507
ISBN 0-7432-4506-7

7. AUTHOR AND EDITOR BOTH NAMED

Bangs, Lester. *Psychotic Reactions and Carburetor Dung*. Ed. Greil

Marcus. New York: Knopf, 1988. Print.

NOTE: To cite the editor's contribution instead, begin the entry with the editor's name.

Marcus, Greil, ed. *Psychotic Reactions and Carburetor Dung*. By

Lester Bangs. New York: Knopf, 1988. Print.

8. EDITOR, NO AUTHOR NAMED

Wall, Cheryl A., ed. *Changing Our Own Words: Essays on Criticism,*

Theory, and Writing by Black Women. New Brunswick: Rutgers

UP, 1989. Print.

9. ANTHOLOGY. Cite an entire anthology the same way you would cite a book with an editor and no named author (see model 8).

Walker, Dale L., ed. *Westward: A Fictional History of the American*

West. New York: Forge, 2003. Print.

10. WORK IN AN ANTHOLOGY OR CHAPTER IN A BOOK WITH AN EDITOR. List the author(s) of the selection or chapter; its title; the title of the book; the abbreviation *Ed.* and the name(s) of the editor(s); the publication information; and the inclusive page numbers of the selection or chapter.

Komunyakaa, Yusef. "Facing It." *The Seagull Reader*. Ed. Joseph

Kelly. New York: Norton, 2000. 126-27. Print.

Use the following format to provide original publication information for a reprinted selection. *Rpt.* is the abbreviation for *Reprinted*.

Byatt, A. S. "The Thing in the Forest." *New Yorker* 3 June 2002:

80-89. Rpt. in *The O. Henry Prize Stories 2003*. Ed. Laura

Furman. New York: Anchor, 2003. 3-22. Print.

11. TWO OR MORE ITEMS FROM THE SAME ANTHOLOGY. List the anthology as one entry (see model 9). Also list each selection separately with a cross-reference.

Estleman, Loren D. "Big Tim Magoon and the Wild West." Walker

391-404.

Salzer, Susan K. "Miss Libbie Tells All." Walker 199-212.

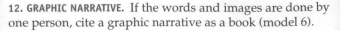
12. GRAPHIC NARRATIVE. If the words and images are done by one person, cite a graphic narrative as a book (model 6).

> Bechdel, Alison. *Fun Home.* New York: Houghton Mifflin, 2006.
>
> Print.

If the work is a collaboration, indicate the author(s) or illustrator(s) who are most important to your research before the title of the work. List other contributors after the title, in the order of their appearance on the title page. Label each person's contribution to the work.

> Stavans, Ilan, writer. *Latino USA: A Cartoon History.* Illus. Lalo
>
> Alcaraz. New York: Basic, 2000. Print.

13. TRANSLATION

> Boethius, Anicius M. S. *The Consolation of Philosophy.* Trans. V. E.
>
> Watts. London: Penguin, 1969. Print.

14. BOOK WITH BOTH TRANSLATOR AND EDITOR. List the editor's and translator's names after the title, in the order they appear on the title page.

> Kant, Immanuel. *"Toward Perpetual Peace" and Other Writings*
>
> *on Politics, Peace, and History.* Ed. Pauline Kleingeld. Trans.
>
> David L. Colclasure. New Haven: Yale UP, 2006. Print.

15. TRANSLATION OF A SECTION OF A BOOK. If different translators have worked on various parts of the book, identify the translator of the part you are citing.

> García Lorca, Federico. "The Little Mad Boy." Trans. W. S. Merwin.
>
> *The Selected Poems of Federico García Lorca.* Ed. Francisco
>
> García Lorca and Donald M. Allen. London: Penguin, 1969.
>
> Print.

16. TRANSLATION OF A BOOK BY AN UNKNOWN AUTHOR

> *Grettir's Saga.* Trans. Denton Fox and Hermann Palsson. Toronto:
>
> U of Toronto P, 1974. Print.

17. BOOK IN A LANGUAGE OTHER THAN ENGLISH. If necessary, provide a translation of the book's title in brackets.

> Benedetti, Mario. *La borra del café [The Coffee Grind].* Buenos
>
> Aires: Sudamericana, 2000. Print.

18. EDITION OTHER THAN THE FIRST. If both an author and an editor are listed (see model 7), give the edition after the editor's name.

> Walker, John A. *Art in the Age of Mass Media*. 3rd ed. London:
>
> > Pluto, 2001. Print.

19. ONE VOLUME OF A MULTIVOLUME WORK. Give the volume number after the title.

> Ch'oe, Yong-Ho, Peter Lee, and William Theodore De Barry, eds.
>
> > *Sources of Korean Tradition*. Vol. 2. New York: Columbia UP,
> >
> > 2000. Print. 2 vols.

20. TWO OR MORE VOLUMES OF A MULTIVOLUME WORK

> Ch'oe, Yong-Ho, Peter Lee, and William Theodore De Barry, eds.
>
> > *Sources of Korean Tradition*. 2 vols. New York: Columbia UP,
> >
> > 2000. Print.

21. PREFACE, FOREWORD, INTRODUCTION, OR AFTERWORD. After the writer's name, describe the contribution. After the title, indicate the book's author (with *By*) or editor (with *Ed.*).

> Atwan, Robert. Foreword. *The Best American Essays 2002*. Ed.
>
> > Stephen Jay Gould. Boston: Houghton, 2002. viii-xii. Print.

22. ENTRY IN A REFERENCE BOOK. For a well-known encyclopedia, note the edition (if identified) and year of publication. If the entries are alphabetized, omit publication information and page number.

> Kettering, Alison McNeil. "Art Nouveau." *World Book Encyclopedia*.
>
> > 2002 ed. Print.

23. BOOK THAT IS PART OF A SERIES. After the medium, cite the series name (and number, if any) from the title page.

> Nichanian, Marc, and Vartan Matiossian, eds. *Yeghishe Charents:*
>
> > *Poet of the Revolution*. Costa Mesa: Mazda, 2003. Print.
> >
> > Armenian Studies Ser. 5.

24. REPUBLICATION (MODERN EDITION OF AN OLDER BOOK). Indicate the original publication date after the title.

> Austen, Jane. *Sense and Sensibility*. 1813. New York: Dover, 1996.
>
> > Print.

25. PUBLISHER'S IMPRINT. If the title page gives a publisher's imprint, hyphenate the imprint and the publisher's name.

> Hornby, Nick. *About a Boy*. New York: Riverhead-Penguin Putnam,
>
> 1998. Print.

26. BOOK WITH A TITLE WITHIN THE TITLE. Do not italicize a book title within a title. For an article title within a title, italicize as usual and place the article title in quotation marks.

> Mullaney, Julie. *Arundhati Roy's* The God of Small Things: *A*
>
> *Reader's Guide*. New York: Continuum, 2002. Print.

> Rhynes, Martha. *"I, Too, Sing America": The Story of Langston*
>
> *Hughes*. Greensboro: Morgan, 2002. Print.

27. SACRED TEXT. To cite individual published editions of sacred books, begin the entry with the title. If you are not citing a particular edition, sacred texts should not appear in the works-cited list.

Print periodicals. Begin with the author name(s). (See models 1–5.) Then include the article title, the title of the periodical, the date or volume information, and the page numbers.

✔ CHECKLIST

Formatting Print Periodical Entries

- Put titles of articles from periodicals in quotation marks. Place the period inside the closing quotation mark.

- Give the title of the periodical as it appears on the magazine's or journal's cover or newspaper's front page; omit any initial *A, An,* or *The.* Italicize the title.

- For journals, follow the journal title with the volume number, then a period and the issue number (if any). Put the year in parentheses after the volume or issue number.

- For magazines and newspapers, give the date in this order: day (if given), month, year. Abbreviate months except for May, June, and July.

- List inclusive page numbers if the article appears on consecutive pages. If it skips pages, give only the first page number and a plus sign.

- Give the medium (*Print*) and a period.

Source Map: Journals, MLA Style

A citation for the journal on p. 227 would include the following elements:

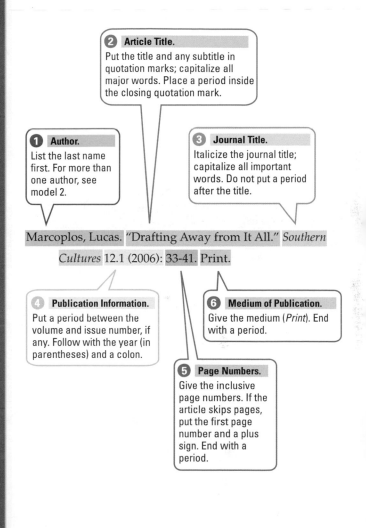

2 Article Title.
Put the title and any subtitle in quotation marks; capitalize all major words. Place a period inside the closing quotation mark.

1 Author.
List the last name first. For more than one author, see model 2.

3 Journal Title.
Italicize the journal title; capitalize all important words. Do not put a period after the title.

Marcoplos, Lucas. "Drafting Away from It All." *Southern Cultures* 12.1 (2006): 33-41. Print.

4 Publication Information.
Put a period between the volume and issue number, if any. Follow with the year (in parentheses) and a colon.

6 Medium of Publication.
Give the medium (*Print*). End with a period.

5 Page Numbers.
Give the inclusive page numbers. If the article skips pages, put the first page number and a plus sign. End with a period.

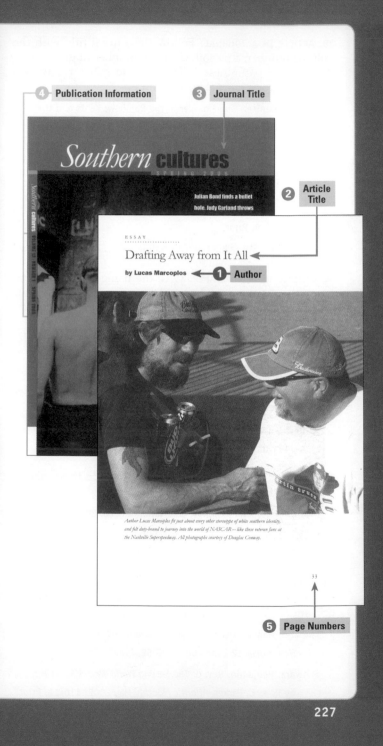

4 Publication Information

3 Journal Title

Southern **cultures**
SPRING 2006

Julian Bond finds a bullet
hole. Judy Garland throws

2 Article Title

ESSAY

Drafting Away from It All

by Lucas Marcoplos ◄— **1** Author

Author Lucas Marcoplos fit just about every other stereotype of white southern identity, and felt duty-bound to journey into the world of NASCAR—like these veteran fans at the Nashville Superspeedway. All photographs courtesy of Douglas Conway.

33

5 Page Numbers

28. ARTICLE IN A JOURNAL. Follow the journal title with the volume number, a period, the issue number (if given), and the year (in parentheses). The basic format for a works-cited entry for a journal appears on pp. 226–27.

> Gigante, Denise. "The Monster in the Rainbow: Keats and the
> Science of Life." *PMLA* 117.3 (2002): 433-48. Print.

29. ARTICLE IN A MAGAZINE. Provide the date from the magazine cover instead of volume or issue numbers. Abbreviate months other than May, June, and July.

> Surowiecki, James. "The Stimulus Strategy." *New Yorker* 25 Feb.
> 2008: 29. Print.
>
> Taubin, Amy. "All Talk?" *Film Comment* Nov.-Dec. 2007: 45-47. Print.

30. ARTICLE IN A NEWSPAPER. Give the name of the newspaper without any initial *A, An,* or *The.* Give the date and the edition (if listed), and the section number or letter (if listed). End with the medium of publication (*Print*).

> Bernstein, Nina. "On Lucille Avenue, the Immigration Debate."
> *New York Times* 26 June 2006, late ed.: A1+. Print.

31. ARTICLE THAT SKIPS PAGES. When an article skips pages, give only the first page number and a plus sign.

> Tyrnauer, Matthew. "Empire by Martha." *Vanity Fair* Sept. 2002:
> 364+. Print.

32. EDITORIAL OR LETTER TO THE EDITOR. Include the author's name and the title, if given.

> "California Dreaming." Editorial. *Nation* 25 Feb. 2008: 4. Print.
>
> Galbraith, James K. "JFK's Plans to Withdraw." Letter. *New York
> Review of Books* 6 Dec. 2007: 77-78. Print.

33. REVIEW. List the reviewer's name and the title of the review, if any, followed by *Rev. of* ("Review of") and the title and author, director, or other creator of the work.

> Franklin, Nancy. "Dead On." Rev. of *Deadwood,* by David Milch.
> *New Yorker* 12 June 2006: 158-59. Print.
>
> Schwarz, Benjamin. Rev. of *The Second World War: A Short History,*
> by R. A. C. Parker. *Atlantic Monthly* May 2002: 110-11. Print.

34. UNSIGNED ARTICLE

"Performance of the Week." *Time* 6 Oct. 2003: 18. Print.

Electronic sources. Electronic sources such as Web sites differ from print sources in the ease with which they can be changed, updated, or eliminated. In addition, the various electronic media do not organize their works the same way.

35. WORK FROM AN ONLINE DATABASE. The basic format for citing a work from a database appears on pp. 230–31.

✓ CHECKLIST

Citing Electronic Sources

The entry for an electronic source may include up to six basic elements.

- **AUTHOR.** For variations on author, see models 1–5.
- **TITLE.** Italicize the titles of books or entire sites. Put shorter titles in quotation marks. Capitalize all important words.
- **PRINT PUBLICATION INFORMATION.** For an online book or journal article from a database that provides information about the work's publication in print, include the volume and issue number with the year in parentheses, then a colon and the inclusive page numbers, or *n. pag.* if no page numbers are listed. (For articles taken from online newspapers and magazines, however, omit the print publication information.)
- **ELECTRONIC PUBLICATION INFORMATION.** For a work from a Web site, including online magazines and newspapers, list all of the following that you can find: the title of the site, italicized; the site's editor(s), if given, preceded by *Ed.*; and the name of any sponsor. (The sponsor's name usually appears at the bottom of the home page.) Then add the date of electronic publication or latest update. For a work from a database such as InfoTrac or LexisNexis, give the name of the database, italicized.
- **MEDIUM OF PUBLICATION.** List the medium (*Web*).
- **DATE OF ACCESS.** Give the most recent date you accessed the source.

The *MLA Handbook* does not usually require a URL. If you think your readers will have difficulty finding the source without one, put it after the period following the date of access, enclosed in angle brackets. Put a period after the closing bracket.

Source Map: Articles from Databases, MLA Style

Follow this model for a journal article from an electronic database such as InfoTrac. For information on citing online newspaper or magazine articles, see model 37. A citation for the article on p. 231 would include the following elements:

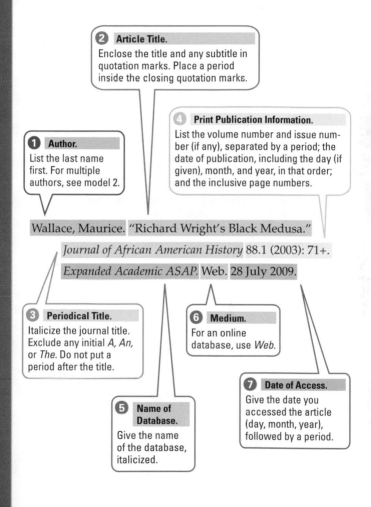

2 Article Title.
Enclose the title and any subtitle in quotation marks. Place a period inside the closing quotation marks.

4 Print Publication Information.
List the volume number and issue number (if any), separated by a period; the date of publication, including the day (if given), month, and year, in that order; and the inclusive page numbers.

1 Author.
List the last name first. For multiple authors, see model 2.

Wallace, Maurice. "Richard Wright's Black Medusa."

   Journal of African American History 88.1 (2003): 71+.

   Expanded Academic ASAP. Web. 28 July 2009.

3 Periodical Title.
Italicize the journal title. Exclude any initial *A, An,* or *The.* Do not put a period after the title.

6 Medium.
For an online database, use *Web.*

5 Name of Database.
Give the name of the database, italicized.

7 Date of Access.
Give the date you accessed the article (day, month, year), followed by a period.

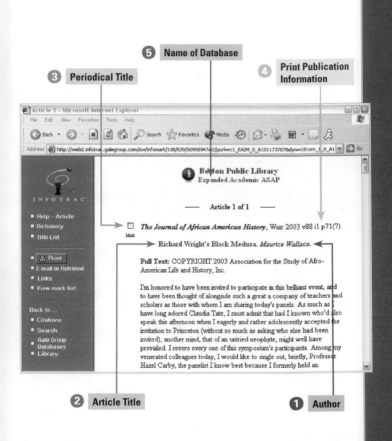

❸ Periodical Title

❺ Name of Database

❹ Print Publication Information

❷ Article Title

❶ Author

Article 1 - Microsoft Internet Explorer

File   Edit   View   Favorites   Tools   Help

Back   ▼   Search   Favorites   Media

Address   http://web2.infotrac.galegroup.com/itw/infomark/108/539/50958947v2/purl=rc1_EAIM_0_A101173707&dyn=18!xrn_1_0_A1   Go

INFOTRAC

- Help - Article
- Dictionary
- Title List

- Print
- E-mail or Retrieval
- Links
- View mark list

Back to ...
- Citations
- Search
- Gale Group
  Databases
- Library

Boston Public Library
Expanded Academic ASAP

—— Article 1 of 1 ——

☐ *The Journal of African American History*, Wntr 2003 v88 i1 p71(7)

Mark

Richard Wright's Black Medusa. *Maurice Wallace.*

Full Text: COPYRIGHT 2003 Association for the Study of Afro-American Life and History, Inc.

I'm honored to have been invited to participate in this brilliant event, and to have been thought of alongside such a great a company of teachers and scholars as those with whom I am sharing today's panels. As much as I have long adored Claudia Tate, I must admit that had I known who'd also speak this afternoon when I eagerly and rather adolescently accepted the invitation to Princeton (without so much as asking who else had been invited), another mind, that of an untried neophyte, might well have prevailed. I revere every one of this symposium's participants. Among my venerated colleagues today, I would like to single out, briefly, Professor Hazel Carby, the panelist I know best because I formerly held an

231

For a work from an online database, provide all of the following elements that are available: the author's name; the title of the work, in quotation marks; any print publication information; the name of the online database, italicized; the medium consulted (*Web*); and the date of access.

Goldman, William. "*The Princess Bride* Shooting Draft." 1987.

    Internet Movie Script Database. Web. 12 June 2008.

For a work from a subscription service such as InfoTrac, include the same information as for an online database: after the information about the work, give the name of the database, italicized; the medium consulted (*Web*); and the date of access.

Collins, Ross F. "Cattle Barons and Ink Slingers: How Cow Country

    Journalists Created a Great American Myth." *American*

    Journalism 24.3 (2007): 7-29. *Communication and Mass*

    Media Complete. Web. 7 Feb. 2008.

36. ARTICLE IN AN ONLINE JOURNAL. Cite an online journal article as you would a print journal article (see model 28), using inclusive page numbers, if possible, or the first page number and a plus sign. If an online article does not have page numbers, use *n. pag.* Then end the entry with the medium consulted (*Web*) and the date of access.

Gallagher, Brian. "Greta Garbo Is Sad: Some Historical Reflections

    on the Paradoxes of Stardom in the American Film Industry,

    1910-1960." *Images: A Journal of Film and Popular Culture* 3

    (1997): n. pag. Web. 7 Aug. 2006.

37. ARTICLE IN AN ONLINE MAGAZINE OR NEWSPAPER. For an online magazine or newspaper article, give the author, the title of the article in quotation marks, the name of the magazine or newspaper (italicized), the sponsor of the Web site, the date of publication, the medium consulted (*Web*), and the date of access.

Burt, Stephen. "Paper Trail: The True Legacy of Marianne Moore,

    Modernist Monument." *Slate*. Washingtonpost.Newsweek

    Interactive, 11 Nov. 2003. Web. 12 Nov. 2003.

Shea, Christopher. "Five Truths about Tuition." *New York Times*.

    New York Times, 9 Nov. 2003. Web. 11 Nov. 2003.

38. ONLINE EDITORIAL OR LETTER TO THE EDITOR. Include the word *Editorial* or *Letter* after the author (if given) and title (if any). Then follow with the name of the journal, magazine, or newspaper; the sponsor of the Web site; the date of publication; the medium consulted (*Web*); and the date of access.

> "The Funding Gap." Editorial. *Washington Post*. Washington Post,
>
> 5 Nov. 2003. Web. 9 Nov. 2003.

> Moore, Paula. "Go Vegetarian." Letter. *New York Times*. New York
>
> Times, 25 Feb. 2008. Web. 6 Mar. 2008.

39. ONLINE REVIEW. Cite an online review as you would a print review: give the reviewer's name and title of the review, if any; then add *Rev. of* and the title of the work being reviewed and the author, director, or other creator of the work. End with the name of the Web site, the sponsor of the site, the date of publication, the medium consulted (*Web*), and the date of access.

> O'Hehir, Andrew. "The Nightmare in Iraq." Rev. of *Gunner Palace,*
>
> dir. Michael Tucker and Petra Epperlein. *Salon*. Salon Media
>
> Group, 4 Mar. 2005. Web. 24 Mar. 2005.

40. ONLINE BOOK. Cite an online book as you would a print book (see models 6–27). After the print publication information (city, publisher, and year), if any, give the title of the Web site or database in which the book appears; the medium (*Web*); and the date of access.

> Euripides. *The Trojan Women*. Trans. Gilbert Murray. New York:
>
> Oxford UP, 1915. *Internet Sacred Text Archive*. Web. 12 Oct.
>
> 2003.

Cite a part of an online book as you would a part of a print book (see models 10 and 15). Give the available print and electronic publication information, the medium (*Web*), and the date of access.

> Riis, Jacob. "The Genesis of the Gang." *The Battle with the Slum*.
>
> New York: Macmillan, 1902. *Bartleby.com: Great Books Online*.
>
> 2000. Web. 31 Mar. 2005.

41. ONLINE POEM. Include the poet's name and the title of the poem, followed by the print publication information for the poem (if applicable). End with the title of the Web site or

database in which the poem appears, the medium (*Web*), and the date of access.

> Dickinson, Emily. "The Grass." *Poems: Emily Dickinson*. Boston:
>
> Roberts Brothers, 1891. *Humanities Text Initiative American*
>
> *Verse Project*. 1995. Web. 6 Jan. 2006.

42. ENTRY IN AN ONLINE REFERENCE WORK. List the author of the entry, if known, or begin with the title of the entry in quotation marks. Follow with the name of the Web site, the sponsor of the site, the date of publication, the medium consulted (*Web*), and the date of access.

> "Tour de France." *Encyclopaedia Britannica Online*. Encyclopaedia
>
> Britannica, 2006. Web. 21 May 2006.

43. WORK FROM A WEB SITE. For basic information on citing a work from a Web site, see pp. 236–37. Include all of the following elements that are available: the author; the title of the document in quotation marks; the name of the Web site, italicized; the name of the publisher or sponsor (if none is available, use *N.p.*); the date of publication (if not available, use *n.d.*); the medium consulted (*Web*); and the date of access.

> "Hands Off Public Broadcasting." *Media Matters for America*. Media
>
> Matters for America, 24 May 2005. Web. 31 May 2005.

> Stauder, Ellen Keck. "Darkness Audible: Negative Capability and
>
> Mark Doty's 'Nocturne in Black and Gold.'" *Romantic Circles*
>
> *Praxis Series*. U of Maryland, 2003. Web. 28 Sept. 2003.

44. ARTICLE DOWNLOADED FROM THE WEB. If you download a work from the Web, determine what kind of source it is (such as a journal article or part of a book) and include the information necessary for citing such a source. In place of the medium of publication, give the digital file format (*PDF file*). Omit the access date.

> Grant, Donna M., Alisha D. Malloy, and Marianne C. Murphy. "A
>
> Comparison of Student Perceptions of Their Computer Skills
>
> to Their Actual Abilities." *Journal of Information Technology*
>
> *Education* 8 (2009): 141-60. PDF file.

45. ENTIRE WEB SITE. Follow the guidelines for a specific work from the Web, beginning with the name of the author or

editor, followed by the title of the Web site, italicized; the name of the sponsor or publisher (if none, use *N.p.*); the date of publication or last update; the medium of publication (*Web*); and the date of access.

Bernstein, Charles, Kenneth Goldsmith, Martin Spinelli, and

Patrick Durgin, eds. *Electronic Poetry Corner*. SUNY Buffalo,

2003. Web. 26 Sept. 2006.

Weather.com. Weather Channel Interactive, 2006. Web. 13 Mar.

2006.

For a personal Web site, include the name of the person who created the site; the title, italicized, or (if there is no title) a description such as *Home page*; the publisher or sponsor of the site (if none, use *N.p.*); the date of the last update; the medium of publication (*Web*); and the date of access.

Ede, Lisa. Home page. Oregon State U, 2007. Web. 17 May 2009.

46. WEB LOG (BLOG). For an entire Web log, give the author's last name; the title of the Web log, italicized; the sponsor or publisher of the Web log (if there is none, use *N.p.*); the date of the most recent update; the medium (*Web*); and the date of access.

Atrios. *Eschaton*. N.p., 27 June 2009. Web. 27 June 2009.

47. POST OR COMMENT ON A WEB LOG (BLOG). Follow the guidelines for a short work from a Web site: give the author's name; the title of the post or comment, in quotation marks (if there is no title, use the description *Web log post* or *Web log comment*); the title of the Web log, italicized; the sponsor of the Web log (if there is none, use *N.p.*); the date of the most recent update; the medium (*Web*); and the date of access.

Parker, Randall. "Growth Rate for Electric Hybrid Vehicle Market

Debated." *FuturePundit*. N.p., 20 May 2005. Web. 24 May 2005.

48. ENTRY IN A WIKI. Because wiki content is collectively edited, do not include an author. Treat a wiki as you would a work from a Web site (model 43). Include the title of the entry; the name of the wiki, italicized; the sponsor or publisher of the wiki (use *N.p.* if there is no sponsor); the date of the latest update; the medium (*Web*); and the date

Source Map: Works from Web Sites, MLA Style

You may need to browse other parts of a site to find some of the following elements, and some sites may omit elements. Uncover as much information as you can. A citation for the work on p. 237 would include the following elements:

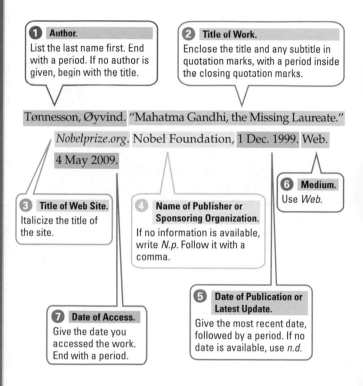

1 Author.
List the last name first. End with a period. If no author is given, begin with the title.

2 Title of Work.
Enclose the title and any subtitle in quotation marks, with a period inside the closing quotation marks.

Tønnesson, Øyvind. "Mahatma Gandhi, the Missing Laureate."

Nobelprize.org. Nobel Foundation, 1 Dec. 1999. Web.

4 May 2009.

6 Medium.
Use *Web.*

3 Title of Web Site.
Italicize the title of the site.

4 Name of Publisher or Sponsoring Organization.
If no information is available, write *N.p.* Follow it with a comma.

5 Date of Publication or Latest Update.
Give the most recent date, followed by a period. If no date is available, use *n.d.*

7 Date of Access.
Give the date you accessed the work. End with a period.

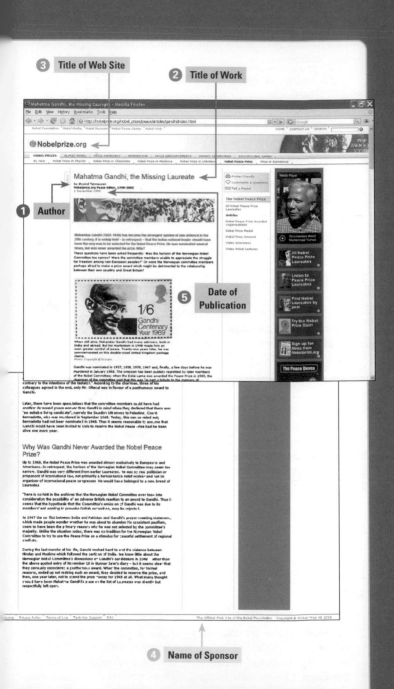

3 Title of Web Site

2 Title of Work

1 Author

5 Date of Publication

4 Name of Sponsor

of access. Check with your instructor before using a wiki as a source.

"Fédération Internationale de Football Association." *Wikipedia.*

Wikimedia Foundation, 27 June 2006. Web. 27 June 2006.

49. POSTING TO A DISCUSSION GROUP. Begin with the author's name and the title of the posting in quotation marks or, if the posting has no title, use *Online posting* (not italicized or in quotation marks). Follow with the name of the Web site, the sponsor or publisher of the site (use *N.p.* if there is no sponsor), the date of publication, the medium (*Web*), and the date of access.

Daly, Catherine. "PoetrySlams." *Poetics Discussion List.* SUNY

Buffalo, 29 Aug. 2003. Web. 1 Oct. 2003.

50. EMAIL. Include the writer's name; the subject line, in quotation marks; *Message to* (not italicized or in quotation marks) followed by the recipient's name; the date of the message; and the medium of delivery (*E-mail*). (MLA style hyphenates *e-mail*.)

Harris, Jay. "Thoughts on Impromptu Stage Productions." Message

to the author. 16 July 2006. E-mail.

51. POSTING TO A SOCIAL NETWORKING SITE. Include the writer's name, a description of the posting, the date of the message, and the medium of delivery. (The MLA does not provide guidelines for citing postings on such sites; this model is based on guidelines for citing email.)

Ferguson, Sarah. Posting on author's wall. 6 Mar. 2008. Facebook

posting.

52. CD-ROM

Cambridge Advanced Learner's Dictionary. 3rd ed. Cambridge:

Cambridge UP, 2008. CD-ROM.

Multimedia sources (including online versions)

53. FILM, VIDEO, OR DVD. If you cite a particular person's work, start with that name. If not, start with the title; then name the director, distributor, the year of release, and the medium. Other contributors, such as writers or performers, may follow the director. If you cite a DVD or video instead

of a theatrical release, include the original film release date and the label *DVD* or *Videocassette*. For material found on a Web site, give the name of the site, italicized; the medium (*Web*); and the access date.

Jenkins, Tamara, dir. *The Savages*. Perf. Laura Linney and Philip

Seymour Hoffman. 2007. *Fox Searchlight*. Web. 4 Mar. 2008.

Spirited Away. Dir. Hayao Miyazaki. 2001. Walt Disney Video,

2003. DVD.

There Will Be Blood. Dir. Paul Thomas Anderson. Perf. Daniel Day-

Lewis. Paramount Vantage/Miramax, 2007. Film.

54. TELEVISION OR RADIO PROGRAM. In general, begin with the title of the program, italicized. Then list important contributors (narrator, writer, director, actors); the network; the local station and city, if any; the broadcast date; and the medium (*Television, Radio*). To cite a particular person's work, begin with that name. To cite a particular episode from a series, begin with the episode title, in quotation marks.

The American Experience: Buffalo Bill. Writ., dir., prod. Rob

Rapley. PBS. Thirteen/WNET, New York. 25 Feb. 2008.

Television.

"The Fleshy Part of the Thigh." *The Sopranos*. Writ. Diane Frolov

and Andrew Schneider. Dir. Alan Taylor. HBO. 2 Apr. 2006.

Television.

Komando, Kim. "E-mail Hacking and the Law." WCBS Radio. WCBS,

New York. 28 Oct. 2003. Radio.

NOTE: Treat an online version as a short work from a Web site (model 43). Give the name of the Web site, italicized. Then give the publisher or sponsor, a comma, and the date posted. End with the medium (*Web*) and the access date.

Roy, Sandip. "A Brain Drain in Reverse, Back to India." *NPR.org*.

NPR, 19 May 2009. Web. 21 May 2009.

55. BROADCAST INTERVIEW. List the person interviewed and then the title, if any. If the interview has no title, use the label *Interview* and name the interviewer, if relevant. Then identify the source. To cite a broadcast interview, end with information about the program, the date(s) the interview took place, and the medium.

Revkin, Andrew. Interview with Terry Gross. *Fresh Air.* Natl. Public

Radio. WNYC, New York, 14 June 2006. Radio.

NOTE: If you listened to an archived version online, after the site's sponsor (if known), add the date of the interview, the medium (*Web*), and the access date. For a podcast interview, see model 61.

Revkin, Andrew. Interview with Terry Gross. *Fresh Air. NPR.org.*

NPR, 14 June 2006. Web. 12 Jan. 2008.

56. UNPUBLISHED OR PERSONAL INTERVIEW. List the person interviewed; the label *Telephone interview, Personal interview,* or *E-mail interview*; and the date the interview took place.

Freedman, Sasha. Personal interview. 10 Nov. 2006.

57. SOUND RECORDING. List the name of the person or group you wish to emphasize (such as the composer, conductor, or band); the title of the recording or composition; the artist, if appropriate; the manufacturer; and the year of issue. Give the medium (such as *MP3 file, CD,* or *LP*) at the end. If you are citing a particular song or selection, include its title, in quotation marks, before the title of the recording.

Bach, Johann Sebastian. *Bach: Violin Concertos.* Perf. Itzhak

Perlman and Pinchas Zukerman. English Chamber Orchestra.

EMI, 2002. CD.

Sonic Youth. "Incinerate." *Rather Ripped.* Geffen, 2006. MP3 file.

✓ CHECKLIST

Citing Sources without Models in MLA Style

To cite a source for which you cannot find a model, collect as much information as you can find—about the creator, title, sponsor, date of posting or latest update, and the date you accessed the site—with the goal of helping your readers find the source for themselves, if possible. Then look at the models in this section to see which one most closely matches the type of source you are using. For example, a YouTube video might resemble a Web log posting (model 47), a film (model 53), a television show (model 54), a broadcast interview (model 55), or a speech (model 59).

Before citing an electronic source for which you have no model in an academic writing project, ask your instructor for help.

NOTE: If you are citing instrumental music that is identified only by form, number, and key, do not italicize or enclose it in quotation marks.

> Grieg, Edvard. Concerto in A minor, op. 16. Cond. Eugene
>
> Ormandy. Philadelphia Orch. RCA, 1989. LP.

58. MUSICAL COMPOSITION. When you are not citing a specific published version, first give the composer's name, followed by the title.

> Mozart, Wolfgang Amadeus. *Don Giovanni,* K527.

> Mozart, Wolfgang Amadeus. Symphony no. 41 in C major, K551.

NOTE: Cite a published score as you would a book. If you include the date the composition was written, do so immediately after the title.

> Schoenberg, Arnold. *Chamber Symphony No. 1 for 15 Solo*
>
> *Instruments, Op. 9.* 1906. New York: Dover, 2002. Print.

59. LECTURE OR SPEECH. List the speaker; title, in quotation marks; sponsoring institution or group; place; and date. If the speech is untitled, use a label such as *Lecture.*

> Eugenides, Jeffrey. Portland Arts and Lectures. Arlene Schnitzer
>
> Concert Hall, Portland, OR. 30 Sept. 2003. Lecture.

NOTE: If you watched an archived version online, after the site's sponsor (if known), add the date of the lecture or speech, the medium (*Web*), and the access date.

> Colbert, Stephen. Speech at the White House Correspondents'
>
> Association Dinner. *YouTube.* YouTube, 29 Apr. 2006. Web.
>
> 20 May 2008.

60. LIVE PERFORMANCE. List the title, italicized; appropriate names (such as writer or performer); place; and date. To cite a particular person's work, begin the entry with that name. End with the medium (*Performance*).

> *Anything Goes.* By Cole Porter. Perf. Klea Blackhurst. Shubert
>
> Theater, New Haven. 7 Oct. 2003. Performance.

61. PODCAST. Treat a podcast as a short work from a Web site (model 43). Include all of the following that are relevant and available: the speaker, the title of the podcast, the title

of the program, the host or performers, the title of the site, the date of posting, the site's sponsor, and the medium (*MP3 file*). Omit the access date.

> "Seven Arrested in U.S. Terror Raid." *Morning Report*. Host
>
> Krishnan Guru-Murthy. *4 Radio*. Channel 4 News, 23 June
>
> 2006. MP3 file.

62. WORK OF ART OR PHOTOGRAPH. List the artist or photographer; the work's title, italicized; the date of composition (if unknown, use *n.d.*); and the medium of composition (*Oil on canvas, Bronze*). Then cite the name of the museum or other location and the city. To cite a reproduction in a book, add the publication information. To cite artwork found online, omit the medium of composition and after the location add the title of the database or Web site, italicized; the medium consulted (*Web*); and the date of access.

> Chagall, Marc. *The Poet with the Birds*. 1911. Minneapolis Inst. of
>
> Arts. *artsmia.org*. Web. 6 Oct. 2009.

> *General William Palmer in Old Age*. 1810. Oil on canvas. National
>
> Army Museum, London. *White Mughals: Love and Betrayal*
>
> *in Eighteenth-Century India*. William Dalrymple. New York:
>
> Penguin, 2002. 270. Print.

> Kahlo, Frida. *Self-Portrait with Cropped Hair*. 1940. Oil on canvas.
>
> Museum of Mod. Art, New York.

63. MAP OR CHART. Cite a map or chart as you would a book or a short work within a longer work and include the word *Map* or *Chart* after the title. Add the medium of publication. For an online source, end with the date of access.

> "Australia." Map. *Perry-Castaneda Library Map Collection*. U of
>
> Texas, 1999. Web. 4 Nov. 2008.

> *California*. Map. Chicago: Rand, 2002. Print.

64. CARTOON OR COMIC STRIP. List the artist's name; the title (if any) of the cartoon or comic strip, in quotation marks; the label *Cartoon* or *Comic strip*; and the usual publication information for a print periodical (models 28–31) or a work from a Web site (model 43).

> Johnston, Lynn. "For Better or Worse." Comic strip. *FBorFW.com*.
>
> Lynn Johnston Publications, 30 June 2009. Web. 20 July 2009.

Lewis, Eric. "The Unpublished Freud." Cartoon. *New Yorker* 11 Mar.
2002: 80. Print.

65. ADVERTISEMENT. Include the label *Advertisement* after the
name of the item or organization being advertised.

Microsoft. Advertisement. *Harper's* Oct. 2003: 2-3. Print.

Microsoft. Advertisement. *New York Times.* New York Times,
11 Nov. 2006. Web. 11 Nov. 2006.

66. VIDEO OR COMPUTER GAME. Include the medium.

Grand Theft Auto: San Andreas. New York: Rockstar Games, 2004.
DVD-ROM.

Other sources (including online versions). If an online
version is not shown here, use the appropriate model for
the source and then end with the medium and the date of
access.

67. REPORT OR PAMPHLET. Cite a report or pamphlet by following the guidelines for a print or an online book.

Allen, Katherine, and Lee Rainie. *Parents Online.* Washington: Pew
Internet and Amer. Life Project, 2002. Print.

Environmental Working Group. *Dead in the Water.* Washington:
Environmental Working Group, 2006. Web. 24 Apr. 2009.

68. GOVERNMENT PUBLICATION. Begin with the author, if identified. Otherwise, start with the name of the government, followed by the agency and any subdivision. Use abbreviations
if they can be readily understood. Then give the title, italicized. For congressional documents, cite the number, session,
and house of Congress (using *S* for Senate and *HR* for House
of Representatives); the type (*Bill, Report, Resolution, Document*) in abbreviated form; and the number of the material.
If you cite the *Congressional Record,* give only the date and
page number(s). For print sources, end with the publication
information (place, publisher, date) and the medium (*Print*).
For online sources, follow the models for a work from a Web
site (model 43) or an entire Web site (model 45).

Gregg, Judd. *Report to Accompany the Genetic Information
Act of 2003.* US 108th Cong., 1st sess. S. Rept. 108-22.
Washington: GPO, 2003. Print.

Kinsella, Kevin, and Victoria Velkoff. *An Aging World: 2001*. US

Bureau of the Census. Washington: GPO, 2001. Print.

United States. Environmental Protection Agency. Office of

Emergency and Remedial Response. *This Is Superfund*.

Environmental Protection Agency, Jan. 2000. Web. 16 Aug.

2004.

69. PUBLISHED PROCEEDINGS OF A CONFERENCE. Cite proceedings as you would a book. If the title doesn't include enough information about the conference, add necessary information after the title.

Cleary, John, and Gary Gurtler, eds. *Proceedings of the Boston*

Area Colloquium in Ancient Philosophy 2002. Boston: Brill

Academic, 2003. Print.

70. DISSERTATION. Enclose the title in quotation marks. Add the label *Diss.*, the school, the year the work was accepted, and the medium.

LeCourt, Donna. "The Self in Motion: The Status of the (Student)

Subject in Composition Studies." Diss. Ohio State U, 1993.

Print.

NOTE: Cite a published dissertation as a book, adding the identification *Diss.* and the university.

Onley, James. *The Arabian Frontier of the British Raj: Merchants,*

Rulers, and the British in the Nineteenth-Century Gulf. Diss. U

of Oxford, 2001. Oxford: Oxford UP, 2007. Print.

71. DISSERTATION ABSTRACT. To cite the abstract of a dissertation using *Dissertation Abstracts International* (*DAI*), include the *DAI* volume and issue number, year (in parentheses), page number, and medium.

Huang-Tiller, Gillian C. "The Power of the Meta-Genre: Cultural,

Sexual, and Racial Politics of the American Modernist

Sonnet." Diss. U of Notre Dame, 2000. *DAI* 61.4 (2000):

1401. Print.

72. PUBLISHED INTERVIEW. List the person interviewed and then the title of the interview. If the interview has no title,

use the label *Interview* and name the interviewer, if relevant. Then identify the source.

> Ebert, Roger. Interview by Matthew Rothschild. *Progressive.*
>
> Progressive Magazine, Aug. 2003. Web. 5 Oct. 2003.
>
> Taylor, Max. "Max Taylor on Winning." *Time* 13 Nov. 2000: 66.
>
> Print.

73. UNPUBLISHED LETTER. Cite a published letter as a work in an anthology (see model 10). If the letter is unpublished, follow this form, ending with the form of the material:

> Anzaldúa, Gloria. Letter to the author. 10 Sept. 2002. MS.

74. MANUSCRIPT OR OTHER UNPUBLISHED WORK. Begin with the author's name and the title or, if there is no title, a description of the material. Then note the form of the material (such as *MS* for *manuscript* or *TS* for *typescript*) and any identifying numbers assigned to it. End by giving the name and location of the library or research institution housing the material, if applicable.

> Woolf, Virginia. "The Searchlight." TS Ser. III, Box 4, Item
>
> 184. Papers of Virginia Woolf, 1902-1956. Smith Coll.,
>
> Northampton.

75. LEGAL SOURCE. To cite a legal case, give the name of the case, the number of the case (using the abbreviation *No.*), the name of the court, the date of the decision, and the medium.

> Eldred v. Ashcroft. No. 01-618. Supreme Ct. of the US. 15 Jan.
>
> 2003. Print.

To cite an act, give the name of the act followed by its Public Law (*Pub. L.*) number, its Statutes at Large (*Stat.*) cataloging number, the date the act was enacted, and the medium.

> Museum and Library Services Act of 2003. Pub. L. 108-81. 117
>
> Stat. 991. 25 Sept. 2003. Print.

42e ## Sample Student Research Essay, MLA Style

SAMPLE STUDENT RESEARCH ESSAY, MLA STYLE

Craig 1

1 David Craig

Professor Turkman

English 219

8 December 2008

2 Messaging and the Language of Youth Literacy

3 The English language is under attack. At least, that is what many people seem to believe. From concerned parents to local librarians, everyone seems to have a negative comment on the state of youth literacy today. They fear that the current generation of grade school students will graduate with an extremely low level of literacy, and they point out that although language education hasn't changed, kids are having more trouble reading and writing than **4** in the past. When asked about the cause of this situation, many adults pin the blame on new technology such as e-mail, texting, and instant messaging, arguing that electronic shortcuts create and compound undesirable reading and writing habits and discourage students from learning conventionally correct ways to use language. But although the arguments against messaging are passionate, **5** evidence suggests that they may not hold up.

The disagreements about messaging shortcuts are profound, even among academics. John Briggs, an English professor at the **6** University of California, Riverside, says, "Americans have always been informal, but now the informality of precollege culture is so ubiquitous that many students have no practice in using language in any formal setting at all" (qtd. in McCarroll). Such objections

1 Name, instructor, course, date, aligned in left margin **2** Title, centered
3 Opens with attention-getting statement **4** Background on the problem
5 Thesis statement **6** Quotation used as evidence

Annotations indicate MLA-style formatting **and effective writing.**

are not new; Sven Birkerts of Mount Holyoke College argued in 1999 that "[students] read more casually. They strip-mine what they read" online and consequently produce "quickly generated, casual prose" (qtd. in Leibowitz A67). However, academics are also among the defenders of texting and instant messaging (IM), with some suggesting that messaging may be a beneficial force in the development of youth literacy because it promotes regular contact with words and the use of a written medium for communication.

Regardless of one's views on texting and IMing, the phenomenon of electronic communication is certainly widespread among the young. According to the Pew Internet & American Life ⑧ Project, 81% of those aged 15-17 regularly send text messages (Lenhart, Madden, Macgill, and Smith 21). In 2001, the most conservative estimate based on Pew numbers showed that American youths spent, at a minimum, nearly three million hours per day on instant messaging services (Lenhart and Lewis 20). These IM numbers hold steady today, and they may even be expanding thanks to popular Web 2.0 sites such as Facebook and Gmail, which incorporate chat functions. What's more, young messagers seem to be using a new vocabulary.

To establish the existence of a messaging language, I analyzed ⑨ 11,341 lines of text from IM conversations between U.S. residents aged twelve to seventeen. Young messagers voluntarily sent me chat logs. I went through all of the logs, recording the number of times IM language was used in place of conventional English. During the course of my study, I identified four types of IM language: phonetic

---

⑦ Last name and page number in upper right corner ⑧ Statistical evidence cited
⑨ Writer's field research introduced

Annotations indicate MLA-style formatting and effective writing.

Craig 3

replacements, acronyms, abbreviations, and inanities. An example of phonetic replacement is using *ur* for *you are*. Another popular type of IM language is the acronym; a common one is *lol*, for *laughing out loud*. Abbreviations are also common in IM, but I discovered that typical abbreviations, such as *etc.*, are not new to the English language. Finally, inanities include completely new expressions and nonsensical variations of other words.

In the chat transcripts that I analyzed, the best display of typical IM lingo came from conversations between two thirteen-year-old Texan girls who are avid IM users. Figure 1 graphs how often they used certain phonetic replacements and abbreviations. The *y*-axis plots frequency of replacement, comparing the number of times a word or **⑩** phrase is used in IM language with the total number of times that it is communicated. The *x*-axis lists specific IM words and phrases.

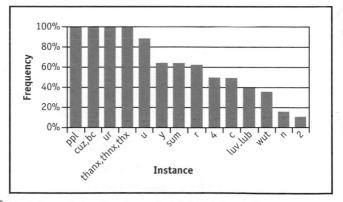

⑪ *Fig. 1. Usage of phonetic replacements and abbreviations in IM.*

⑩ **Figure explained in text** **⑪** **Figure labeled and titled**

Annotations indicate MLA-style formatting and effective writing.

Craig 4

My research shows that the Texan girls used the first ten phonetic replacements or abbreviations at least 50% of the time in their normal messaging. For example, for every time one of them wrote *see*, there was a parallel time when *c* was used in its place. It appears that the popular IM culture contains at least some elements of its own language. Much of this language seems new: no formal dictionary yet identifies the most common IM words and phrases.

While messaging is widespread and does seem to have its own vocabulary, these two factors alone do not mean it has a damaging **⑫** influence on youth literacy. Scholars of metalinguistics, in fact, support the claim that IM is not damaging to those who use it. One of the most prominent components of IM language is phonetic replacement, in which a word such as *everyone* becomes *every1*. This type of wordplay has a special importance in the development of an advanced literacy. According to David Crystal, an internationally recognized scholar of linguistics, as young children learn how words **⑬** string together to express ideas, they go through many phases of language play. The rhymes and nonsensical chants of preschoolers are vital to their learning language, and a healthy appetite for wordplay leads to a better command of language later in life (182).

Crystal uses *metalinguistics* to refer to the ability to "step back" and analyze how language works. "If we are good at stepping back," he says, "at thinking in a more abstract way about what we hear and what we say, then we are more likely to be good at acquiring those skills which depend on just such a stepping back in order to be successful—and this means, chiefly, reading and writing. . . . [T]he **⑭**

⑫ **Writer returns to opposing argument** ⑬ **Linguistic authority cited in support of thesis** ⑭ **Ellipses indicate omission in quotation**

Annotations indicate MLA-style formatting and effective writing.

Craig 5

greater our ability to play with language, . . . the more advanced will be our command of language as a whole" (181).

Metalinguistics also involves our ability to write in a variety of distinct styles and tones. Many critics assume that *either* IM *or* academic literacy will eventually win out and that the two modes cannot exist side by side. However, human beings ordinarily develop a large range of language abilities, from the formal to the relaxed. Mark Twain, for example, employed local speech when writing dialogue for *Huckleberry Finn*. Yet few people would argue that Twain's knowledge of this form of English had a negative impact on his ability to write in standard English.

15 Of course, just as Mark Twain used dialects carefully in dialogue, writers must pay careful attention to the kind of language they use in any setting. The anonymous owner of the language Web site The Discouraging Word backs up this idea in an email message:

16 What is necessary, we feel, is that students learn how to shift between different styles of writing—that, in other words, the abbreviations and shortcuts of IM should be used online . . . but that they should not be used in an essay submitted to a teacher. . . . IM might even be considered . . . a different way of reading and writing, one that requires specific and unique skills shared by certain communities.

17 The analytical ability necessary for writers to choose an appropriate tone and style in their writing is metalinguistic in nature because it involves the comparison of language systems. Thus, young

15 Evidence supporting connection between wordplay and literacy **16** Email correspondence cited as a block quotation **17** Writer synthesizes evidence

Annotations indicate MLA-style formatting and effective writing.

Craig 6

people who possess both IM and traditional skills stand to be better off than their peers who have been trained only in traditional or conventional systems.

Youth literacy does seem to be declining. But the possibility of instant messaging causing the decline seems unlikely when there is evidence of other possible causes. According to the College Board, which collects data from its test takers, enrollment in English composition and grammar classes has decreased in the last decade by 14% (Carnahan and Coletti 11). Simply put, schools in the United States are not teaching English as much as they used to. Rather than blaming IM alone for the decline in literacy and test scores, we must look toward our schools' lack of focus on the teaching of conventional English skills.

I found that the use of instant messaging does not threaten the **18** development or maintenance of formal language skills. The current decline in youth literacy is not due to the rise of instant messaging; rather, fewer young students seem to be receiving an adequate education in the use of conventional English. Unfortunately, it may always be fashionable to blame new tools for old problems, but in the case of instant messaging, that blame is not warranted. Although IM may expose literacy problems, it does not create them.

18 Conclusion sums up argument

Annotations indicate MLA-style formatting **and effective writing.**

(19)   Works Cited

(20) Carnahan, Kristin, and Chiara Coletti. *10-Year Trend in SAT Scores*

(21)   *Indicates Increased Emphasis on Math Is Yielding Results;*

     Reading and Writing Are Causes for Concern. New York: College

     Board, 2002. Print.

(22) Crystal, David. *Language Play*. Chicago: U of Chicago P, 1998. Print.

(23) The Discouraging Word. "Re: Instant Messaging and Literacy."

     Message to the author. 13 Nov. 2008. E-mail.

(24) Leibowitz, Wendy R. "Technology Transforms Writing and the

     Teaching of Writing." *Chronicle of Higher Education* 26 Nov.

     1999: A67-68. Print.

(25) Lenhart, Amanda, and Oliver Lewis. *Teenage Life Online: The Rise of*

     the Instant-Message Generation and the Internet's Impact on

     Friendships and Family Relationships. Washington: Pew Internet

     & American Life Project, 2001. Web. 8 Oct. 2008.

     Lenhart, Amanda, Mary Madden, Alexandra Rankin Macgill, and Aaron

     Smith. *Teens and Social Media.* Washington: Pew Internet &

     American Life Project, 2007. Web. 8 Oct. 2008.

(26) McCarroll, Christina. "Teens Ready to Prove Text-Messaging Skills Can

     Score SAT Points." *Christian Science Monitor* 11 Mar. 2005. Web.

     12 Oct. 2008.

▶ bedfordstmartins.com/easywriter To read a longer version of this essay, click
on **Student Writing**.

---

(19) **Heading centered** **(20)** **First line of each entry flush left; subsequent lines indented** **(21)** **Report** **(22)** **Book** **(23)** **Email** **(24)** **Newspaper article** **(25)** **Online report** **(26)** **Online newspaper article**

Annotations indicate MLA-style formatting **and effective writing.**

43 APA Style

Many fields in the social sciences ask students to follow the basic guidelines prescribed by the American Psychological Association (APA) for formatting manuscripts and documenting various kinds of sources. For more information, consult the *Publication Manual of the American Psychological Association*, Sixth Edition (2010).

43a APA manuscript format

The following formatting guidelines are adapted from the APA recommendations for preparing manuscripts for publication in journals. However, check with your instructor before preparing your final draft.

Title page. APA does not provide any specific title-page guidelines. Be sure to center the title and include your name, the course name and number, the instructor's name, and the date. If your instructor wants you to include a running head, place it flush left on the first line. Write the words *Running head*, a colon, and a short version of the title (fifty characters or fewer, including spaces) using all capital letters. On the same line, flush with the right margin, type the number *1*.

Margins and spacing. Leave margins of at least one inch at the top and bottom and on both sides of the page. Do not justify the right margin. Double-space the entire text, including headings, set-off quotations (23a), content notes, and the list of references. Indent one-half inch, or five spaces, from the left margin for the first line of a paragraph and all lines of a quotation over forty words long.

Short title and page numbers. Type the running head and the short title in the upper left corner of each page. Type the page number in the upper right corner of each page, in the same position as on the title page.

Long quotations. For a long, set-off quotation (one having more than forty words), indent it one-half inch (or five

---

bedfordstmartins.com/easywriter To access the advice in this chapter online, click on **Documenting Sources**.

to seven spaces) from the left margin, and do not use quotation marks. Place the page reference in parentheses one space after the final punctuation.

Abstract. If your instructor asks for an abstract with your paper, the abstract should go immediately after the title page, with the word *Abstract* centered about an inch from the top of the page. Double-space the text of the abstract. For most papers, a one-paragraph abstract of about one hundred words will be sufficient to introduce readers to your topic and provide a brief summary of your major thesis and supporting points.

Headings. Headings are used within the text of many APA-style papers. In papers with only one or two levels of headings, center the main headings; italicize the subheadings and position them flush with the left margin. Capitalize all major words; however, do not capitalize **articles**, short **prepositions**, and **coordinating conjunctions** unless they are the first word or follow a colon.

Visuals. Tables should be labeled *Table*, numbered, and captioned. All other visuals (charts, graphs, photographs, and drawings) should be labeled *Figure*, numbered, and captioned with a description and the source information. Remember to refer to each visual in your text, stating how

DIRECTORY TO APA STYLE FOR IN-TEXT CITATIONS

1. Basic format for a quotation *255*
2. Basic format for a paraphrase or summary *255*
3. Two authors *255*
4. Three to five authors *256*
5. Six or more authors *256*
6. Corporate or group author *256*
7. Unknown author *256*
8. Two or more authors with the same last name *257*
9. Two or more works by an author in a single year *257*
10. Two or more sources in one parenthetical reference *257*
11. Indirect source *257*
12. Personal communication *257*
13. Electronic document *257*
14. Table or figure reproduced in the text *258*

it contributes to the point(s) you are making. Tables and figures should generally appear near the relevant text; check with your instructor for guidelines on placement of visuals.

43b In-text citations

APA style requires parenthetical references in the text to document quotations, paraphrases, summaries, and other material from a source. These citations correspond to full bibliographic entries in a list of references at the end of the text.

Note that APA style generally calls for using the past tense or present perfect tense for signal verbs: *Baker (2003) showed* or *Baker (2003) has shown.* Use the present tense only to discuss results *(the experiment demonstrates)* or widely accepted information *(researchers agree).*

An in-text citation in APA style always indicates *which source* on the references page the writer is referring to, and it explains *in what year* the material was published; for quoted material, the in-text citation also indicates *where* in the source the quotation can be found.

1. BASIC FORMAT FOR A QUOTATION. Generally, use the author's name in a signal phrase to introduce the cited material, and place the date, in parentheses, immediately after the author's name. The page number, preceded by *p.,* appears in parentheses after the quotation.

> Gitlin (2001) pointed out that "political critics, convinced that the media are rigged against them, are often blind to other substantial reasons why their causes are unpersuasive" (p. 141).

If the author is not named in a signal phrase, place the author's name, the year, and the page number in parentheses after the quotation: (Gitlin, 2001, p. 141).

2. BASIC FORMAT FOR A PARAPHRASE OR SUMMARY. Include the author's last name and the year as in model 1, but omit the page or paragraph number unless the reader will need it to find the material in a long work.

> Gitlin (2001) has argued that critics sometimes overestimate the influence of the media on modern life.

3. TWO AUTHORS. Use both names in all citations. Use *and* in a signal phrase, but use an ampersand (&) in parentheses.

Babcock and Laschever (2003) have suggested that many women do not negotiate their salaries and pay raises as vigorously as their male counterparts do.

A recent study has suggested that many women do not negotiate their salaries and pay raises as vigorously as their male counterparts do (Babcock & Laschever, 2003).

4. THREE TO FIVE AUTHORS. List all the authors' names for the first reference.

Safer, Voccola, Hurd, and Goodwin (2003) reached somewhat different conclusions by designing a study that was less dependent on subjective judgment than were previous studies.

In subsequent references, use just the first author's name plus *et al.*

Based on the results, Safer et al. (2003) determined that the apes took significant steps toward self-expression.

5. SIX OR MORE AUTHORS. Use only the first author's name and *et al.* in every citation.

As Soleim et al. (2002) demonstrated, advertising holds the potential for distorting and manipulating "free-willed" consumers.

6. CORPORATE OR GROUP AUTHOR. If the name of the organization or corporation is long, spell it out the first time you use it, followed by an abbreviation in brackets. In later references, use the abbreviation only.

FIRST CITATION (Centers for Disease Control and Prevention [CDC], 2006)

LATER CITATIONS (CDC, 2006)

7. UNKNOWN AUTHOR. Use the title or its first few words in a signal phrase or in parentheses. A book's title is italicized, as in the following example; an article's title is placed in quotation marks.

The employment profiles for this time period substantiated the trend (*Federal Employment,* 2001).

8. TWO OR MORE AUTHORS WITH THE SAME LAST NAME. If your list of references includes works by different authors with the same last name, include the authors' initials in each citation.

S. Bartolomeo (2000) conducted the groundbreaking study on teenage childbearing.

9. TWO OR MORE WORKS BY AN AUTHOR IN A SINGLE YEAR. Assign lowercase letters (*a, b,* and so on) alphabetically by title, and include the letters after the year.

Gordon (2004b) examined this trend in more detail.

10. TWO OR MORE SOURCES IN ONE PARENTHETICAL REFERENCE. List sources by different authors in alphabetical order by authors' last names, separated by semicolons: (Cardone, 1998; Lai, 2002). List works by the same author in chronological order, separated by commas: (Lai, 2000, 2002).

11. INDIRECT SOURCE. Use the phrase *as cited in* to indicate that you are reporting information from a secondary source. Name the original source in a signal phrase, but list the secondary source in your list of references.

Amartya Sen developed the influential concept that land reform was necessary for "promoting opportunity" among the poor (as cited in Driver, 2007, para. 2).

12. PERSONAL COMMUNICATION. Cite any personal letters, email messages, electronic postings, telephone conversations, or interviews as shown. Do not include personal communications in the reference list.

R. Tobin (personal communication, November 4, 2006) supported his claims about music therapy with new evidence.

13. ELECTRONIC DOCUMENT. Cite a Web or electronic document as you would a print source, using the author's name and date.

Link and Phelan (2005) argued for broader interventions in public health that would be accessible to anyone, regardless of individual wealth.

14. TABLE OR FIGURE REPRODUCED IN THE TEXT. Number figures (graphs, charts, illustrations, and photographs) and tables separately.

For a table, place the label (*Table 1*) and an informative heading (*Hartman's Key Personality Traits*) above the table; below, provide information about its source.

Table 1
Hartman's Key Personality Traits

Trait category	Color			
	Red	Blue	White	Yellow
Motive	Power	Intimacy	Peace	Fun
Strengths	Loyal to tasks	Loyal to people	Tolerant	Positive
Limitations	Arrogant	Self-righteous	Timid	Uncommitted

Note. Table is adapted from information found at *The Hartman Personality Profile,* by N. Hayden. Retrieved February 24, 2009, from http://students.cs.byu.edu/~nhayden/Code/index.php

For a figure, place the label (*Figure 3*) and a caption indicating the source below the image. If you do not cite the source of the table or figure elsewhere in your text, you do not need to include the source on your list of references.

The APA recommends the following for electronic sources without names, dates, or page numbers:

Author unknown

Use a shortened form of the title in a signal phrase or in parentheses (see model 7). If an organization is the author, see model 6.

Date unknown

Use the abbreviation *n.d.* (for "no date") in place of the year: (*Hopkins, n.d.*).

No page numbers

Many works found online or in electronic databases lack stable page numbers. (Use the page numbers for an electronic work in a format, such as PDF, that has stable pagination.) If paragraph numbers are included in such a source, use the abbreviation *para:* (*Giambetti, 2006, para. 7*). If no paragraph numbers are included but the source includes headings, give the heading and identify the paragraph in the section.

Jacobs and Johnson (2007) have argued that "the South African media is still highly concentrated and not very diverse in terms of race and class" (South African Media after Apartheid, para. 3).

43c Content notes

APA style allows you to use content notes to expand or supplement your text. Indicate such notes in your text by superscript numbers ([1]). Type the notes themselves on a separate page after the last page of the text, under the heading *Footnotes*, which should be centered at the top of the page. Double-space all entries. Indent the first line of each note one-half inch, or five spaces, but begin subsequent lines at the left margin.

SUPERSCRIPT NUMERAL IN TEXT

The age of the children involved was an important factor in the selection of items for the questionnaire.[1]

FOOTNOTE

[1]Marjorie Youngston Forman and William Cole of the Child Study Team provided great assistance in identifying appropriate items for the questionnaire.

43d List of references

The alphabetical list of the sources cited in your document is called *References*. (If your instructor asks that you list everything you have read—not just the sources you cite—call the list *Bibliography*.)

The following sample entries use hanging indent format, in which the first line aligns on the left and the subsequent lines indent one-half inch, or five spaces. This is the customary APA format for final copy, including student papers.

Guidelines for author listings

List authors' last names first, and use only initials for first and middle names. The in-text citations in your text point readers toward particular sources in your list of references.

NAME CITED IN SIGNAL PHRASE IN TEXT

Driver (2007) has noted. . . .

DIRECTORY TO APA STYLE FOR A LIST OF REFERENCES

Guidelines for Author Listings

1. One author *261*
2. Multiple authors *261*
3. Corporate or group author *262*
4. Unknown author *262*
5. Two or more works by the same author *262*

Books

6. Basic format for a book *262*
   SOURCE MAP *264–65*
7. Editor *262*
8. Selection in a book with an editor *262*
9. Translation *263*
10. Edition other than the first *263*
11. Multivolume work *263*
12. Article in a reference work *268*
13. Republished book *268*

Print Periodicals

14. Article in a journal paginated by volume *268*
15. Article in a journal paginated by issue *268*
16. Article in a magazine *268*
    SOURCE MAP *266–67*
17. Article in a newspaper *268*
18. Editorial or letter to the editor *268*
19. Unsigned article *269*
20. Review *269*
21. Published interview *269*

Electronic Sources

22. Article from an online periodical *269*
23. Article from a database *269*
    SOURCE MAP *270–71*
24. Document from a Web site *272*
    SOURCE MAP *274–75*
25. Chapter or section of a Web document *272*
26. Email message or real-time communication *272*
27. Online posting *272*
28. Web log (blog) post *276*
29. Wiki entry *276*
30. Software *276*

continued

continued

Other Sources (including online versions)

31. Government publication *276*
32. Dissertation *277*
33. Technical or research report *277*
34. Conference proceedings *277*
35. Paper presented at a meeting or symposium, unpublished *277*
36. Poster session *277*
37. Film, video, or DVD *278*
38. Television program, single episode *278*
39. Television feature video podcast *278*
40. Audio podcast *278*
41. Video Web post *278*
42. Recording *278*

NAME IN PARENTHETICAL CITATION IN TEXT

. . . (Driver, 2007).

BEGINNING OF ENTRY IN LIST OF REFERENCES

Driver, T. (2007).

Models 1–5 below explain how to arrange author names. The information that follows the name of the author depends on the type of work you are citing—a book (models 6–13); a print periodical (models 14–21); an electronic source (models 22–30); or another kind of source (models 31–42). Consult the model that most closely resembles the kind of source you are using.

1. ONE AUTHOR. Give the last name, a comma, the initial(s), and the date in parentheses.

Lightman, A. P. (2002).

2. MULTIPLE AUTHORS. List up to seven authors, last name first, with commas separating authors' names and an ampersand (&) before the last author's name.

Walsh, M. E., & Murphy, J. A. (2003).

NOTE: For a work with more than seven authors, list the first six, then give three ellipses and the final author's name.

3. CORPORATE OR GROUP AUTHOR

Resources for Rehabilitation. (2003).

4. UNKNOWN AUTHOR. Begin with the work's title.

National Geographic atlas of the Middle East. (2003).

5. TWO OR MORE WORKS BY THE SAME AUTHOR. List two or more works by the same author in chronological order. Repeat the author's name in each entry.

Goodall, J. (1999).

Goodall, J. (2002).

If the works appeared in the same year, list them alphabetically by title, and assign lowercase letters (*a, b,* etc.) after the dates.

Shermer, M. (2002a). On estimating the lifetime of civilizations. *Scientific American, 287*(2), 33.

Shermer, M. (2002b). Readers who question evolution. *Scientific American, 287*(1), 37.

Books

6. BASIC FORMAT FOR A BOOK. Begin with the author name(s). (See models 1–5.) Then include the publication year, the title and subtitle, the city of publication (and state or country, if the city is unfamiliar), and the publisher. The source map on pp. 264–65 shows where to find this information in a typical book.

Levick, S. E. (2003). *Clone being: Exploring the psychological and social dimensions.* Lanham, MD: Rowman & Littlefield.

7. EDITOR

Dickens, J. (Ed.). (1995). *Family outing: A guide for parents of gays, lesbians and bisexuals.* London, England: Peter Owen.

8. SELECTION IN A BOOK WITH AN EDITOR

Burke, W. W., & Nourmair, D. A. (2001). The role of personality assessment in organization development. In J. Waclawski

& A. H. Church (Eds.), *Organization development: A data-driven approach to organizational change* (pp. 55–77). San Francisco, CA: Jossey-Bass.

9. TRANSLATION

Al-Farabi, A. N. (1998). *On the perfect state* (R. Walzer, Trans.). Chicago, IL: Kazi.

10. EDITION OTHER THAN THE FIRST

Moore, G. S. (2002). *Living with the earth: Concepts in environmental health science* (2nd ed.). New York, NY: Lewis.

11. MULTIVOLUME WORK

Barnes, J. (Ed.). (1995). *Complete works of Aristotle* (Vols. 1-2). Princeton, NJ: Princeton University Press.

NOTE: If you cite just one volume of a multivolume work, list the volume used, instead of the complete span of volumes, in parentheses after the title.

✓ CHECKLIST

Formatting a List of References

- Start the list on a new page after the text of the document. Continue consecutive page numbering.

- Center the heading *References* one inch from the top of the paper.

- Begin each entry flush with the left margin, but indent subsequent lines one-half inch or five spaces. Double-space the entire list.

- List sources alphabetically by the author's last name. If no author is given, alphabetize by the first word of the title other than *A, An,* or *The.*

- Italicize titles and subtitles of books and periodicals. Titles of articles should not be italicized or enclosed in quotation marks.

- For titles of books and articles, capitalize only the first word of the title and subtitle and any proper nouns or proper adjectives. For titles of periodicals, capitalize all major words.

Source Map: Books, APA Style

Take information from the book's title page and copyright page (on the reverse side of the title page), not from the cover or a library catalog. A citation for the book on p. 265 would include the following elements:

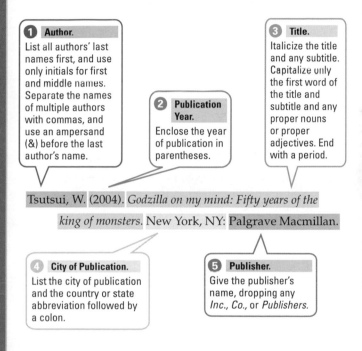

1 Author.
List all authors' last names first, and use only initials for first and middle names. Separate the names of multiple authors with commas, and use an ampersand (&) before the last author's name.

2 Publication Year.
Enclose the year of publication in parentheses.

3 Title.
Italicize the title and any subtitle. Capitalize only the first word of the title and subtitle and any proper nouns or proper adjectives. End with a period.

Tsutsui, W. (2004). *Godzilla on my mind: Fifty years of the*

king of monsters. New York, NY: Palgrave Macmillan.

4 City of Publication.
List the city of publication and the country or state abbreviation followed by a colon.

5 Publisher.
Give the publisher's name, dropping any *Inc., Co.,* or *Publishers.*

2 Publication Year

GODZILLA ON MY MIND
Copyright © William Tsutsui, 2004.
All rights reserved. No part of this book may be used or
reproduced in any manner whatsoever without written permission
except in the case of brief quotations embodied in critical articles
or reviews.

First published 2004 by
PALGRAVE MACMILLAN™
175 Fifth Avenue, New York, N.Y. 10010 and
Houndmills, Basingstoke, Hampshire, England RG21 6XS.
Companies and representatives throughout the world.

4 City of Publication

PALGR...
the Palgr...
Palgrave...
the Unite...
is a regis...
countries...

ISBN 1–...

Library o...
Tsutsui, ...
Godzilla ...
Tsutsui.
   p. ...
   Includ...
   ISBN ...
   1. Go...

PN1995.9...
791.43'65...

A catalo...
Library.

Design b...

10 9 8 ...

Printed i...

3 Title

GODZILLA®
ON MY MIND

*

*Fifty Years of the
King of Monsters*

3 Subtitle

WILLIAM TSUTSUI

1 Author

palgrave
macmillan

5 Publisher

Source Map: Articles from Periodicals, APA Style

A citation for the article on p. 267 would include the following elements:

② Publication Date.
Enclose the date in parentheses, followed by a period. For journals, use only the year. For magazines and newspapers, use the year, month, and day, if given.

① Author.
List all authors' last names first, and use only initials for first and middle names. For more about citing authors, see models 1–5.

Luers, W., Pickering, T., & Walsh, J. (2008, March 20).

A solution for the US-Iran nuclear standoff.

The New York Review of Books, 55(4), 19-22.

③ Article Title.
Do not italicize or enclose in quotation marks. Capitalize only the first word of the title and any subtitle and any proper nouns or proper adjectives. End with a period.

④ Periodical Title.
Italicize the periodical title and capitalize all major words. End with a comma.

⑥ Page Numbers.
Give the inclusive page numbers of the article. For newspapers only, include the abbreviation *p.* ("page") or *pp.* ("pages") before the page numbers. End with a period.

⑤ Publication Information.
Give the volume number (italicized) and the issue number (if the issue begins on p. 1) in parentheses.

Volume LV, Number 4

A Solution for the US–Iran Nuclear Impasse
by William Luers, Thomas Pickering & Jim Walsh

Volume LV, Number 4   March 20, 2008 $5.50

The New York Review
of Books
CAN$6.90

Nicholson Baker:
Why WIKIPEDIA Wins

A Solution for the US–Iran Nuclear Standoff

William Luers, Thomas Pickering, and Jim Walsh

Mahmoud Ahmadinejad announcing the expansion of Iran's nuclear program at a nuclear enrichment facility in Natanz, April 2007

12. ARTICLE IN A REFERENCE WORK

> Dean, C. (1994). Jaws and teeth. In *The Cambridge encyclopedia of human evolution* (pp. 56–59). Cambridge, England: Cambridge University Press.

If no author is listed, begin with the title.

13. REPUBLISHED BOOK

> Piaget, J. (1952). *The language and thought of the child.* London, England: Routledge & Kegan Paul. (Original work published 1932)

Print periodicals

Begin with the author name(s). (See models 1–5.) Then include the publication date (year only for journals, and year, month, and day for other periodicals); the article title; the periodical title; the volume and issue numbers, if any; and the page numbers. The source map on pp. 266–67 shows where to find this information in a sample periodical.

14. ARTICLE IN A JOURNAL PAGINATED BY VOLUME

> O'Connell, D. C., & Kowal, S. (2003). Psycholinguistics: A half century of monologism. *The American Journal of Psychology, 116,* 191-212.

15. ARTICLE IN A JOURNAL PAGINATED BY ISSUE. If each issue begins with page 1, include the issue number after the volume number.

> Hall, R. E. (2000). Marriage as vehicle of racism among women of color. *Psychology: A Journal of Human Behavior, 37*(2), 29-40.

16. ARTICLE IN A MAGAZINE

> Ricciardi, S. (2003, August 5). Enabling the mobile work force. *PC Magazine, 22,* 46.

17. ARTICLE IN A NEWSPAPER

> Faler, B. (2003, August 29). Primary colors: Race and fundraising. *The Washington Post,* p. A5.

18. EDITORIAL OR LETTER TO THE EDITOR

> Zelneck, B. (2003, July 18). Serving the public at public universities [Letter to the editor]. *The Chronicle Review,* p. B18.

19. UNSIGNED ARTICLE

Annual meeting announcement. (2003, March). *Cognitive Psychology, 46,* 227.

20. REVIEW

Ringel, S. (2003). [Review of the book *Multiculturalism and the therapeutic process*]. *Clinical Social Work Journal, 31,* 212-213.

21. PUBLISHED INTERVIEW

Smith, H. (2002, October). [Interview with A. Thompson]. *The Sun,* pp. 4-7.

Electronic sources

Updated guidelines for citing various kinds of electronic resources are maintained at the APA's Web site (www.apa .org).

22. ARTICLE FROM AN ONLINE PERIODICAL. Give the author, date, title, and publication information as you would for a print document. Include both the volume and issue numbers (if given) for all journal articles. If the article has a digital object identifier (DOI), include it. If there is no DOI, include the URL for the periodical's home page or for the article (if the article is difficult to find from the periodical's home page). For newspaper articles accessible from a searchable Web site, give the site URL only.

Cleary, J. M., & Crafti, N. (2007). Basic need satisfaction, emotional eating, and dietary restraint as risk factors for recurrent overeating in a community sample. *E-Journal of Applied Psychology, 2*(3), 27-39. Retrieved from http:// ojs.lib.swin.edu.au/index.php/ejap

23. ARTICLE FROM A DATABASE. Give the information as you would for a print document. Include both the volume and issue numbers for all journal articles. If the article has a DOI, include it. If there is no DOI, write *Retrieved from* and the URL of the journal's home page, not the URL of the database. (A Web search for the journal will give the URL.) The source map on pp. 270–71 shows where to find this information for a typical article from a database.

Hazleden, R. (2003, December). Love yourself: The relationship of the self with itself in popular self-help texts. *Journal of*

Source Map: Articles from Databases, APA Style

A citation for the article on p. 271 would include the following elements:

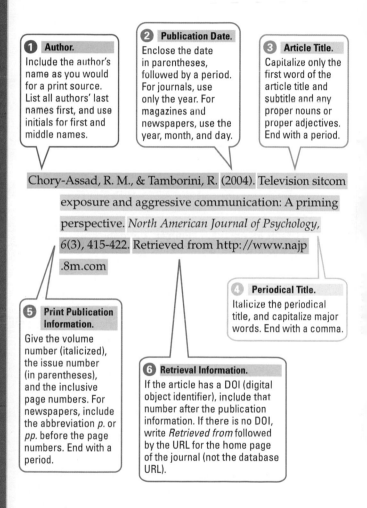

1 Author.
Include the author's name as you would for a print source. List all authors' last names first, and use initials for first and middle names.

2 Publication Date.
Enclose the date in parentheses, followed by a period. For journals, use only the year. For magazines and newspapers, use the year, month, and day.

3 Article Title.
Capitalize only the first word of the article title and subtitle and any proper nouns or proper adjectives. End with a period.

Chory-Assad, R. M., & Tamborini, R. (2004). Television sitcom exposure and aggressive communication: A priming perspective. *North American Journal of Psychology, 6*(3), 415-422. Retrieved from http://www.najp .8m.com

4 Periodical Title.
Italicize the periodical title, and capitalize major words. End with a comma.

5 Print Publication Information.
Give the volume number (italicized), the issue number (in parentheses), and the inclusive page numbers. For newspapers, include the abbreviation *p.* or *pp.* before the page numbers. End with a period.

6 Retrieval Information.
If the article has a DOI (digital object identifier), include that number after the publication information. If there is no DOI, write *Retrieved from* followed by the URL for the home page of the journal (not the database URL).

1 Author

2 Publication Date

3 Article Title

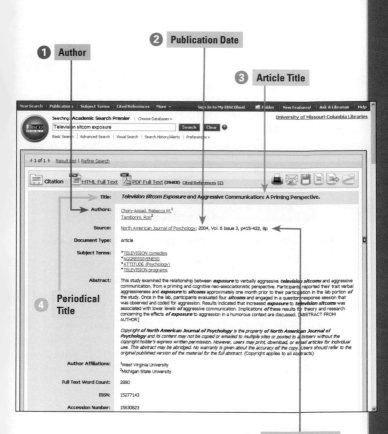

New Search | Publications | Subject Terms | Cited References | More ▾   Sign In to My EBSCOhost | 📁 Folder | New Features! | Ask A Librarian | Help

University of Missouri-Columbia Libraries

Searching: **Academic Search Premier** | Choose Databases »

`Television sitcom exposure`   Search   Clear ❓

Basic Search | Advanced Search | Visual Search | Search History/Alerts | Preferences »

◀ 1 of 1 ▶   Result List | Refine Search

📄 Citation   📄 HTML Full Text   📄 PDF Full Text (394KB)   Cited References (2)   🖨 ✉ 💾 📄 📄 🖊

Title:	*Television Sitcom Exposure* and Aggressive Communication: A Priming Perspective.
Authors:	Chory-Assad, Rebecca M.[1]
	Tamborini, Ron[2]
Source:	North American Journal of Psychology; 2004, Vol. 6 Issue 3, p415-422, 8p
Document Type:	Article
Subject Terms:	*TELEVISION comedies
	*AGGRESSIVENESS
	*ATTITUDE (Psychology)
	*TELEVISION programs
Abstract:	This study examined the relationship between *exposure* to verbally aggressive *television sitcoms* and aggressive communication, from a priming and cognitive neo-associationistic perspective. Participants reported their trait verbal aggressiveness and *exposure* to *sitcoms* approximately one month prior to their participation in the lab portion *of* the study. Once in the lab, participants evaluated four *sitcoms* and engaged in a question-response session that was observed and coded for aggression. Results indicated that increased *exposure* to *television sitcoms* was associated with lower levels *of* aggressive communication. Implications *of* these results for theory and research concerning the effects *of exposure* to aggression in a humorous context are discussed. [ABSTRACT FROM AUTHOR]
	Copyright of ***North American Journal of Psychology*** is the property of ***North American Journal of Psychology*** and its content may not be copied or emailed to multiple sites or posted to a listserv without the copyright holder's express written permission. However, users may print, download, or email articles for individual use. This abstract may be abridged. No warranty is given about the accuracy of the copy. Users should refer to the original published version of the material for the full abstract. (Copyright applies to all Abstracts)
Author Affiliations:	[1]West Virginia University
	[2]Michigan State University
Full Text Word Count:	2880
ISSN:	15277143
Accession Number:	15630823

4 Periodical Title

5 Print Publication Information

271

Sociology, 39(4), 413-428. Retrieved from http://jos.sagepub
.com

Morley, N. J., Ball, L. J., & Ormerod, T. C. (2006). How

the detection of insurance fraud succeeds and fails.

Psychology, Crime, & Law, 12(2), 163-180. doi:10.1080

/10683160512331316325

24. DOCUMENT FROM A WEB SITE. Include all of the following information that you can find: the author's name; the publication date (or *n.d.* if no date is available); the title of the document; the title of the site or larger work, if any; any publication information available in addition to the date; *Retrieved from* and the URL. Provide your date of access only if no publication date is given. The source map on pp. 274–75 shows where to find this information for an article from a Web site.

Behnke, P. C. (2006, February 22). The homeless are everyone's

problem. *Authors' Den.* Retrieved from http://

www.authorsden.com/visit/viewArticle.asp?id=21017

What parents should know about treatment of behavioral and

emotional disorders in preschool children. (2006). *APA*

Online. Retrieved from http://www.apa.org/releases

/kidsmed.html

25. CHAPTER OR SECTION OF A WEB DOCUMENT. Follow model 24. After the chapter or section title, type *In* and give the document title, with identifying information, if any, in parentheses. End with the date of access and the URL.

Salamon, Andrew. (n.d.). War in Europe. In *Childhood in times*

of war (chap. 2). Retrieved April 11, 2008, from http://

remember.org/jean

26. EMAIL MESSAGE OR REAL-TIME COMMUNICATION. Because the APA stresses that any sources cited in your list of references be retrievable by your readers, you should not include entries for email messages, real-time communications (such as text messages), or any other postings that are not archived. Instead, cite these sources in your text as forms of personal communication.

27. ONLINE POSTING. Include an online posting in the references list only if you are able to retrieve the message from

---

✓ CHECKLIST

Citing Electronic Sources

When citing sources accessed online or from an electronic database, include as many of the following elements as you can find:

- **AUTHOR.** Give the author's name, if available.

- **PUBLICATION DATE.** Include the date of electronic publication or of the latest update, if available. When no publication date is available, use *n.d.* ("no date"). You will need to include the date you accessed the source in your retrieval information.

- **TITLE.** List the document title, neither italicized nor in quotation marks.

- **PRINT PUBLICATION INFORMATION.** For articles from online journals, newspapers, or reference databases, give the publication title and other publishing information as you would for a print periodical. (See models 14–17.)

- **RETRIEVAL INFORMATION.** For a work from a database, do the following: if the article has a DOI (digital object identifier), include that number after the publication information. If there is no DOI, write *Retrieved from* followed by the URL for the journal's home page (not the database URL). For a work found on a Web site, write *Retrieved from* and include the URL. If the work seems likely to be updated or has no date of publication, include the retrieval date. If the URL is longer than one line, break it only before a punctuation mark; do not break *http://*.

---

an archive. Provide the author's name, the date of posting, and the subject line. Include other identifying information in square brackets. End with the retrieval statement, including the name of the newsgroup, online forum, or discussion group, if any, and the URL of the archived message. For a newsgroup posting, end with the name of the newsgroup.

> Troike, R. C. (2001, June 21). Buttercups and primroses [Msg 8]. Message posted to the American Dialect Society's electronic mailing list, archived at http://listserv.linguistlist.org /archives/ads-l.html

> Wittenberg, E. (2001, July 11). Gender and the Internet [Msg 4]. Message posted to news://comp.edu.composition

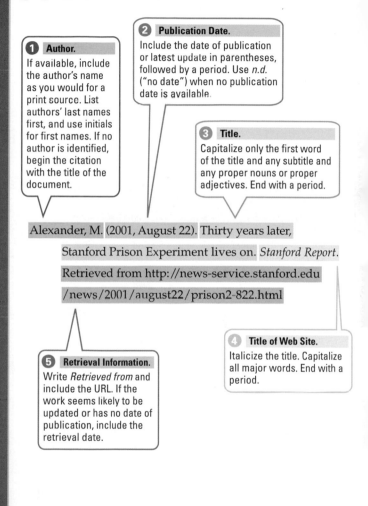

Source Map: Works from Web Sites, APA Style

A citation for the work on p. 275 would include the following elements:

2 Publication Date.
Include the date of publication or latest update in parentheses, followed by a period. Use *n.d.* ("no date") when no publication date is available.

1 Author.
If available, include the author's name as you would for a print source. List authors' last names first, and use initials for first names. If no author is identified, begin the citation with the title of the document.

3 Title.
Capitalize only the first word of the title and any subtitle and any proper nouns or proper adjectives. End with a period.

Alexander, M. (2001, August 22). Thirty years later,

Stanford Prison Experiment lives on. *Stanford Report*.

Retrieved from http://news-service.stanford.edu

/news/2001/august22/prison2-822.html

5 Retrieval Information.
Write *Retrieved from* and include the URL. If the work seems likely to be updated or has no date of publication, include the retrieval date.

4 Title of Web Site.
Italicize the title. Capitalize all major words. End with a period.

5 Retrieval Information

4 Title of Web Site

2 Publication Date

http://news-service.stanford.edu/news/2001/august22/prison2-822.html

HOME

Stanford Report, August 22, 2001

Thirty years later, Stanford Prison Experiment lives on

BY MEREDITH ALEXANDER

Thirty years ago, a group of young men were rounded up by Palo Alto police and dropped off at a new jail -- in the Stanford Psychology Department. Strip searched, sprayed for lice and locked up with chains around their ankles, the "prisoners" were part of an experiment to test people's reactions to power dynamics in social situations. Other college student volunteers -- the "guards" -- were given authority to dictate 24-hour-a-day rules. They were soon humiliating the "prisoners" in an effort to break their will. Psychology Professor Philip Zimbardo's Stanford Prison Experiment of August 1971 quickly became a classic. Using realistic methods, Zimbardo and others were able to create a prison atmosphere that transformed its participants. The young men who played prisoners and guards revealed how much circumstances can distort individual personalities -- and how anyone, when given complete control over others, can act like a monster.

"In a few days, the role dominated the person," Zimbardo -- now president-elect of the American Psychological Association -- recalled. "They *became* guards and prisoners." So disturbing was the transformation that Zimbardo ordered the experiment abruptly ended.

A "guard" leads a "prisoner" down the hall in a 1971 Stanford psychology experiment. The experiment explored power dynamics by creating false distinctions among college student volunteers. Credit: Chuck Painter

Related Information

- **Prison Experiment Website**

- **Psychologist puts the 'real'**

1 Author

3 Article Title

275

✓ CHECKLIST

Citing Sources without Models in APA Style

You may sometimes need to cite a source for which you cannot find a model in APA style. To do so, collect as much information as you can find—about the creator, title, sponsor, date of creation or update—with the goal of helping your readers find the source for themselves, if possible. Then look at the models in this section to see which one most closely matches the type of source you are using. For example, you might consider whether the source is most like an article (look for the appropriate print or electronic model), a work taken from a Web site (model 24), an online posting (model 27), a video (models 37 and 41), a podcast (models 39–40), or some other kind of source.

In an academic writing project, before citing an electronic source for which you have no model, also be sure to ask your instructor's advice.

---

28. WEB LOG (BLOG) POST

> Spaulding, P. (2008, April 16). I did laundry rather than
> watch tonight's debate. Message posted to http://
> pandagon.blogsome.com/

29. WIKI ENTRY. Use the date of posting, if there is one, or *n.d.* for "no date" if there is none. Include the retrieval date because wiki content can change frequently.

> Happiness. (2007, June 14). Retrieved March 24, 2008, from
> PsychWiki: http://www.psychwiki.com/wiki/Happiness

30. SOFTWARE

> PsychMate [Software]. (2003). Available from Psychology
> Software Tools: http://pstnet.com/products/psychmate

Other sources (including online versions)

31. GOVERNMENT PUBLICATION

> Office of the Federal Register. (2003). *The United States*
> *government manual 2003/2004.* Washington, DC: U.S.
> Government Printing Office.

Cite an online government document as you would a printed government work, adding the date of access and the URL. If there is no date, use *n.d.*

U.S. Public Health Service. (1999). *The surgeon general's call
to action to prevent suicide*. Retrieved November 5, 2003,
from http://www.mentalhealth.org/suicideprevention
/calltoaction.asp

32. DISSERTATION. If you retrieved the dissertation from a
database, give the database name and the accession number, if one is assigned.

Lengel, L. L. (1968). *The righteous cause: Some religious aspects
of Kansas populism*. Retrieved from ProQuest Digital
Dissertations. (6900033)

If you retrieve a dissertation from a Web site, give the type
of dissertation, the institution, and year after the title, and
provide a retrieval statement.

Meeks, M. G. (2006). *Between abolition and reform: First-year
writing programs, e-literacies, and institutional change*
(doctoral dissertation, University of North Carolina,
2006). Retrieved from http://dc.lib.unc.edu/cgi-bin
/showfile.exe?CISOROOT=/etd&CISOPTR=212

33. TECHNICAL OR RESEARCH REPORT

McCool, R., Fikes, R., & McGuinness, D. (2003). *Semantic Web
tools for enhanced authoring* (Report No. KSL-03-07).
Stanford, CA: Knowledge Systems Laboratory.

34. CONFERENCE PROCEEDINGS

Mama, A. (2001). Challenging subjects: Gender and power in
African contexts. In *Proceedings of Nordic African Institute
Conference: Rethinking power in Africa*. Uppsala, Sweden, 9-18.

35. PAPER PRESENTED AT A MEETING OR SYMPOSIUM, UNPUBLISHED.
Cite the month of the meeting if it is available.

Jones, J. G. (1999, February). *Mental health intervention in mass
casualty disasters*. Paper presented at the Rocky Mountain
Region Disaster Mental Health Conference, Laramie, WY.

36. POSTER SESSION

Barnes Young, L. L. (2003, August). *Cognition, aging, and
dementia*. Poster session presented at the 2003 Division 40
APA Convention, Toronto, Ontario, Canada.

37. FILM, VIDEO, OR DVD

Mottola, G. (Director). (2007). *Superbad* [Motion picture]. United
    States: Sony.

38. TELEVISION PROGRAM, SINGLE EPISODE

Imperioli, M. (Writer), & Buscemi, S. (Director). (2002).
    Everybody hurts [Television series episode]. In D. Chase
    (Executive Producer), *The Sopranos*. New York, NY: Home Box
    Office.

39. TELEVISION FEATURE VIDEO PODCAST. Include as much of the
following information as you can find: the writer or producer; the date produced or posted; the title of the podcast;
identifying information, if necessary, in brackets; the title of
the series, if any; and the retrieval information.

Allen, D. (Producer). (2005). Deep jungle: New frontiers
    [Television series episode]. In F. Kaufman (Executive
    Producer), *Nature*. Podcast retrieved from WNET:
    http://www.pbs.org/wnet/nature/podcasts.html

40. AUDIO PODCAST. Include as much information as you can
find, as for a video podcast (see model 39).

O'Brien, K. (Writer). (2008, January 31). Developing countries.
    KUSP's life in the fast lane [Audio podcast]. Retrieved from
    http://www.kusp.org/shows/fast.html

41. VIDEO WEB POST

Klusman, P. (2008, February 13). An engineer's guide to cats
    [Video file]. Video posted to http://www.youtube.com
    /watch?v=mHXBL6bzAR4

42. RECORDING

The Avalanches. (2001). Frontier psychiatrist. On *Since I left you*
    [CD]. Los Angeles, CA: Elektra/Asylum Records.

43e **Sample APA pages**

SAMPLE STUDENT RESEARCH ESSAY, APA STYLE

SAMPLE APA TITLE PAGE

Running head: LEADERSHIP ROLES   1 ❶

                                                                        ❷

Leadership Roles in a Small-Group Project   ❸

Merlla McLaughlin
Oregon State University

❶ Running head (fifty characters or fewer) sets flush left on first line of title page
❷ Page number sets flush right on first line of every page   ❸ Title, name, and
affiliation, centered and double-spaced

Annotations indicate APA-style formatting and effective writing.

SAMPLE APA ABSTRACT

                                   Abstract

Using the interpersonal communications research of J. K. Brilhart and G. J. Galanes as well as that of W. Wilmot and J. Hocker, along with T. Hartman's Personality Assessment, I observed and analyzed the leadership roles and group dynamics of my project collaborators in a communications course. Based on results of the Hartman Personality Assessment, I predicted that a single leader would emerge. However, complementary individual strengths and gender differences encouraged a distributed leadership style, in which the group experienced little confrontation. Conflict, because it was handled positively, was crucial to the group's progress.

4 Heading centered **5** No indentation **6** Study described **7** Key points of report discussed **8** Double-spaced text

Annotations indicate APA-style formatting and effective writing.

SAMPLE APA FIRST TEXT PAGE

Running head: LEADERSHIP ROLES   3

Leadership Roles in a Small-Group Project ⑨

Although classroom lectures provide students with volumes of ⑩
information, many experiences can be understood only by living
them. So it is with the workings of a small, task-focused group.
What observations can I make after working with a group of peers ⑪
on a class project? And what have I learned as a result?

Leadership Expectations and Emergence ⑫

The six members of this group were selected by the instructor;
half were male and half were female. By performing the Hartman
Personality Assessment (Hartman, 1998) in class, we learned that ⑬
Hartman has associated key personality traits with the colors red,
blue, white, and yellow (see Table 1). The assessment identified most
of us as "Blues," concerned with intimacy and caring. ⑭

Table 1 ⑮

Hartman's Key Personality Traits

Trait category	Color			
	Red	Blue	White	Yellow
Motive	Power	Intimacy	Peace	Fun
Strengths	Loyal to tasks	Loyal to people	Tolerant	Positive
Limitations	Arrogant	Self-righteous	Timid	Uncommitted

Note. Table is adapted from information found at *The Hartman* ⑯
Personality Profile, by N. Hayden. Retrieved February 24, 2009, from
http://students.cs.byu.edu/~nhayden/Code/index.php

⑨ **Full title, centered** ⑩ **Paragraphs indented** ⑪ **Questions indicate the focus of the essay** ⑫ **Headings help organize the report** ⑬ **APA-style parenthetical reference** ⑭ **Background information about team members' personality types** ⑮ **Table referred to in preceding text** ⑯ **Source of table identified** Annotations indicate APA-style formatting and effective writing.

SAMPLE APA LIST OF REFERENCES

Running head: LEADERSHIP ROLES   7

⑰   References

⑱ Brilhart, J. K., & Galanes, G. J. (1998). *Effective group discussion*
        (9th ed.). Boston, MA: McGraw-Hill.

   Hartman, T. (1998). *The color code: A new way to see yourself, your*
        relationships, and your life. New York, NY: Scribner.

⑲ Hayden, N. (n.d.). *The Hartman Personality Profile*. Retrieved February
        15, 2009, from http://students.cs.byu.edu/~nhayden/Code
        /index.php

⑳ Wilmot, W., & Hocker, J. (2007). *Interpersonal conflict* (7th ed.).

㉑   Boston, MA: McGraw-Hill.

⬤ bedfordstmartins.com/easywriter To read this essay in its entirety, click on
Student Writing.

---

⑰ **References start on new page** ⑱ **Book** ⑲ **Web site** ⑳ **Entries alphabetized**
㉑ **First line of each entry flush left; subsequent lines indented**

Annotations indicate APA-style formatting **and effective writing.**

The style guide of the University of Chicago Press has long been used in history and some other fields in the humanities. *The Chicago Manual of Style,* Fifteenth Edition (2003), provides a complete guide to *Chicago* style, including two systems for citing sources. This chapter presents the notes and bibliography system.

44a *Chicago* manuscript format

Title page.   About halfway down the title page, center the full title of your paper and your name. Unless otherwise instructed, at the bottom of the page also list the course name, the instructor's name, and the date submitted. Do not type a number on this page. Check your instructor's preference on whether to count the title page as part of the text (if so, the first text page will be page 2) or as part of the frontmatter (if so, the first text page will be page 1).

Margins and spacing.   Leave one-inch margins at the top, bottom, and sides of your pages. Double-space the entire text, including block quotations, notes, and bibliography.

Page numbers.   Number all pages (except the title page) in the upper right-hand corner. Also use a short title or your name before page numbers.

Long quotations.   For a long quotation, indent one-half inch (or five spaces) from the left margin and do not use quotation marks. In general, *Chicago* defines a long quotation as one hundred words or eight lines, though you may decide to set off shorter quotes for emphasis (23a).

Headings.   *Chicago* style allows, but does not require, headings. Many students and instructors find them helpful. (See 6c for guidelines on using headings and subheadings.)

Visuals.   Visuals (photographs, drawings, charts, graphs, and tables) should be placed as near as possible to the

---

bedfordstmartins.com/easywriter   To access the advice in this chapter online, click on **Documenting Sources**.

relevant text. (See 40b for guidelines on incorporating visuals into your text.) Tables should be labeled *Table*, numbered, and captioned. All other visuals should be labeled *Figure* (abbreviated *Fig.*), numbered, and captioned. Remember to refer to each visual in your text, pointing out how it contributes to the point(s) you are making.

Notes.   Notes can be footnotes (each appearing at the bottom of the page on which its citation appears in the text) or endnotes (all appearing on a separate page at the end of the text under the heading *Notes*). Be sure to check your instructor's preference. The first line of each note is indented one-half inch, or five spaces, and begins with a number followed by a period and one space before the first word. All remaining lines of the entry are flush with the left margin. Single-space footnotes with a double space between each note; double-space endnotes.

Bibliography.   Begin the list of sources on a separate page after the main text and any endnotes. Continue numbering the pages consecutively. Center the title *Bibliography* (without underlining, italics, or quotation marks) one inch below the top of the page. Double-space, and then begin each entry at the left margin. Indent the second and subsequent lines of each entry one-half inch, or five spaces.

List sources alphabetically by authors' last names or by the first major word in the title if the author is unknown. See page 300 for an example of a *Chicago*-style bibliography.

44b In-text citations, notes, and bibliography

In *Chicago* style, use superscript numbers (^{1}) to mark citations in the text. Place the superscript number for each note just after the relevant quotation, sentence, clause, or phrase. Type the number after any punctuation mark except the dash; do not leave a space before the superscript. Number citations sequentially throughout the text. When you use signal phrases to introduce quotations or other source material, note that *Chicago* style requires you to use the present tense (*citing Bebout's studies, Meier points out . . .*).

IN THE TEXT

> Sweig argues that Castro and Che Guevara were not the only key players in the Cuban Revolution of the late 1950s.[19]

IN THE FIRST NOTE REFERRING TO THE SOURCE

19. Julia Sweig, *Inside the Cuban Revolution* (Cambridge, MA: Harvard University Press, 2002), 9.

IN SUBSEQUENT NOTES. After giving complete information the first time you cite a work, shorten any additional references to that work: list only the author's name, a comma, a shortened version of the title, a comma, and the page number. If the reference is to the same source cited in the previous note, you can use the Latin abbreviation *Ibid.* (for "in the same place") instead of the name and title.

19. Julia Sweig, *Inside the Cuban Revolution* (Cambridge, MA: Harvard University Press, 2002), 9.

20. Ibid., 13.

21. Ferguson, "Comfort of Being Sad," 63.

22. Sweig, *Cuban Revolution,* 21.

Bibliography

The alphabetical list of the sources used is usually titled *Bibliography* in *Chicago* style. If *Sources Consulted, Works Cited,* or *Selected Bibliography* better describes your list, however, any of these titles is acceptable.

In the bibliographic entry for a source, include the same information as in the first note for that source, but omit the specific page reference. However, give the first author's name last name first, followed by a comma and the first name; separate the main elements of the entry with periods rather than commas; and do not enclose the publication information for books in parentheses. List sources alphabetically by authors' last names (or by the first major word in the title if the author is unknown).

IN THE BIBLIOGRAPHY

Sweig, Julia. *Inside the Cuban Revolution.* Cambridge, MA: Harvard University Press, 2002.

Start the bibliography on a separate page after the main text and any endnotes. Continue the consecutive numbering of pages. Center the title *Bibliography* (without italics or quotation marks). Begin each entry at the left margin. Indent subsequent lines of each entry five spaces or one-half inch. Double-space the entire list.

DIRECTORY TO *CHICAGO*-STYLE NOTES AND BIBLIOGRAPHIC ENTRIES

Books

1. One author *287*
2. Multiple authors *287*
3. Corporate or group author *287*
4. Unknown author *287*
5. Editor *288*
6. Selection in an anthology or chapter in a book with an editor *288*
7. Edition other than the first *288*
8. Multivolume work *288*
9. Reference work *288*

Periodicals

10. Article in a journal *288*
11. Article in a magazine *289*
12. Article in a newspaper *289*

Electronic Sources

13. Article from a database *289*
    SOURCE MAP *290–91*
14. Article in an electronic journal *289*
15. Article in an online magazine *289*
16. Work from a Web site *292*
    SOURCE MAP *294–95*
17. Entry in a Web log (blog) *292*
18. Online book *292*
19. Email and other personal communication *293*

Other Sources

20. Published or broadcast interview *293*
21. Podcast *293*
22. Video or DVD *293*
23. CD-ROM *296*
24. Pamphlet, report, or brochure *296*
25. Government publication *296*

44c Notes and bibliographic entries

For easy reference, the following examples demonstrate how to format both notes and bibliographic entries according to *Chicago* style.

Books

1. ONE AUTHOR

1. James S. Hirsch, *Riot and Remembrance: The Tulsa Race War and Its Legacy* (Boston: Houghton Mifflin, 2002), 119.

Hirsch, James S. *Riot and Remembrance: The Tulsa Race War and Its Legacy*. Boston: Houghton Mifflin, 2002.

2. MULTIPLE AUTHORS

2. Margaret Macmillan and Richard Holbrooke, *Paris 1919: Six Months That Changed the World* (New York: Random House, 2003), 384.

Macmillan, Margaret, and Richard Holbrooke. *Paris 1919: Six Months That Changed the World*. New York: Random House, 2003.

When there are more than three authors, you may list the first author followed by *et al.* or *and others* in the note. In the bibliography, however, list all the authors' names.

2. Stephen J. Blank and others, *Conflict, Culture, and History: Regional Dimensions* (Miami: University Press of the Pacific, 2002), 276.

Blank, Stephen J., Lawrence E. Grinter, Karl P. Magyar, Lewis B. Ware, and Bynum E. Weathers. *Conflict, Culture, and History: Regional Dimensions*. Miami: University Press of the Pacific, 2002.

3. CORPORATE OR GROUP AUTHOR

3. World Intellectual Property Organization, *Intellectual Property Profile of the Least Developed Countries* (Geneva: World Intellectual Property Organization, 2002), 43.

World Intellectual Property Organization. *Intellectual Property Profile of the Least Developed Countries*. Geneva: World Intellectual Property Organization, 2002.

4. UNKNOWN AUTHOR

4. *Broad Stripes and Bright Stars* (Kansas City, MO: Andrews McMeel, 2002), 10.

Broad Stripes and Bright Stars. Kansas City, MO: Andrews McMeel, 2002.

5. EDITOR

5. James H. Fetzer, ed., *The Great Zapruder Film Hoax: Deceit and Deception in the Death of JFK* (Chicago: Open Court, 2003), 56.

Fetzer, James H., ed. *The Great Zapruder Film Hoax: Deceit and Deception in the Death of JFK.* Chicago: Open Court, 2003.

6. SELECTION IN AN ANTHOLOGY OR CHAPTER IN A BOOK WITH AN EDITOR

6. Denise Little, "Born in Blood," in *Alternate Gettysburgs,* ed. Brian Thomsen and Martin H. Greenberg (New York: Berkley Publishing Group, 2002), 245.

Little, Denise. "Born in Blood." In *Alternate Gettysburgs,* edited by Brian Thomsen and Martin H. Greenberg, 242-55. New York: Berkley Publishing Group, 2002.

7. EDITION OTHER THAN THE FIRST

7. Charles G. Beaudette, *Excess Heat: Why Cold Fusion Research Prevailed,* 2nd ed. (South Bristol, ME: Oak Grove Press, 2002), 313.

Beaudette, Charles G. *Excess Heat: Why Cold Fusion Research Prevailed.* 2nd ed. South Bristol, ME: Oak Grove Press, 2002.

8. MULTIVOLUME WORK

8. John Watson, *Annals of Philadelphia and Pennsylvania in the Olden Time,* vol. 2 (Washington, DC: Ross & Perry, 2003), 514.

Watson, John. *Annals of Philadelphia and Pennsylvania in the Olden Time.* Vol. 2. Washington, DC: Ross & Perry, 2003.

9. REFERENCE WORK. Cite well-known reference works in your notes, but do not list them in your bibliography. Use *s.v.,* the abbreviation for the Latin *sub verbo* ("under the word") to help your reader find the entry.

9. *Encarta World Dictionary,* s.v. "carpetbagger."

Periodicals

10. ARTICLE IN A JOURNAL

10. Karin Lützen, "The Female World: Viewed from Denmark," *Journal of Women's History* 12, no. 3 (2000): 36.

Lützen, Karin. "The Female World: Viewed from Denmark." *Journal of Women's History* 12, no. 3 (2000): 34-38.

11. ARTICLE IN A MAGAZINE

11. Douglas Brinkley and Anne Brinkley, "Lawyers and Lizard-Heads," *Atlantic Monthly,* May 2002, 56.

Brinkley, Douglas, and Anne Brinkley. "Lawyers and Lizard-Heads."
   Atlantic Monthly, May 2002, 55-61.

12. ARTICLE IN A NEWSPAPER

12. Caroline E. Mayer, "Wireless Industry to Adopt Voluntary Standards," *Washington Post,* September 9, 2003, sec. E.

Mayer, Caroline E. "Wireless Industry to Adopt Voluntary Standards."
   Washington Post, September 9, 2003, sec. E.

Electronic sources

13. ARTICLE FROM A DATABASE. The source map on pp. 290–91 indicates where to find necessary information for citing an article from a database.

13. Peter DeMarco, "Holocaust Survivors Lend Voice to History," *Boston Globe,* November 2, 2003, http://www.lexisnexis.com (accessed November 19, 2003).

DeMarco, Peter. "Holocaust Survivors Lend Voice to History." *Boston
   Globe,* November 2, 2003. http://www.lexisnexis.com (accessed
   November 19, 2003).

14. ARTICLE IN AN ELECTRONIC JOURNAL

14. Damian Bracken, "Rationalism and the Bible in Seventh-Century Ireland," *Chronicon* 2 (1998), http://www.ucc.ie/chronicon/bracfra.htm (accessed November 1, 2005).

Bracken, Damian. "Rationalism and the Bible in Seventh-Century
   Ireland." *Chronicon* 2 (1998). http://www.ucc.ie/chronicon/
   bracfra.htm (accessed November 1, 2005).

15. ARTICLE IN AN ONLINE MAGAZINE

15. Kim Iskyan, "Putin's Next Power Play," *Slate,* November 4, 2003, http://slate.msn.com/id/2090745 (accessed November 7, 2008).

Iskyan, Kim. "Putin's Next Power Play." *Slate,* November 4, 2003.
   http://slate.msn.com/id/2090745 (accessed November 7, 2008).

Citations for the article on p. 291 would include the following elements:

Endnote

2 Article Title.
Enclose title and subtitle (if any) in quotation marks, and capitalize major words. In the notes section, put a comma before and after the title. In the bibliography, put a period before and after.

1 Author.
In a note, list author's first name first. In the bibliographic entry, list the first author last name first; list other authors first name first.

1. Howard Schuman, Barry Schwartz, and Hannah D'Arcy, "Elite Revisionists and Popular Beliefs: Christopher Columbus, Hero or Villain?" *Public Opinion Quarterly* 69, no. 1 (2005), http://elibrary.bigchalk.com (accessed October 15, 2007).

4 Publication Information.
For journals, follow the title with the volume number, a comma, the abbreviation *no.,* the issue number, and the publication year in parentheses. For other periodicals, give the month, day (if given), and year. End with a comma (in a note) or a period (in a bibliography).

3 Periodical Title.
Italicize the title and subtitle, and capitalize all major words. Follow with a comma, unless it is a journal.

5 Retrieval Information.
Give the brief URL for the database, then, in parentheses, the word *accessed* and the access date. End with a period.

Bibliographic entry

Schuman, Howard, Barry Schwartz, and Hannah D'Arcy. "Elite Revisionists and Popular Beliefs: Christopher Columbus, Hero or Villain?" *Public Opinion Quarterly* 69, no. 1 (2005). http://elibrary.bigchalk.com (accessed October 15, 2007).

Document Page: ELITE REVISIONISTS AND POPULAR BELIEFS: CHRISTOPHER COLUMBUS: HERO OR VILLAIN? - Microsoft Internet Explorer

File   Edit   View   Favorites   Tools   Help

Back | Search | Favorites | Media

Address | http://www.elibrary.com.proxy.dbrl.org/libweb/jullo/do/document?set=search&groupId=1&requestId=lib_standard&browseId=1&action=8to=PC647PCF484F256 ▼ | Go

eLibrary

search   topics   reference   my list   bookcart   quiz   help exit

◼ return to search results

◉ to best part   printer friendly version : document info : email : add to my list ✚

ELITE REVISIONISTS AND POPULAR BELIEFS: CHRISTOPHER COLUMBUS, HERO OR VILLAIN?; Schuman, Howard;
Schwartz, Barry; D'Arcy, Hannah
Public Opinion Quarterly   04-01-2005

ELITE REVISIONISTS AND POPULAR BELIEFS: CHRISTOPHER COLUMBUS, HERO OR VILLAIN?

Byline: Schuman, Howard; Schwartz, Barry; D'Arcy, Hannah
Volume: 69
Number: 1
ISSN: 0033362X
Publication Date: 04-01-2005
Page: 2
Type: Periodical
Language: English

Abstract According to revisionist historians and American Indian activists, Christopher Columbus deserves condemnation for
having brought slavery, disease, and death to America's indigenous peoples. We ask whether the general public's beliefs
about Columbus show signs of reflecting these critical accounts, which increased markedly as the 1992 Quincentenary
approached. Our national surveys, using several different question wordings, indicate that most Americans continue to
admire Columbus because, as tradition puts it, "he discovered America," though only a small number of mainly older
respondents speak of him in the heroic terms common in earlier years. At the same time, the percentage of Americans who
reject traditional beliefs about Columbus is also small and is divided between those who simply acknowledge the priority of
Indians as the "First Americans" and those who go further to view Columbus as a villain. The latter group of respondents, we
find, show a critical stance toward modal American beliefs much more broadly.

We also analyze American history school textbooks for evidence of influence from revisionist writings, and we consider
representations of Columbus in the mass media as well. Revisionist history can be seen as one consequence of the "minority
rights revolution" that began after World War II and has achieved considerable success, but the endurance of Columbus's
reputation—to a considerable extent even among the minorities who have the least reason to respect him—raises important
questions about the inertia of tradition, the politics of collective memory, and the difference between elite and popular
beliefs.

The revolution in minority rights over the past half century has not only changed the attitudes of the American public
regarding race, gender, and other social divisions, but has also spurred attempts to revise beliefs about important
individuals and events from the past. For example, Abraham Lincoln is now viewed less as the savior of the Union—the
emphasis during the Civil War and for more than half a century afterward (Blight 2001)—and much more for his actions in

> ✔ CHECKLIST
>
> ### Citing Sources without Models in *Chicago* Style
>
> *Chicago* currently provides no guidelines or models for citing newer kinds of electronic sources, such as MP3 files, YouTube videos, and the like. To cite a source for which you cannot find a model, collect as much information as you can find—about the creator, title, sponsor, date of creation or update—with the goal of helping your readers find the source for themselves, if possible. Then look at the models in this section to see which one most closely matches the type of source you are using. For example, a YouTube video might resemble an entry in a Web log (model 17), a broadcast interview (model 20), a podcast (model 21), or a video (model 22).
>
> In an academic writing project, before citing an electronic source for which you have no model, also be sure to ask your instructor's advice.

16. WORK FROM A WEB SITE. The source map on pp. 294–95 shows where to find important information for a typical work from a Web site.

16. Rutgers University, "Picture Gallery," *The Rutgers Oral History Archives of World War II,* http://fas-history.rutgers.edu/oralhistory/orlhom.htm (accessed November 7, 2007).

Rutgers University. "Picture Gallery." *The Rutgers Oral History Archives of World War II.* http://fas-history.rutgers.edu/oralhistory/orlhom.htm (accessed November 7, 2007).

17. ENTRY IN A WEB LOG (BLOG)

17. Josh Marshall, "Neologism Watch," *Talking Points Memo,* http://talkingpointsmemo.com/archives/182621.php.

Marshall, John. "Neologism Watch." *Talking Points Memo.* http://talkingpointsmemo.com/archives/182621.php.

18. ONLINE BOOK

18. Janja Bec, *The Shattering of the Soul* (Los Angeles: Simon Wiesenthal Center, 1997), http://motlc.wiesenthal.com/resources/books/shatteringsoul/index.html (accessed December 2, 2007).

Bec, Janja. *The Shattering of the Soul.* Los Angeles: Simon Wiesenthal
   Center, 1997. http://motlc.wiesenthal.com/resources/books/
   shatteringsoul/index.html (accessed December 2, 2007).

19. EMAIL AND OTHER PERSONAL COMMUNICATION. Cite email
messages and other personal communications (letters, text
messages, postings on social networking sites such as Facebook, telephone calls, and so on) in the text or in a note. Do
not cite personal communications in the bibliography.

   19. Kareem Adas, email message to author, February 11, 2008.

Other sources

20. PUBLISHED OR BROADCAST INTERVIEW

   20. Warren Buffett, interview by Charlie Rose, *The Charlie Rose
Show,* PBS, June 26, 2006.

Buffett, Warren. Interview by Charlie Rose. *The Charlie Rose Show.*
   PBS, June 26, 2006.

Interviews you conduct are personal communications (see
model 19).

21. PODCAST. Treat a podcast like a work from a Web site (see
model 16), and include as much of the following information as you can find: the author (or speaker); the title of the
podcast; the title of the site on which it appears; the site
sponsor; and the URL.

   21. Kelly O'Brien, "Developing Countries," *KUSP's Life in the Fast
Lane.* Central Coast Public Radio, http://www.kusp.org/shows/fast.html
(accessed October 10, 2008).

O'Brien, Kelly. "Developing Countries." *KUSP's Life in the Fast Lane.*
   Central Coast Public Radio. http://www.kusp.org/shows/fast.html
   (accessed October 10, 2008).

22. VIDEO OR DVD

   22. Denzel Washington and Forest Whitaker, *The Great Debaters,*
DVD, directed by Denzel Washington (2007; Los Angeles: MGM, 2008).

Washington, Denzel, and Forest Whitaker. *The Great Debaters.* DVD.
   Directed by Denzel Washington, 2007. Los Angeles: MGM, 2008.

Source Map: Works from Web Sites, *Chicago* Style

Citations for the Web site on p. 295 would include the following elements:

Endnote

1 **Author.**
In a note, list author first name first. In the bibliographic entry, list the first author last name first and additional authors first name first.

2 **Document Title.**
Enclose the title in quotation marks, and capitalize all major words. In a note, put a comma before and after the title. In the bibliography, put a period before and after.

1. Douglas Linder, "The Scopes Trial: An Introduction," *Famous Trials,* http://www.law.umkc.edu/faculty/projects/ FTrials/scopes/scopes.htm (accessed September 24, 2009).

3 **Title of Web Site.**
Italicize the title, and capitalize all major words. In the notes section, put a comma after the title. In the bibliography, put a period after the title.

4 **Retrieval Information.**
Give the URL for the Web site, followed, in parentheses, by the word *accessed* and the access date. End with a period.

Bibliographic entry

Linder, Douglas. "The Scopes Trial: An Introduction." *Famous Trials.* http://www.law.umkc.edu/faculty/projects/FTrials/ scopes/scopes.htm (accessed September 24, 2009).

Retrieval Information

Famous Trials in American History

Tennessee vs. John Scopes
The "Monkey Trial"

1925

Clarence Darrow and William Jennings Bryan during the trial
Photo Credit: CORBIS/Bettmann

The Scopes Trial: An Introduction

by Douglas Linder (c) 2003

The early 1920s found social patterns in chaos. Traditionalists, the older Victorians, worried that everything valuable was ending. Younger modernists no longer asked whether society would approve of their behavior, only whether their behavior met the approval of their intellect. Intellectual experimentation flourished. Americans danced to the sound of the Jazz Age, showed their contempt for alcoholic prohibition, debated abstract art and Freudian theories. In a response to the new social patterns set in motion by modernism, a wave of revivalism developed, becoming especially strong in the American South.

Who would dominate American culture—the modernists or the traditionalists? Journalists were looking for a showdown, and they found one in a Dayton, Tennessee courtroom in the summer of 1925 ...[CONTINUED]

Famous Trials Homepage

THIS SITE LAST UPDATED 4/23/03

Navigation menu (left):
Anti-Evolution Statute
Genesis Stories
Excerpts from Scopes Trial Transcript
Observer's Account
Mencken's Trial Account
Biographies of Key Figures
Text Used by Scopes
Dayton, Tennessee
Trial Pictures and Cartoons
Darrow Page
Appellate Decisions
Scopes Trial Satire
Chronology & Year 1925
Trial of the Century?
Evolution Controversy
Inherit the Wind
Expert's Impressions
John Scopes Reflects
Hell & High Schools
Links & Bibliography
Trial Video
Trial Jeopardy
Send Comments

1 Author

2 Document Title

3 Title of Web Site

295

23. CD-ROM

> 23. *The Civil War,* CD-ROM (Fogware, 2000).

The Civil War. CD-ROM. Fogware, 2000.

24. PAMPHLET, REPORT, OR BROCHURE. Information about the author or publisher may not be readily available, but give enough information to identify your source.

> 24. Jamie McCarthy, *Who Is David Irving?* (San Antonio, TX: Holocaust History Project, 1998).

McCarthy, Jamie. *Who Is David Irving?* San Antonio, TX: Holocaust
> History Project, 1998.

25. GOVERNMENT PUBLICATION

> 25. U.S. House Committee on Ways and Means, *Report on Trade Mission to Sub-Saharan Africa,* 108th Cong., 1st sess. (Washington, DC: U.S. Government Printing Office, 2003), 28.

U.S. House Committee on Ways and Means. *Report on Trade Mission to
> Sub-Saharan Africa.* 108th Cong., 1st sess. Washington, DC: U.S.
> Government Printing Office, 2003.

44d Sample *Chicago* pages

SAMPLE *CHICAGO* TITLE PAGE

Sweet Home Chicago: Preserving the Past,

Protecting the Future of the Windy City

Amanda Rinder

Twentieth-Century U.S. History

Professor Goldberg

November 27, 2006

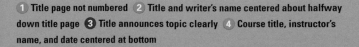

1 Title page not numbered **2** Title and writer's name centered about halfway down title page **3** Title announces topic clearly **4** Course title, instructor's name, and date centered at bottom

Annotations indicate *Chicago*-style formatting and effective writing.

SAMPLE *CHICAGO* FIRST TEXT PAGE

⑤   Rinder 2

Only one city has the "Big Shoulders" described by Carl

⑥ Sandburg: Chicago (fig. 1). So renowned are its skyscrapers and

celebrated building style that an entire school of architecture is

named for Chicago. Presently, however, the place that Frank Sinatra

called "my kind of town" is beginning to lose sight of exactly what

kind of town it is. Many of the buildings that give Chicago its

distinctive character are being torn down in order to make room for

⑦ new growth. Both preserving the classics and encouraging new

creation are important; the combination of these elements gives

⑧ Chicago architecture its unique flavor. Witold Rybczynski, a professor

of urbanism, told Tracie Rozhon of the *New York Times,* "Of all the

cities we can think of . . . we associate Chicago with new things,

with building new. Combining that with preservation is a difficult

⑨ task, a tricky thing. It's hard to find the middle ground in Chicago."[1]

⑩ *Fig. 1. Chicago skyline, circa 1940s. (Postcard courtesy of Minnie Dangburg.)*

⑤ **Author and page number in upper right corner of each page after the title page**
⑥ **Writer refers to each figure by number** ⑦ **Thesis introduced** ⑧ **Double-spaced text** ⑨ **Source cited using superscript numeral** ⑩ **Figure caption includes number, short title, source**
Annotations indicate *Chicago-style formatting* **and effective writing.**

SAMPLE *CHICAGO* ENDNOTES

Rinder 12

Notes

1. Tracie Rozhon, "Chicago Girds for Big Battle over Its Sky-line," *New York Times,* November 12, 2000, http://www.lexisnexis.com (accessed November 7, 2006). ⑪

2. David Garrard Lowe, *Lost Chicago* (New York: Watson-Guptill Publications, 2000), 112.

3. *Microsoft Encarta Encyclopedia 2000,* s.v. "Sullivan, Louis Henri." ⑫

4. Lowe, *Lost Chicago,* 123. ⑬

5. Daniel Bluestone, *Constructing Chicago* (New Haven: Yale University Press, 1991), 105.

6. Alan J. Shannon, "When Will It End?" *Chicago Tribune,* September 11, 1987, quoted in Karen J. Dilibert, *From Landmark to Landfill* (Chicago: Chicago Architectural Foundation, 2000), 11.

7. Steve Kerch, "Landmark Decisions," *Chicago Tribune,* March 18, 1990, sec. 16.

8. Patrick T. Reardon, "'No' Vote Makes It a Landmark Day for the Berghoff," *Chicago Tribune,* April 5, 1991, sec 1.

9. Ibid. ⑭

10. John W. Stamper, *Chicago's North Michigan Avenue* (Chicago: University of Chicago Press, 1991), 215.

11. Nancy Stuenkel, "Success Spoiling the Magnificent Mile?" *Chicago Sun-Times,* April 9, 1995, http://www.lexisnexis.com (accessed November 8, 2006).

12. Paul Gapp, "McCarthy Building Puts Landmark Law on a Collision Course with Developers," *Chicago Tribune,* April 20, 1986, http://www.chicagotribune.com (accessed November 8, 2006).

---

⑪ Note number indented; subsequent lines flush left ⑫ Encyclopedia entry appears in notes but not in bibliography ⑬ Second reference to source ⑭ Reference to preceding source

Annotations indicate *Chicago*-style formatting and effective writing.

SAMPLE *CHICAGO* BIBLIOGRAPHY

(15) Bibliography

(16) Bluestone, Daniel. *Constructing Chicago*. New Haven: Yale University Press, 1991.

(17) Dilibert, Karen J. *From Landmark to Landfill*. Chicago: Chicago Architectural Foundation, 2000.

(18) Gapp, Paul. "McCarthy Building Puts Landmark Law on a Collision Course with Developers." *Chicago Tribune,* April 20, 1986. http://www.chicagotribune.com (accessed November 8, 2006).

(19) Kerch, Steve. "Landmark Decisions." *Chicago Tribune,* March 18, 1990, sec. 16.

Lowe, David Garrard. *Lost Chicago*. New York: Watson-Guptill Publications, 2000.

Reardon, Patrick T. " 'No' Vote Makes It a Landmark Day for the Berghoff." *Chicago Tribune,* April 5, 1991, sec. 1.

(20) Rozhon, Tracie. "Chicago Girds for Big Battle over Its Skyline." *New York Times,* November 12, 2000. http://www.lexisnexis.com (accessed November 7, 2006).

(21) Stamper, John W. *Chicago's North Michigan Avenue*. Chicago: University of Chicago Press, 1991.

Stuenkel, Nancy. "Success Spoiling the Magnificent Mile?" *Chicago Sun-Times,* April 9, 1995. http://www.lexisnexis.com (accessed November 8, 2006).

---

(15) Bibliography starts on new page **(16)** Book **(17)** Pamphlet **(18)** Work from a Web site **(19)** Newspaper article **(20)** Article from database **(21)** First line of each entry flush left; subsequent lines indented

Annotations indicate Chicago-style formatting and effective writing.

Writers in the physical sciences, the life sciences, and mathematics often use the documentation style set forth by the Council of Science Editors (CSE). Guidelines for citing print sources can be found in *Scientific Style and Format: The CSE Manual for Authors, Editors, and Publishers,* Seventh Edition (2006).

45a CSE manuscript format

Title page.   Center the title of your paper. Beneath it, center your name. Include other relevant information, such as the course name and number, the instructor's name, and the date submitted.

Margins and spacing.   Leave standard margins at the top and bottom and on both sides of each page. Double-space the text and the references list.

Page numbers.   Type a short version of the paper's title and the page number in the upper right-hand corner of each page.

Abstract.   CSE style often calls for a one-paragraph abstract (about one hundred words). The abstract should be on a separate page, right after the title page, with the title *Abstract* centered one inch from the top of the page.

Headings.   CSE style does not require headings, but it notes that they can help readers quickly find the contents of a section of the paper.

Tables and figures.   Tables and figures must be labeled *Table* or *Figure* and numbered separately, one sequence for tables and one for figures. Give each table and figure a short, informative title. Be sure to introduce each table and figure in your text, and comment on its significance.

---

 bedfordstmartins.com/easywriter To access the advice in this chapter online, click on **Documenting Sources**.

List of references. Start the list of references on a new page at the end of the essay, and continue to number the pages consecutively. Center the title *References* one inch from the top of the page, and double-space before beginning the first entry.

45b In-text citations

In CSE style, citations within an essay follow one of three formats.

- The *citation-sequence format* calls for a superscript number or a number in parentheses after any mention of a source. The sources are numbered in the order they appear. Each number refers to the same source every time it is used. The first source mentioned in the paper is numbered *1*, the second source is numbered *2*, and so on.

- The *citation-name format* also calls for a superscript number or a number in parentheses after any mention of a source. The numbers are added after the list of references is completed and alphabetized, so that the source numbered *1* is alphabetically first in the list of references, *2* is alphabetically second, and so on.

- The *name-year format* calls for the last name of the author and the year of publication in parentheses after any mention of a source. If the last name appears in a signal phrase, the name-year format allows for giving only the year of publication in parentheses.

Before deciding which system to use, ask your instructor's preference.

1. CITATION-SEQUENCE OR CITATION-NAME FORMAT

VonBergen[12] provides the most complete discussion of this phenomenon.

For the citation-sequence and citation-name formats, you would use the same superscript ([12]) for each subsequent citation of this work by VonBergen.

2. NAME-YEAR FORMAT

VonBergen (2003) provides the most complete discussion of this phenomenon. Hussar's two earlier studies of juvenile obesity (1995, 1999) examined only children with diabetes.

The classic examples of such investigations (Morrow 1968; Bridger et al. 1971; Franklin and Wayson 1972) still shape the assumptions of current studies.

DIRECTORY TO CSE STYLE FOR A LIST OF REFERENCES

Books

1. One author *304*
2. Two or more authors *305*
3. Corporate or group author *305*
4. Book prepared by editor(s) *305*
5. Section of a book with an editor *306*
6. Chapter of a book *306*
7. Paper or abstract in conference proceedings *306*

Periodicals

8. Article in a journal *307*
   SOURCE MAP *308–09*
9. Article in a weekly journal *307*
10. Article in a magazine *307*
11. Article in a newspaper *307*

Electronic Sources

12. Material from an online database *311*
    SOURCE MAP *312–13*
13. Article in an online journal *311*
14. Article in an online newspaper *311*
15. Online book *311*
16. Web site *311*
17. Government Web site *314*

45c List of references

The citations in the text of an essay correspond to items on a list called *References.*

- If you use the citation-sequence format, number and list the references in the order in which the references are *first* cited in the text.
- If you use the citation-name format, list and number the references in alphabetical order.
- If you use the name-year format, list the references, unnumbered, in alphabetical order.

In the following examples, you will see that the citation-sequence and citation-name formats call for listing the date after the publisher's name in references for books and after the periodical name in references for articles. The name-year format calls for listing the date immediately after the author's name in any kind of reference.

CSE style also specifies the treatment and placement of the following basic elements:

- AUTHOR. List all authors last name first, and use only initials for first and middle names. Do not place a comma after the author's last name, and do not place periods after or spaces between the initials. Use a period after the last initial of the last author listed.
- TITLE. Do not italicize or underline titles and subtitles of books and periodicals. Do not enclose titles of articles in quotation marks. For books and articles, capitalize only the first word of the title and any proper nouns or proper adjectives. Abbreviate and capitalize all major words in a periodical title.

As you refer to the following sample entries, pay attention to how publication information (publishers for books, details about periodicals for articles) and other specific elements are punctuated.

Books

1. ONE AUTHOR

Citation-sequence and citation-name

1. Buchanan M. Nexus: small worlds and the groundbreaking theory of networks. New York: Norton; 2003.

Name-Year

Buchanan M. 2003. Nexus: small worlds and the groundbreaking theory of networks. New York: Norton.

2. TWO OR MORE AUTHORS
Citation-sequence and citation-name

2. Wojciechowski BW, Rice NM. Experimental methods in kinetic studies. 2nd ed. St. Louis (MO): Elsevier Science; 2003.

Name-Year

Wojciechowski BW, Rice NM. 2003. Experimental methods in kinetic studies. 2nd ed. St. Louis (MO): Elsevier Science.

3. CORPORATE OR GROUP AUTHOR
Citation-sequence and citation-name

3. World Health Organization. The world health report 2002: reducing risks, promoting healthy life. Geneva (Switzerland): The Organization; 2002.

Place the organization's abbreviation at the beginning of the name-year entry, and use the abbreviation in the corresponding in-text citation. Alphabetize the entry by the first word of the full name, not by the abbreviation.

Name-Year

[WHO] World Health Organization. 2002. The world health report 2002: reducing risks, promoting healthy life. Geneva (Switzerland): The Organization.

4. BOOK PREPARED BY EDITOR(S)
Citation-sequence and citation-name

4. Torrence ME, Isaacson RE, editors. Microbial food safety in animal agriculture: current topics. Ames: Iowa State University Press; 2003.

Name-Year

Torrence ME, Isaacson RE, editors. 2003. Microbial food safety in animal agriculture: current topics. Ames: Iowa State University Press.

5. SECTION OF A BOOK WITH AN EDITOR
Citation-sequence and citation-name

> 5. Kawamura A. Plankton. In: Perrin MF, Wursig B, Thewissen JGM, editors. Encyclopedia of marine mammals. San Diego (CA): Academic Press; 2002. p. 939-942.

Name-Year

> Kawamura A. 2002. Plankton. In: Perrin MF, Wursig B, Thewissen JGM, editors. Encyclopedia of marine mammals. San Diego (CA): Academic Press. p. 939-942.

6. CHAPTER OF A BOOK
Citation-sequence and citation-name

> 6. Honigsbaum M. The fever trail: in search of the cure for malaria. New York: Picador; 2003. Chapter 2, The cure; p. 19-38.

Name-Year

> Honigsbaum M. 2003. The fever trail: in search of the cure for malaria. New York: Picador. Chapter 2, The cure; p. 19-38.

7. PAPER OR ABSTRACT IN CONFERENCE PROCEEDINGS
Citation-sequence and citation-name

> 7. Gutierrez AP. Integrating biological and environmental factors in crop system models [abstract]. In: Integrated Biological Systems Conference; 2003 Apr 14-16: San Antonio, TX. Beaumont (TX): Agroeconomics Research Group; 2003. p. 14-15.

Name-Year

> Gutierrez AP. 2003. Integrating biological and environmental factors in crop system models [abstract]. In: Integrated Biological Systems Conference; 2003 Apr 14-16; San Antonio, TX. Beaumont (TX): Agroeconomics Research Group. p. 14-15.

Periodicals

For the basic format for an article from a periodical, see pp. 308–09. For newspaper and magazine articles, include the section designation and column number, if any, in addition to the date and the inclusive page numbers. For rules on

abbreviating journal titles, consult the CSE manual, or ask an instructor to suggest other examples.

8. ARTICLE IN A JOURNAL
Citation-sequence and citation-name

> 8. Mahmud K, Vance ML. Human growth hormone and aging. New Engl J Med. 2003;348(2):2256-2257.

Name-Year

> Mahmud K, Vance ML. 2003. Human growth hormone and aging. New Engl J Med. 348(2):2256-2257.

9. ARTICLE IN A WEEKLY JOURNAL
Citation-sequence and citation-name

> 9. Holden C. Future brightening for depression treatments. Science. 2003 Oct 31:810-813.

Name-Year

> Holden C. 2003. Future brightening for depression treatments. Science. Oct 31:810-813.

10. ARTICLE IN A MAGAZINE
Citation-sequence and citation-name

> 10. Livio M. Moving right along: the accelerating universe holds secrets to dark energy, the Big Bang, and the ultimate beauty of nature. Astronomy. 2002 Jul:34-39.

Name-Year

> Livio M. 2002 Jul. Moving right along: the accelerating universe holds secrets to dark energy, the Big Bang, and the ultimate beauty of nature. Astronomy. 34-39.

11. ARTICLE IN A NEWSPAPER
Citation-sequence and citation-name

> 11. Kolata G. Bone diagnosis gives new data but no answers. New York Times (National Ed.). 2003 Sep 28;Sect. 1:1 (col. 1).

Name-Year

> Kolata G. 2003 Sep 28. Bone diagnosis gives new data but no answers. New York Times (National Ed.). Sect. 1:1 (col. 1).

Source Map: Articles from Periodicals, CSE Style

Note that data placement will vary, depending on whether you are using the citation-sequence or citation-name format or the name-year format. Citations for the article on p. 309 would include the following elements:

Citation-sequence or citation-name format

1 Author.
List all authors' last names first, and use only initials for first and middle names. End with a period.

2 Title and Subtitle of Article.
Capitalize only the first word of the title and any proper nouns or proper adjectives. End with a period.

1. Narechania A. Hearing is believing: ivory-billed sightings leave field biologists wanting to hear more. Am Scholar. 2005;74(3):84-97.

3 Periodical Title.
Capitalize all major words, and end with a period. Abbreviate journal titles.

4 Publication Date.
For journals, use only the year; use the year and month (and day) for publications without volume numbers.

5 Publication Information.
For journal articles, give the volume number, the issue number if available (in parentheses), and a colon. Give the inclusive page numbers, and end with a period.

Name-year format

Narechania A. 2005. Hearing is believing: ivory-billed sightings leave field biologists wanting to hear more. Am Scholar. 74(3):84-97.

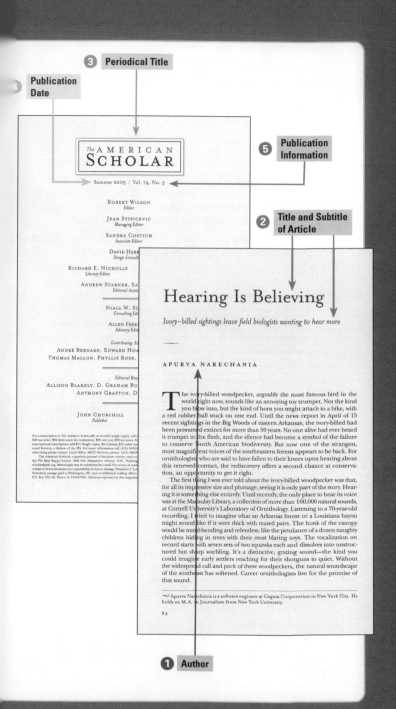

3 Periodical Title

Publication Date

5 Publication Information

2 Title and Subtitle of Article

The AMERICAN
SCHOLAR

Summer 2005 | Vol. 74, No. 3

ROBERT WILSON
Editor

JEAN STIPICEVIC
Managing Editor

SANDRA COSTICH
Associate Editor

DAVID HERB
Design Consult

RICHARD E. NICHOLLS
Literary Editor

ANDREW STARNER, SA
Editorial Assist

NIALL W. SL
Consulting Edi

ALLEN FREE
Advisory Edit

Contributing Ed
ANDRÉ BERNARD, EDWARD HOA
THOMAS MALLON, PHYLLIS ROSE,

Editorial Boa
ALLISON BLAKELY, D. GRAHAM BU
ANTHONY GRAFTON, D

JOHN CHURCHILL
Publisher

Hearing Is Believing

Ivory-billed sightings leave field biologists wanting to hear more

APURVA NARECHANIA

The ivory-billed woodpecker, arguably the most famous bird in the world right now, sounds like an annoying toy trumpet. Not the kind you blow into, but the kind of horn you might attach to a bike, with a red rubber ball stuck on one end. Until the news report in April of 15 recent sightings in the Big Woods of eastern Arkansas, the ivory-billed had been presumed extinct for more than 50 years. No one alive had ever heard it trumpet in the flesh, and the silence had become a symbol of the failure to conserve North American biodiversity. But now one of the strangest, most magnificent voices of the southeastern forests appears to be back. For ornithologists who are said to have fallen to their knees upon hearing about this renewed contact, the rediscovery offers a second chance at conservation, an opportunity to get it right.

The first thing I was ever told about the ivory-billed woodpecker was that, for all its impressive size and plumage, seeing it is only part of the story. Hearing it is something else entirely. Until recently, the only place to hear its voice was at the Macaulay Library, a collection of more than 160,000 natural sounds, at Cornell University's Laboratory of Ornithology. Listening to a 70-year-old recording, I tried to imagine what an Arkansas forest or a Louisiana bayou might sound like if it were thick with mated pairs. The honk of the canopy would be mind-bending and relentless, like the petulance of a dozen naughty children hiding in trees with their most blaring toys. The vocalization on record starts with seven sets of two squawks each and dissolves into unstructured but sharp warbling. It's a distinctive, grating sound—the kind you could imagine early settlers reaching for their shotguns to quiet. Without the widespread call and peck of these woodpeckers, the natural soundscape of the southeast has softened. Career ornithologists live for the promise of that sound.

~ Apurva Narechania is a software engineer at Cognia Corporation in New York City. He holds an M.A. in Journalism from New York University.

84

1 Author

Electronic sources

The examples below use the citation-sequence or citation-name system. To adapt them to the name-year system, delete the note number and place the update date immediately after the author's name.

The basic entry for most sources accessed through the Internet should include the following elements:

- AUTHOR. Give the author's name, if available, last name first, followed by the initial(s) and a period.

- TITLE. For book, journal, and article titles, follow the style for print materials. For all other types of electronic material, reproduce the title that appears on the screen.

- MEDIUM. Indicate, in brackets, that the source is not in print format by using designations such as [*Internet*].

- PLACE OF PUBLICATION. The city usually should be followed by the two-letter abbreviation for state. No state abbreviation is necessary for well-known cities such as New York, Chicago, Boston, and London or for a publisher whose location is part of its name (for example, University of Oklahoma Press). If the city is inferred, put the city and state in brackets. If the city cannot be inferred, use the words *place unknown* in brackets.

- PUBLISHER. For Web sites, pages on Web sites, and online databases, include the individual or organization that produces or sponsors the site. If no publisher can be determined, use the words *publisher unknown* in brackets. No publisher is necessary for online journals or journals accessed online.

- DATES. Cite three important dates if possible: the date the publication was placed on the Internet or the copyright date; the latest date of any update or revision; and the date you accessed the publication.

- PAGE, DOCUMENT, VOLUME, AND ISSUE NUMBERS. When citing a portion of a larger work or site, list the inclusive page numbers or document numbers of the specific item being cited. For journals or journal articles, include volume and issue numbers. If exact page numbers are not available, include in brackets the approximate length in computer screens, paragraphs, or bytes.

- ADDRESS. Include the URL or other electronic address; use the phrase *Available from:* to introduce the address. Only URLs that end with a slash are followed by a period.

12. MATERIAL FROM AN ONLINE DATABASE. For the basic format for citing an article from a database, see pp. 312–13. (Because CSE does not provide guidelines for citing an article from an online database, this model has been adapted from CSE guidelines for citing an online journal article.)

12. Shilts E. Water wanderers. Can Geographic [Internet].

2002 [cited 2004 Jan 27]; 122(3); 72-77. Expanded Academic

ASAP. Farmington Hills (MI): Thomson Gale. Available from:

http://web4.infotrac.galegroup.com/itw/. Document No.:

A86207443.

13. ARTICLE IN AN ONLINE JOURNAL

13. Perez P, Calonge TM. Yeast protein kinase C. J Biochem

[Internet]. 2002 Oct [cited 2003 Nov 3];132(4):513-517.

Available from: http://edpex104.bcasj.or.jp/jb-pdf/132-4/

jb132-4-513.pdf

14. ARTICLE IN AN ONLINE NEWSPAPER

14. Yoon CK. Genes offer new clues in old debate on species'

origins. New York Times [Internet]. 2009 Feb 9 [cited 2009

Mar 30]. Available from: http://www.nytimes.com/2009/02/

10/science/10species.html

15. ONLINE BOOK

15. Patrick TS, Allison JR, Krakow GA. Protected plants of

Georgia [Internet]. Social Circle (GA): Georgia Department of

Natural Resources; c1995 [cited 2003 Dec 3]. Available from:

http://www.georgiawildlife.com/content/displaycontent

.asp?txtDocument=89&txtPage=9

To cite a portion of an online book, give the name of the part after the publication information: *Chapter 6, Encouraging germination.* See model 6.

16. WEB SITE

16. Geology and public policy [Internet]. Boulder (CO): Geological

Society of America; c2009 [updated 2009 May 18; cited 2009 May

20]. Available from http://www.geosociety.org/geopolicy/

Source Map: Articles from Databases, CSE Style

Note that date placement will vary depending on whether you are using the citation-sequence or citation-name format or the name-year format. A citation for the article on p. 313 would include the following elements:

Citation-sequence or citation-name format

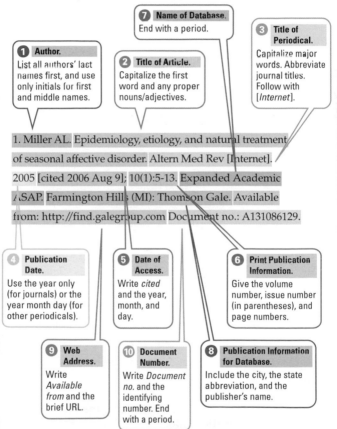

7 Name of Database. End with a period.

1 Author. List all authors' last names first, and use only initials for first and middle names.

2 Title of Article. Capitalize the first word and any proper nouns/adjectives.

3 Title of Periodical. Capitalize major words. Abbreviate journal titles. Follow with [*Internet*].

1. Miller AL. Epidemiology, etiology, and natural treatment of seasonal affective disorder. Altern Med Rev [Internet]. 2005 [cited 2006 Aug 9]; 10(1):5-13. Expanded Academic ASAP. Farmington Hills (MI): Thomson Gale. Available from: http://find.galegroup.com Document no.: A131086129.

4 Publication Date. Use the year only (for journals) or the year month day (for other periodicals).

5 Date of Access. Write *cited* and the year, month, and day.

6 Print Publication Information. Give the volume number, issue number (in parentheses), and page numbers.

9 Web Address. Write *Available from* and the brief URL.

10 Document Number. Write *Document no.* and the identifying number. End with a period.

8 Publication Information for Database. Include the city, the state abbreviation, and the publisher's name.

Name-year format

Miller AL. 2005. Epidemiology, etiology, and natural treatment of seasonal affective disorder. Altern Med Rev [Internet]. [cited 2006 Aug 9]; 10(1):5-13. Expanded Academic ASAP. Farmington Hills (MI): Thomson Gale. Available from: http:// find.galegroup.com Document No.: A131086129.

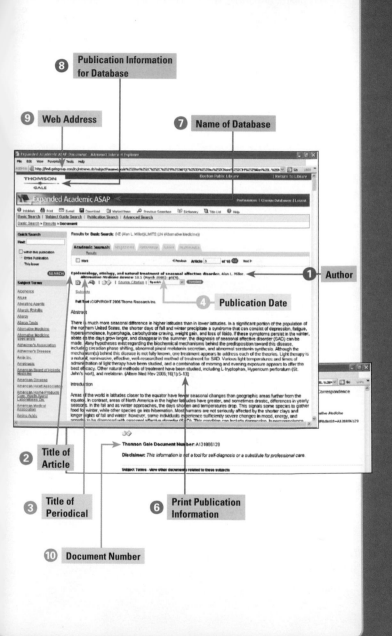

8 Publication Information for Database

9 Web Address

7 Name of Database

1 Author

4 Publication Date

2 Title of Article

3 Title of Periodical

6 Print Publication Information

10 Document Number

17. GOVERNMENT WEB SITE

17. Health disparities [Internet]. Atlanta (GA): Centers for Disease Control and Prevention (US); [updated 2008 Nov 20; cited 2009 May 1]. Available from: http://www.cdc.gov/aging/healthdisparities.htm

45d Sample CSE pages

SAMPLE CSE TITLE PAGE

Field Measurements of
Photosynthesis and Transpiration
Rates in Dwarf Snapdragon
(*Chaenorrhinum minus* Lange);
An Investigation of Water Stress
Adaptations

Tara Gupta

Proposal for a
Summer Research Fellowship
Colgate University
February 25, 2004

1 Specific and informative title, name, and other relevant information centered on title page

Annotations indicate CSE-style formatting and effective writing.

SAMPLE CSE TEXT PAGE

2   Water Stress Adaptations 2

3 _____ Introduction _____

Dwarf snapdragon (*Chaenorrhinum minus*) is a weedy pioneer plant found growing in central New York during spring and summer. **4** Interestingly, the distribution of this species has been limited almost exclusively to the cinder ballast of railroad tracks[1] and to sterile **5** strips of land along highways[2]. In these harsh environments, characterized by intense sunlight and poor soil water retention, one would expect *C. minus* to exhibit anatomical features similar to those of xeromorphic plants (species adapted to arid habitats).

However, this is not the case. T. Gupta and R. Arnold (unpublished) have found that the leaves and stems of *C. minus* are not covered by a thick, waxy cuticle but rather with a thin cuticle that is less effective in inhibiting water loss through diffusion. The root system is not long and thick, capable of reaching deeper, moister soils; instead, it is thin and diffuse, permeating only the topmost (and driest) soil horizon. Moreover, in contrast to many xeromorphic plants, the stomata (pores regulating gas exchange) are not found in sunken crypts or cavities in the epidermis that retard water loss from transpiration.

Despite a lack of these morphological adaptations to water stress, *C. minus* continues to grow and reproduce when morning dew has been its only source of water for up to 5 weeks (2002 letter from **6** R. Arnold to me). Such growth involves fixation of carbon by photosynthesis and requires that the stomata be open to admit sufficient carbon dioxide. Given the dry, sunny environment, the time required for adequate carbon fixation must also mean a significant

---

2 Shortened title next to page number **3** Headings throughout help organize the proposal **4** Introduction states scientific issue, gives background information **5** Documentation follows CSE citation-sequence format **6** Personal communication cited in parentheses within text but not included in references

Annotations indicate CSE-style formatting and effective writing.

SAMPLE CSE LIST OF REFERENCES

Water Stress Adaptations 5

References

1. Wildrlechner MP. Historical and phenological observations of the ⑦ spread of *Chaenorrhinum minus* across North America. Can J Bot. 1983;61(1):179-187.

2. Dwarf snapdragon [Internet]. Olympia (WA): Washington State ⑧ Noxious Weed Control Board; 2001 [updated 2001 Jul 7; cited 2003 Jan 25]. Available from: http://www.wa.gov/agr/weedboard/ weed_info/dwarfsnapdragon.html

3. Boyer JS. Plant productivity and environment. Science. 1982 Nov ⑨ 6:443-448.

4. Manhas JG, Sukumaran NP. Diurnal changes in net photosynthetic ⑩ rate in potato in two environments. Potato Res. 1988;31:375-378.

5. Doley DG, Unwin GL, Yates DJ. Spatial and temporal distribution of photosynthesis and transpiration by single leaves in a rainforest tree, *Argyrodendron peralatum*. Aust J Plant Physiol. 1988;15(3):317-326.

6. Kallarackal J, Milburn JA, Baker DA. Water relations of the banana. III. Effects of controlled water stress on water potential, transpiration, photosynthesis and leaf growth. Aust J Plant Physiol. 1990;17(1):79-90.

7. Idso SB, Allen SG. Kimball BA, Choudhury BJ. Problems with porometry: measuring net photosynthesis by leaf chamber techniques. Agron. 1989;81(4):475-479.

⑦ **Includes all published works cited; numbers correspond to order in which sources are first mentioned** ⑧ **Article for government Web site** ⑨ **Article in weekly magazine** ⑩ **Article in journal**

Annotations indicate CSE-style formatting and effective writing.

Glossary of Terms

absolute phrase See *phrase*.

active voice The form of a verb when the subject performs the action: *Lata <u>sang</u> the chorus again.* See also *voice*.

adjective A word that modifies, quantifies, identifies, or describes a noun or a word or words acting as a noun. Most adjectives precede the noun or other word(s) they modify (*a <u>good</u> book*), but a **predicate adjective** follows the noun or pronoun it modifies (*the book is <u>good</u>*).

adjective clause See *clause*.

adjective forms Changes in an adjective from the **positive** degree (*tall, good*) to the **comparative** (comparing two—*taller, better*) or the **superlative** (comparing more than two—*tallest, best*). Short regular adjectives (*tall*) add *-er* and *-est,* but most adjectives of two syllables or more form the comparative by adding *more* (*more beautiful*) and the superlative by adding *most* (*most beautiful*). A few adjectives have irregular forms (*good, better, best*), and some (*only, forty*) do not change form.

adverb A word that qualifies, modifies, limits, or defines a verb, an adjective, another adverb, or a clause, frequently answering the questions *where? when? how? why? to what extent?* or *under what conditions?* Adverbs derived from adjectives and nouns commonly end in the suffix *-ly. She will <u>soon</u> travel <u>south</u> and will <u>probably</u> visit her <u>very</u> favorite sister.* See also *conjunction*.

adverb clause See *clause*.

adverb forms Changes in an adverb from the **positive** degree (*eagerly*) to the **comparative** (comparing two—*more eagerly*) or the **superlative** (comparing more than two—*most eagerly*). Most adverbs add *more* to form the comparative and *most* to form the superlative, but a few add *-er* and *-est* (*fast, faster, fastest*) or have irregular forms (*little, less, least*).

adverbial particle A word that is used as a preposition but combines with some verbs to form a phrasal (two-word) verb with its own meaning. *He got <u>over</u> her and got <u>on</u> with his life.*

agreement The correspondence of a pronoun with the word it refers to (its antecedent) in person, number, and gender or of a verb with its subject in person and number. See also *antecedent, gender, number, person*.

antecedent The specific noun to which a pronoun refers. A pronoun and its antecedent must agree in person, number, and gender. *<u>Ginger Rogers</u> moved <u>her</u> feet as no one else has.*

appositive A noun or noun phrase that identifies or adds identifying information to a preceding noun phrase. *Zimbardo, <u>an</u>*

innovative researcher, designed the Stanford Prison Experiment. My sister Janet has twin boys.

appositive phrase See *appositive*.

argument A text that makes and supports a **claim**. See also *evidence, warrant*.

article *A, an,* or *the,* the most common adjectives. *A* and *an* are **indefinite**; they do not specifically identify the nouns they modify. *I bought an apple and a peach. The* is **definite**, or specific. *The peach was not ripe.*

auxiliary verb A helping verb that combines with a main verb to form a verb phrase. The primary auxiliaries are forms of *do, have,* and *be. Did he arrive? We have eaten. She is writing.* **Modal** auxiliaries such as *can, may, shall, will, could, might, should, must, would,* and *ought to* have only one form and show possibility, necessity, obligation, and so on.

base form The form of a verb that is listed in dictionaries, such as *go* or *listen.* For all verbs except *be,* it is the same as the first-person singular form in the present tense.

Boolean operator A word like AND or OR that allows for computer database searches using multiple words.

case The form of a noun or pronoun that reflects its grammatical role in a sentence. Nouns and indefinite pronouns can be **subjective**, **possessive**, or **objective**, but they change form only in the possessive case. *The dog* (subjective) *barked. The dog's* (possessive) *tail wagged. The mail carrier feared the dog* (objective). The personal pronouns *I, he, she, we,* and *they,* as well as the relative or interrogative pronoun *who,* have different forms for all three cases. *We* (subjective) *took the train to Chicago. Our* (possessive) *trip lasted a week. Maria met us* (objective) *at the station.* See also *person, pronoun*.

claim An arguable statement.

clause A group of words containing a subject and a predicate. An **independent clause** can stand alone as a sentence. *The car hit the tree.* A **dependent clause** cannot stand alone and is linked to an independent clause by a subordinating conjunction or a relative pronoun. A dependent clause can function as an adjective, an adverb, or a noun. *The car hit the tree that stood at the edge of the road* (**adjective clause**). *The car hit the tree when the driver lost control* (**adverb clause**). *What the driver didn't notice was the bend in the road* (**noun clause**). See also *nonrestrictive element, restrictive element.*

collective noun A noun that refers to a group or collection (*herd, mob*).

comma splice An error resulting from joining two independent clauses with only a comma.

common noun See *noun*.

comparative or comparative degree The form of an adjective or adverb used to compare two things (*happier, more quickly*). See also *adjective forms, adverb forms.*

complement A word or group of words completing the predicate in a sentence. A **subject complement** follows a linking verb and renames or describes the subject. It can be a **predicate noun** (*Anorexia is an illness*) or a **predicate adjective** (*Karen Carpenter was anorexic*). An **object complement** renames or describes a direct object (*We considered her a prodigy and her behavior extraordinary*).

complete predicate See *predicate.*

complete subject See *subject.*

complex sentence See *sentence.*

compound adjective A combination of words that functions as a single adjective (*blue-green sea, ten-story building, get-tough policy, high school outing, north-by-northwest journey*). Most, but not all, compound adjectives need hyphens to separate their individual elements.

compound noun A combination of words that functions as a single noun (*go-getter, in-law, Jack-of-all-trades, oil well, southeast*).

compound predicate See *predicate.*

compound sentence See *sentence.*

compound subject See *subject.*

conjunction A word or words that join words, phrases, clauses, or sentences. **Coordinating conjunctions** (*and, but, for, nor, or, so,* or *yet*) join grammatically equivalent elements (*Marx and Engels* [two nouns]; *Marx wrote one essay, but Engels wrote the other* [two independent clauses]). **Correlative conjunctions** (such as *both . . . and; either . . . or;* or *not only . . . but also*) are used in pairs to connect grammatically equivalent elements (*neither Marx nor Engels; Marx not only studied the world but also changed it*). A **subordinating conjunction** (such as *although, because, if, that,* or *when*) introduces a dependent clause and connects it to an independent clause. *Marx moved to London, where he did most of his work. Marx argued that religion was an "opiate."* A **conjunctive adverb** (such as *consequently, moreover,* or *nevertheless*) modifies an independent clause following another independent clause. A conjunctive adverb generally follows a semicolon and is followed by a comma. *Thoreau lived simply at Walden; however, he regularly joined his aunt for tea in Concord.*

conjunctive adverb See *conjunction.*

coordinating conjunction See *conjunction.*

correlative conjunction See *conjunction.*

count noun See *noun.*

dangling modifier A word, phrase, or clause that does not logically modify any element in the sentence to which it is attached. _Studying Freud, the meaning of my dreams became clear_ is incorrect because _the meaning_ could not have been studying Freud. _Studying Freud, I began to understand the meaning of my dreams_ is correct because now _I_ was doing the studying.

definite article The word _the_. See also _article_.

degree See _adjective forms, adverb forms_.

dependent clause A word group containing a subject and a predicate, but unable to stand alone as a sentence; usually begins with a subordinating conjunction (_because, although_) or a relative pronoun (_that, which_). See also _clause_.

diction Word choice.

direct address Construction that uses a noun or pronoun to name the person or thing being spoken to. _Hey, Jack. You, get moving._

direct discourse A quotation that reproduces a speaker's exact words, marked with quotation marks.

direct object A noun or pronoun receiving the action of a transitive verb. _McKellan recited Shakespearean soliloquies._ See also _indirect object_.

evidence Support for an argument's claim.

expletive A construction that introduces a sentence with _there_ or _it_, usually followed by a form of _be. There are four candidates for this job. It was a dark and stormy night._

first person See _person_.

fragment A group of words that is not a grammatically complete sentence but is punctuated as one. See also _sentence fragment_.

fused sentence A sentence in which two independent clauses are run together without a conjunction or punctuation between them. Also known as a **run-on sentence**.

future tense See _simple tense_.

gender The classification of a noun or pronoun as masculine (_god, he_), feminine (_goddess, she_), or neuter (_godliness, it_).

genre The kind of writing required to meet a particular purpose, such as a personal narrative, researched argument, film review, brochure, lab notebook, and so on.

gerund A verbal form ending in _-ing_ and functioning as a noun. _Sleeping is a bore._

helping verb See _auxiliary verb_.

imperative mood The form of a verb used to express a command or a request. An imperative uses the base form of the verb and may or may not have a stated subject. _Leave. You be quiet. Let's go._ See also _mood_.

indefinite article The words *a* and *an*. See also *article*.

indefinite pronoun A word such as *each, everyone,* or *nobody* that does not refer to a specific person or thing. See also *pronoun*.

independent clause A word group containing a subject and a predicate that can stand alone as a sentence. See also *clause*.

indicative mood The form of a verb used to state a fact or an opinion or to ask a question. *Washington crossed the Delaware. Did he defeat the Hessians?* See also *mood*.

indirect discourse A paraphrased quotation that does not repeat another's exact words and hence is not enclosed in quotation marks. *Coolidge said that if nominated he would not run.*

indirect object A noun or pronoun identifying to whom or to what or for whom or for what a transitive verb's action is performed. The indirect object almost always precedes the direct object. *I handed the dean my application and told her that I needed financial aid.* See also *direct object*.

indirect question A sentence pattern in which a question is the basis of a subordinate clause. An indirect question should end with a period, not a question mark. *Everyone wonders why young people start smoking.* (The question, phrased directly, is "Why do young people start smoking?")

indirect quotation See *indirect discourse*.

infinitive The base form of a verb, preceded by *to* (*to go, to run, to hit*). An infinitive can serve as a noun, an adverb, or an adjective. *To go would be unthinkable* (noun). *We stopped to rest* (adverb). *The company needs space to grow* (adjective). An infinitive can be in either the active (*to hit*) or passive (*to be hit*) voice and in either the present (*to [be] hit*) or perfect (*to have [been] hit*) tense. An **infinitive phrase** consists of an infinitive together with its modifiers, objects, or complements. See *phrase*.

intensifier A modifier that increases the emphasis of the word or words it modifies. *I would very much like to go. I'm so happy.* Despite their name, intensifiers are stylistically weak; they are best avoided in academic and professional writing.

interjection A grammatically independent word or group of words that is usually an exclamation of surprise, shock, dismay, or the like. *Ouch! For heaven's sake, what do you think you're doing?*

intransitive verb A verb that does not need a direct object to complete its meaning. *The children laughed.*

irregular verb A verb whose past tense and past participle are not formed by adding *-ed* or *-d* to the base form, such as *see, saw, seen*.

keyword A word or phrase used to search a computer database.

linking verb A verb that joins a subject with a subject complement or complements (adjectives that follow the noun they modify). Common linking verbs are *appear, be, become, feel,* and *seem. The argument <u>appeared</u> sound. It <u>was</u> actually a trick.* See also *verb.*

main clause An independent clause. See *clause.*

main verb The verb that provides the central meaning in a verb phrase, such as *given* in the phrase *could be given.*

misplaced modifier A word, phrase, or clause positioned so that it appears to modify a word other than the one the writer intended. <u>*With a credit card*</u>*, the traveler paid for the motel room and opened the door.* Unless the writer intended to indicate that the traveler used the credit card to open the door, *with a credit card* should follow *paid* or *room.*

modal See *auxiliary verb.*

modifier A word, phrase, or clause that acts as an adjective or an adverb and qualifies the meaning of another word, phrase, or clause. See also *adjective, adverb, clause, phrase.*

mood The form of a verb that indicates the writer's or speaker's attitude toward the idea expressed by the verb. Different moods are used to state a fact or an opinion or to ask a question (indicative); to give a command or request (imperative); and to express a wish, a suggestion, a request or requirement, or a condition that does not exist (subjunctive). *The sea <u>is</u> turbulent* (indicative). <u>*Stay*</u> *out of the water* (imperative). *I wish the water <u>were</u> calm enough for swimming* (subjunctive). See also *imperative mood, indicative mood, subjunctive mood.*

noncount noun See *noun.*

nonrestrictive element A word, phrase, or clause that modifies but does not change the essential meaning of a sentence element. A nonrestrictive element is set off from the rest of the sentence with commas, dashes, or parentheses. *Quantum physics, <u>which is a difficult subject</u>, is fascinating.* See also *restrictive element.*

noun A word that names a person, place, object, concept, action, or the like. Nouns serve as subjects, objects, complements, and appositives. Most nouns form the plural with the addition of *-s* or *-es* and the possessive with the addition of *'s* (see *number, case*). **Common nouns** (*president, state, month*) name classes or general groups. **Proper nouns** (*Barack Obama, Florida, July*) name particular persons or things and are capitalized. **Collective nouns** (*family, committee, jury*) refer to a group of related elements. **Count nouns** (*women, trees*) refer to things that can be directly counted. **Noncount nouns** (*sand, rain, violence*) refer to collections of things or to ideas that cannot be directly counted.

noun clause See *clause.*

noun phrase See *phrase.*

number The form of a noun or pronoun that indicates whether it is singular (*book, I, he, her, it*) or plural (*books, we, they, them, their*).

object A word or words, usually a noun or pronoun, influenced by a transitive verb, a verbal, or a preposition. See also *direct object, indirect object, object of a preposition*.

object complement See *complement*.

object of a preposition A noun or pronoun connected to a sentence by a preposition. The preposition, the object, and any modifiers make up a **prepositional phrase**. *I went to the party without her*.

objective case See *case*.

participial phrase A phrase consisting of a participle and any modifiers, objects, and complements and acting as an adjective. See also *participle, phrase*.

participle A verbal adjective that can modify a noun or pronoun. The **present participle** of a verb always ends in -*ing* (*going, being*). The **past participle** usually ends in -*ed* (*ruined, injured*), but many verbs have irregular forms (*gone, been, brought*). Present participles are used with the auxiliary verb *be* to form the **progressive tenses** (*I am making, I will be making, I have been making*). Past participles are used with the auxiliary verb *have* to form the **perfect tenses** (*I have made, I had made, I will have made*) and with *be* to form the passive voice (*I am seen, I was seen*). These combinations of auxiliary verbs and participles are known as **verb phrases**. See also *adjective, phrase, tense, verbal, voice*.

parts of speech The eight grammatical categories into which words can be grouped depending on how they function in a sentence. Many words act as different parts of speech in different sentences. The parts of speech are *adjectives, adverbs, conjunctions, interjections, nouns, prepositions, pronouns,* and *verbs*.

passive voice The form of a verb when the subject is being acted on rather than performing the action. *The batter was hit by a pitch*. See also *voice*.

past participle See *participle*.

past perfect or **past perfect tense** The form a verb takes to show that an action or a condition was completed before another event in the past (*The virus had killed six people before investigators learned of its existence*). See also *tense*.

past subjunctive See *subjunctive mood*.

past tense See *simple tense*.

perfect progressive or **perfect progressive tense** The form a verb takes to show an action or a condition that continues up to some point in the past, present, or future (*The workers had been striking for a month before they signed the contract; She has been*

complaining for days; The experiment _will have been continuing_ for a year next May). See also _tense_.

perfect tense The form a verb takes to show a completed action in the past, present, or future (They _had hoped_ to see the parade but ended up stuck in traffic; I _have_ never _understood_ this equation; By tomorrow, the governor _will have vetoed_ the bill). See also _tense_.

person The relation between a subject and its verb, indicating whether the subject is speaking about itself (**first person**—_I_ or _we_), being spoken to (**second person**—_you_), or being spoken about (**third person**—_he, she, it,_ or _they_). _Be_ has several forms depending on the person (_am, is,_ and _are_ in the present tense and _was_ and _were_ in the past tense). Other verbs change form only in the present tense with a third-person singular subject (_I fall, you fall, she falls, we fall, they fall_).

personal pronoun See _pronoun_.

phrasal verb A verb that combines with a preposition. _The plane took off._

phrase A group of words that functions as a single unit but lacks a subject, verb, or both. An **absolute phrase** modifies an entire sentence. It usually includes a noun or pronoun followed by a participle (sometimes implied) or participial phrase. _The party having ended, everyone left._ A **gerund phrase** includes a gerund and its objects, complements, and modifiers. It functions as a noun, acting as a subject, a complement, or an object. _Exercising regularly and sensibly is a key to good health_ (subject). An **infinitive phrase** includes an infinitive and its objects, complements, and modifiers. It functions as an adjective, an adverb, or a noun. _The Pacific Coast is the place to be_ (adjective). _She went to pay her taxes_ (adverb). _To be young again is all I want_ (noun). A **noun phrase** includes a noun and its modifiers. _A long, rough road crossed the barren desert._ A **participial phrase** includes a present or past participle and its objects, complements, and modifiers. It functions as an adjective. _Absentmindedly climbing the stairs, he stumbled._ They bought a house _built in 1895._ A **prepositional phrase** is introduced by a preposition and ends with a noun or pronoun, called the object of the preposition. It functions as an adjective, an adverb, or a noun. _The gas in the laboratory was leaking_ (adjective). _The firefighters went to the lab to check_ (adverb). _The smell came from inside a wall_ (noun). A **verb phrase** is composed of a main verb and one or more auxiliaries, acting as a single verb in the sentence predicate. _I should have come to the review session._

plural The form of a noun, pronoun, or adjective that refers to more than one person or thing, such as _books, we,_ or _those._

positive or **positive degree** The basic form of an adjective or adverb (_cold, quick_). See also _adjective forms, adverb forms_.

possessive or **possessive case** The form of a noun or pronoun that shows possession. Nouns and indefinite pronouns in the

possessive case use apostrophes (*Harold's, the children's, everyone's, your parents'*), while personal pronouns in the possessive case do not (*my, mine, its, yours, hers*). See also *case*.

possessive pronoun A word used in place of a noun that shows possession. See also *possessive, pronoun*.

predicate The verb and related words in a clause or sentence. The predicate expresses what the subject does, experiences, or is. The **simple predicate** is the verb or verb phrase. *For years the YMHA <u>has been</u> a cultural center in New York City.* The **complete predicate** includes the simple predicate and any modifiers, objects, or complements. *John <u>gave Sarah an engagement ring</u>.* A **compound predicate** has more than one simple predicate. *The athletes <u>swam</u> in a relay and <u>ran</u> in a marathon.*

predicate adjective See *complement*.

predicate noun See *complement*.

prefix An addition to the beginning of a word that alters its meaning (<u>*anti*</u>-*French,* <u>*un*</u>*dress*).

preposition A word or group of words that indicates the relationship of a noun or pronoun, called the *object of the preposition*, to another part of the sentence. *He was <u>at</u> the top <u>of</u> the ladder before the others had climbed <u>to</u> the fourth rung.* See also *phrase*.

prepositional phrase A group of words beginning with a preposition and ending with its object (*in the box; under a cloud*). A prepositional phrase can function as an adjective, an adverb, or a noun. See also *phrase*.

present participle See *participle*.

present perfect or **present perfect tense** The form a verb takes to show that an action or a condition has been completed before the present (*The team <u>has worked</u> together well*). See also *tense*.

present progressive The form a verb takes to show an action or a condition that is ongoing in the present (*He <u>is planning</u> a sales presentation*). See also *tense*.

present tense See *simple tense*.

primary source A research source that offers firsthand knowledge of its subject.

progressive tense The form a verb takes to show an action or a condition that is continuing in the past, present, or future (*He <u>was singing</u> too loudly to hear the telephone; The economy <u>is surging;</u> Business schools <u>will be competing</u> for this student*). See also *tense*.

pronoun A word used in place of a noun, usually called the antecedent of the pronoun. **Indefinite pronouns** do not refer to specific nouns and include *any, each, everybody, some,* and similar words. *<u>Many</u> are called, but <u>few</u> are chosen.* **Personal pronouns** (*I, you, he, she, it, we, you,* and *they*) refer to particular people or things. They have different forms (*I, me, my, mine*) depending on

their case. (See also *case*.) **Possessive pronouns** (*my, mine, our, his/her, your, their*) denote possession. **Relative pronouns** (*who, whom, whose, which, that, what, whoever, whomever, whichever*, and *whatever*) connect a dependent clause to a sentence. *I wonder <u>who</u> will win the prize.*

proper noun See *noun*.

regular verb A verb whose past tense and past participle are formed by adding *-d* or *-ed* to the base form (*care, cared, cared; look, looked, looked*). See also *irregular verb*.

relative pronoun See *pronoun*.

restrictive element A word, phrase, or clause that limits the essential meaning of the sentence element it modifies or provides necessary identifying information about it. A restrictive element is not set off from the rest of the sentence with commas, dashes, or parentheses. *The tree <u>that I hit</u> was an oak.* See also *nonrestrictive element*.

rhetorical situation The situation for writing, which requires writers to think carefully about their assignment, audience, purpose, topic, genre, format, tone, and context and to make appropriate choices regarding these elements.

run-on sentence See *fused sentence*.

secondary source A research source that reports information from research done by others. See also *primary source*.

second person See *person*.

sentence A group of words containing a subject and a predicate and expressing a complete thought. In writing, a sentence begins with a capital letter and ends with a period, a question mark, or an exclamation point. A **compound sentence** contains two or more independent clauses linked with a coordinating conjunction, a correlative conjunction, or a semicolon. *I did not wish to go, but she did.* See also *clause*.

sentence fragment A group of words that is not a grammatically complete sentence but is punctuated as one. Usually a fragment lacks a subject, a verb, or both or is a dependent clause that is not attached to an independent clause. In academic and professional writing, fragments should be revised to be complete sentences.

simple past tense See *tense*.

simple predicate See *predicate*.

simple subject See *subject*.

simple tense Past (*It <u>happened</u>*), present (*Things <u>fall</u> apart*), or future (*You <u>will succeed</u>*) forms of verbs. See also *tense*.

singular The form of a noun, a pronoun, or an adjective that refers to one person or thing, such as *book, it,* or *this*.

split infinitive The often awkward intrusion of an adverb between *to* and the base form of the verb in an infinitive (*to better serve* rather than *to serve better*).

squinting modifier A misplaced word, phrase, or clause that could refer equally, but with different meanings, to words either preceding or following it. For example, in *Playing poker often is dangerous*, the position of *often* fails to indicate whether the writer meant that frequent poker playing is dangerous or that poker playing is often dangerous.

subject The noun or pronoun and related words that indicate who or what a sentence is about. The **simple subject** is the noun or pronoun. The **complete subject** is the simple subject and its modifiers. In *The timid gray mouse fled from the owl*, *mouse* is the simple subject; *The timid gray mouse* is the complete subject. A **compound subject** includes two or more simple subjects. *The mouse and the owl heard the fox.*

subject complement See *complement*.

subjective case See *case*.

subjunctive mood The form of a verb used to express a wish, a suggestion, a request or requirement, or a condition that does not exist. The present subjunctive uses the base form of the verb. *I asked that he be present. Long live the Queen!* The past subjunctive uses the same verb form as the past tense except for the verb *be*, which uses *were* for all subjects. *If I were president, I would change things.* See also *mood*.

subordinate clause A dependent clause. See *clause*.

subordinating conjunction A word or phrase such as *although, because,* or *even though* that introduces a dependent clause and joins it to an independent clause. See also *conjunction*.

suffix An addition to the end of a word that alters the word's meaning or part of speech, as in *migrate* (verb) and *migration* (noun) or *late* (adjective or adverb) and *lateness* (noun).

superlative The form of an adjective or adverb used in a comparison of three or more items (*happiest, most gladly*). See also *adjective forms, adverb forms*.

syntax The arrangement of words in a sentence in order to reveal the relation of each to the whole sentence and to one another.

synthesizing, synthesis The process of grouping pieces of data or information, looking for patterns, and identifying main ideas so that the data or information can be smoothly incorporated into the writer's own work.

tense The form of a verb that indicates the time at which an action takes place or a condition exists. The times expressed by tense are basically **present, past,** and **future**. Each tense has **simple** (*I enjoy*), **perfect** (*I have enjoyed*), **progressive** (*I am enjoying*), and **perfect progressive** (*I have been enjoying*) forms.

thesis A statement that indicates the main idea or claim of a piece of writing. Thesis statements should include a topic—the subject matter—and a comment that makes an important point about the topic.

third person See *person*.

tone The result of expressions that reveal a writer's overall attitude toward a topic or audience.

transition A word or phrase that signals a progression from one sentence or part of a sentence to another.

transitive verb A verb that takes a direct object, which receives the action expressed by the verb. A transitive verb may be in the active or passive voice. *The artist <u>drew</u> the sketch. The sketch <u>was drawn</u> by the arist.* See also *verb*.

verb A word or group of words, essential to a sentence, that expresses what action a subject takes or receives or what the subject's state of being is. *Edison <u>invented</u> the incandescent bulb. Gas lighting <u>was becoming</u> obsolete.* Verbs change form to show tense, number, voice, and mood. See also *auxiliary verb, intransitive verb, irregular verb, linking verb, mood, person, regular verb, tense, transitive verb, verbal, voice.*

verbal A verb form that functions as a noun, an adjective, or an adverb. The three kinds of verbals are gerunds, infinitives, and participles. See also *gerund, infinitive, participle.*

verbal phrase A phrase using a gerund, a participle, or an infinitive. See *phrase*.

verb phrase See *phrase*.

verb tense See *tense*.

voice The form of a verb that indicates whether the subject is acting or being acted on. When a verb is in the **active voice**, the subject performs the action. *Parker <u>played</u> the saxophone fantastically.* When a verb is in the **passive voice**, the subject receives the action. *The saxophone <u>was played</u> by Parker.* The passive voice is formed with the appropriate tense of the verb *be* and the past participle of the transitive verb. See also *verb*.

warrant In a Toulmin argument, an assumption, sometimes unstated, that connects an argument's claim to the reason for making the claim.

Glossary of Usage

Conventions of usage might be called the "good manners" of discourse. And just as our notions of good manners vary from culture to culture and time to time, so do conventions of usage. The word *ain't*, for instance, now considered inappropriate in academic and professional discourse, was once widely used by the most proper British speakers and is still commonly used in some spoken U.S. dialects. In short, matters of usage, like other language choices you must make, depend on what your purpose is and on what is appropriate for a particular audience at a particular time. This glossary provides usage guidelines for some commonly confused or otherwise problematic words and phrases.

a, an Use *a* with a word that begins with a consonant (*a* book), a consonant sound such as "y" or "w" (*a* euphoric moment, *a* one-sided match), or a sounded *h* (*a* hemisphere). Use *an* with a word that begins with a vowel (*an* umbrella), a vowel sound (*an* X-ray), or a silent *h* (*an* honor).

accept, except The verb *accept* means "receive" or "agree to." *Except* is usually a preposition that means "aside from" or "excluding." *All the plaintiffs except Mr. Kim decided to accept the settlement.*

advice, advise The noun *advice* means "opinion" or "suggestion"; the verb *advise* means "offer advice." *Charlotte's mother advised her to dress warmly, but Charlotte ignored the advice.*

affect, effect As a verb, *affect* means "influence" or "move the emotions of"; as a noun, it means "emotions" or "feelings." *Effect* is a noun meaning "result"; less commonly, it is a verb meaning "bring about." *The storm affected a large area. Its effects included widespread power failures. The drug effected a major change in the patient's affect.*

aggravate The formal meaning is "make worse." *Having another mouth to feed aggravated their poverty.* In academic and professional writing, avoid using *aggravate* to mean "irritate" or "annoy."

all ready, already *All ready* means "fully prepared." *Already* means "previously." *We were all ready for Lucy's party when we learned that she had already left.*

all right, alright Avoid the spelling *alright*.

all together, altogether *All together* means "all in a group" or "gathered in one place." *Altogether* means "completely" or "everything considered." *When the board members were all together, their mutual distrust was altogether obvious.*

331

allude, elude *Allude* means "refer indirectly." *Elude* means "avoid" or "escape from." *The candidate did not even allude to her opponent. The suspect eluded the police for several days.*

allusion, illusion An *allusion* is an indirect reference. An *illusion* is a false or misleading appearance. *The speaker's allusion to the Bible created an illusion of piety.*

already See *all ready, already.*

alright See *all right, alright.*

altogether See *all together, altogether.*

among, between In referring to two things or people, use *between.* In referring to three or more, use *among. The relationship between the twins is different from that among the other three children.*

amount, number Use *amount* with quantities you cannot count; use *number* for quantities you can count. *A small number of volunteers cleared a large amount of brush.*

an See *a, an.*

and/or Avoid this term except in business or legal writing. Instead of *fat and/or protein,* write *fat, protein, or both.*

any body, anybody, any one, anyone *Anybody* and *anyone* are pronouns meaning "any person." *Anyone* [or *anybody*] *would enjoy this film. Any body* is an adjective modifying a noun. *Any body of water has its own ecology. Any one* is two adjectives or a pronoun modified by an adjective. *Customers could buy only two sale items at any one time. The winner could choose any one of the prizes.*

anyplace In academic and professional discourse, use *anywhere* instead.

anyway, anyways In writing, use *anyway,* not *anyways.*

apt, liable, likely *Likely to* means "probably will," and *apt to* means "inclines or tends to." In many instances, they are interchangeable. *Liable* often carries a more negative sense and is also a legal term meaning "obligated" or "responsible."

as Avoid sentences in which it is not clear if *as* means "when" or "because." For example, does *Carl left town as his father was arriving* mean "at the same time as his father was arriving" or "because his father was arriving"?

as, as if, like In academic and professional writing, use *as* or *as if* instead of *like* to introduce a clause. *The dog howled as if* [not *like*] *it were in pain. She did as* [not *like*] *I suggested.*

assure, ensure, insure *Assure* means "convince" or "promise"; its direct object is usually a person or persons. *She assured voters she would not raise taxes. Ensure* and *insure* both mean "make certain," but *insure* usually refers specifically to protection against financial loss. *When the city rationed water to ensure that the supply would last, the Browns could no longer afford to insure their car-wash business.*

as to Do not use *as to* as a substitute for *about. Karen was unsure about* [not *as to*] *Bruce's intentions.*

at, where See *where*.

awhile, a while Always use *a while* after a preposition such as *for, in,* or *after. We drove <u>awhile</u> and then stopped for <u>a while</u>.*

bad, badly Use *bad* after a linking verb such as *be, feel,* or *seem.* Use *badly* to modify an action verb, an adjective, or another verb. *The hostess felt <u>bad</u> because the dinner was <u>badly</u> prepared.*

because of, due to Use *due to* when the effect, stated as a noun, appears before the verb *be. His illness was <u>due to</u> malnutrition.* (*Illness,* a noun, is the effect.) Use *because of* when the effect is stated as a clause. *He was sick <u>because of</u> malnutrition.* (*He was sick,* a clause, is the effect.)

being as, being that In academic or professional writing, use *because* or *since* instead of these expressions. *<u>Because</u> [not <u>being as</u>] Romeo killed Tybalt, he was banished to Padua.*

beside, besides *Beside* is a preposition meaning "next to." *Besides* can be a preposition meaning "other than" or an adverb meaning "in addition." *No one <u>besides</u> Francesca would sit <u>beside</u> him.*

between See *among, between*.

breath, breathe *Breath* is a noun; *breathe,* a verb. *"<u>Breathe</u>," said the nurse, so June took a deep <u>breath</u>.*

bring, take Use *bring* when an object is moved from a farther to a nearer place; use *take* when the opposite is true. *<u>Take</u> the box to the post office; <u>bring</u> back my mail.*

but, yet Do not use these words together. *He is strong <u>but</u> [not <u>but yet</u>] gentle.*

but that, but what Avoid using these as substitutes for *that* in expressions of doubt. *Hercule Poirot never doubted <u>that</u> [not <u>but that</u>] he would solve the case.*

can, may *Can* refers to ability and *may* to possibility or permission. *Since I <u>can</u> ski the slalom well, I <u>may</u> win the race.*

can't hardly *Hardly* has a negative meaning; therefore, *can't hardly* is a double negative. This expression is commonly used in some varieties of English but is not used in academic English. *Tim <u>can</u> [not <u>can't</u>] <u>hardly</u> wait.*

can't help but This expression is redundant. Use the more formal *I cannot but go* or less formal *I can't help going* rather than *I can't help but go.*

censor, censure *Censor* means "remove that which is considered offensive." *Censure* means "formally reprimand." *The newspaper <u>censored</u> stories that offended advertisers. The legislature <u>censured</u> the official for misconduct.*

complement, compliment *Complement* means "go well with." *Compliment* means "praise." *Guests <u>complimented</u> her on how her earrings <u>complemented</u> her gown.*

comprise, compose *Comprise* means "contain." *Compose* means "make up." *The class comprises twenty students. Twenty students compose the class.*

conscience, conscious *Conscience* means "a sense of right and wrong." *Conscious* means "awake" or "aware." *After lying, Lisa was conscious of a guilty conscience.*

consensus of opinion Use *consensus* instead of this redundant phrase. *The family consensus was to sell the old house.*

consequently, subsequently *Consequently* means "as a result"; *subsequently* means "then." *He quit, and subsequently his wife lost her job; consequently, they had to sell their house.*

continual, continuous *Continual* means "repeated at regular or frequent intervals." *Continuous* means "continuing or connected without a break." *The damage done by continuous erosion was increased by the continual storms.*

could of *Have,* not *of,* should follow *could, would, should,* or *might.* *We could have [not of] invited them.*

criteria, criterion *Criterion* means "standard of judgment" or "necessary qualification." *Criteria* is the plural form. *Image is the wrong criterion for choosing a president.*

data *Data* is the plural form of the Latin word *datum,* meaning "fact." Although *data* is used informally as either singular or plural, in academic or professional writing, treat *data* as plural. *These data indicate that fewer people are smoking.*

different from, different than *Different from* is generally preferred in academic and professional writing, although both phrases are widely used. *Her lab results were no different from [not than] his.*

discreet, discrete *Discreet* means "tactful" or "prudent." *Discrete* means "separate" or "distinct." *The leader's discreet efforts kept all the discrete factions unified.*

disinterested, uninterested *Disinterested* means "unbiased." *Uninterested* means "indifferent." *Finding disinterested jurors was difficult. She was uninterested in the verdict.*

distinct, distinctive *Distinct* means "separate" or "well defined." *Distinctive* means "characteristic." *Germany includes many distinct regions, each with a distinctive accent.*

doesn't, don't *Doesn't* is the contraction for *does not.* Use it with *he, she, it,* and singular nouns. *Don't* stands for *do not;* use it with *I, you, we, they,* and plural nouns.

due to See *because of, due to.*

each other, one another Use *each other* in sentences involving two subjects and *one another* in sentences involving more than two.

effect See *affect, effect.*

elicit, illicit The verb *elicit* means "draw out." The adjective *illicit* means "illegal." *The police elicited from the criminal the names of others involved in illicit activities.*

elude See *allude, elude.*

emigrate from, immigrate to *Emigrate from* means "move away from one's country." *Immigrate to* means "move to another country." *We emigrated from Norway in 1999. We immigrated to the United States.*

ensure See *assure, ensure, insure.*

enthused, enthusiastic Use *enthusiastic* rather than *enthused* in academic and professional writing.

equally as good Replace this redundant phrase with *equally good* or *as good.*

every day, everyday *Everyday* is an adjective meaning "ordinary." *Every day* is an adjective and a noun, meaning "each day." *I wore everyday clothes almost every day.*

every one, everyone *Everyone* is a pronoun. *Every one* is an adjective and a pronoun, referring to each member of a group. *Because he began after everyone else, David could not finish every one of the problems.*

except See *accept, except.*

explicit, implicit *Explicit* means "directly or openly expressed." *Implicit* means "indirectly expressed or implied." *The explicit message of the ad urged consumers to buy the product, while the implicit message promised popularity if they did so.*

farther, further *Farther* refers to physical distance. *How much farther is it to Munich? Further* refers to time or degree. *I want to avoid further delays.*

fewer, less Use *fewer* with nouns that can be counted. Use *less* with general amounts that you cannot count. *The world will be safer with fewer bombs and less hostility.*

finalize *Finalize* is a pretentious way of saying "end" or "make final." *We closed* [not *finalized*] *the deal.*

firstly, secondly, etc. *First, second,* etc., are more common in U.S. English.

flaunt, flout *Flaunt* means to "show off." *Flout* means to "mock" or "scorn." *The drug dealers flouted authority by flaunting their wealth.*

former, latter *Former* refers to the first and *latter* to the second of two things previously mentioned. *Kathy and Anna are athletes; the former plays tennis, and the latter runs.*

further See *farther, further.*

good, well *Good* is an adjective and should not be used as a substitute for the adverb *well. Gabriel is a good host who cooks well.*

good and *Good and* is colloquial for "very"; avoid it in academic and professional writing.

hanged, hung *Hanged* refers to executions; *hung* is used for all other meanings.

hardly See *can't hardly*.

herself, himself, myself, yourself Do not use these reflexive pronouns as subjects or as objects unless they are necessary. *Jane and I* [not *myself*] *agree. They invited John and me* [not *myself*].

he/she, his/her Better solutions for avoiding sexist language are to write out *he or she*, to eliminate pronouns entirely, or to make the subject plural. Instead of writing *Everyone should carry his/ her driver's license,* try *Drivers should carry their licenses* or *People should carry their driver's licenses.*

himself See *herself, himself, myself, yourself*.

hisself Use *himself* instead in academic or professional writing.

hopefully *Hopefully* is often misused to mean "it is hoped," but its correct meaning is "with hope." *Sam watched the roulette wheel hopefully* [not *Hopefully, Sam will win*].

hung See *hanged, hung*.

illicit See *elicit, illicit*.

illusion See *allusion, illusion*.

immigrate to See *emigrate from, immigrate to*.

impact Avoid the colloquial use of *impact* or *impact on* as a verb meaning "affect." *Population control may reduce* [not *impact*] *world hunger.*

implicit See *explicit, implicit*.

imply, infer To *imply* is to suggest indirectly. To *infer* is to guess or conclude on the basis of an indirect suggestion. *The note implied they were planning a small wedding; we inferred we would not be invited.*

inside of, outside of Use *inside* and *outside* instead. *The class regularly met outside* [not *outside of*] *the building.*

insure See *assure, ensure, insure*.

interact, interface *Interact* is a vague word meaning "do something that somehow involves another person." *Interface* is computer jargon; when used as a verb, it means "discuss" or "communicate." Avoid both verbs in academic and professional writing.

irregardless, regardless *Irregardless* is a double negative. Use *regardless*.

is when, is where These vague expressions are often incorrectly used in definitions. *Schizophrenia is a psychotic condition in which* [not *is when* or *is where*] *a person withdraws from reality.*

its, it's *Its* is the possessive form of *it*. *It's* is a contraction for *it is* or *it has*. *It's important to observe the rat before it eats its meal.*

kind, sort, type These singular nouns should be modified with *this* or *that*, not *these* or *those*, and followed by other singular nouns, not plural nouns. *Wear this kind of dress* [not *those kind of dresses*].

kind of, sort of Avoid these colloquialisms in academic and professional writing. *Amy was somewhat* [not *kind of*] *tired*.

later, latter *Later* means "after some time." *Latter* refers to the second of two items named. *Juan and Chad won all their early matches, but the latter was injured later in the season*.

latter See *former, latter* and *later, latter*.

lay, lie *Lay* means "place" or "put." Its main forms are *lay, laid, laid*. It generally has a direct object, specifying what has been placed. *She laid her books on the desk*. *Lie* means "recline" or "be positioned" and does not take a direct object. Its main forms are *lie, lay, lain*. *She lay awake until two*.

leave, let *Leave* means "go away." *Let* means "allow." *Leave alone* and *let alone* are interchangeable. *Let me leave now, and leave* [or *let*] *me alone from now on!*

lend, loan In academic and professional writing, do not use *loan* as a verb; use *lend* instead. *Please lend me your pen so that I may fill out this application for a loan*.

less See *fewer, less*.

let See *leave, let*.

liable See *apt, liable, likely*.

lie See *lay, lie*.

like See *as, as if, like*.

likely See *apt, liable, likely*.

literally *Literally* means "actually" or "exactly as stated." Use it to stress the truth of a statement that might otherwise be understood as figurative. Do not use *literally* as an intensifier in a figurative statement. *Mirna was literally at the edge of her seat* may be accurate, but *Mirna is so hungry that she could literally eat a horse* is not.

loan See *lend, loan*.

loose, lose *Lose* is a verb meaning "misplace." *Loose* is an adjective that means "not securely attached." *Sew on that loose button before you lose it*.

lots, lots of Avoid these informal expressions meaning "much" or "many" in academic or professional discourse.

man, mankind Replace these terms with *people, humans, humankind, men and women*, or similar wording.

may See *can, may*.

may be, maybe *May be* is a verb phrase. *Maybe* is an adverb that means "perhaps." *He may be the head of the organization, but maybe someone else would handle a crisis better.*

media *Media* is the plural form of the noun *medium* and takes a plural verb. *The media are* [not *is*] *obsessed with scandals.*

might of See *could of.*

moral, morale A *moral* is a succinct lesson. *The moral of the story is that generosity is rewarded. Morale* means "spirit" or "mood." *Office morale was low.*

myself See *herself, himself, myself, yourself.*

nor, or Use *either* with *or* and *neither* with *nor.*

number See *amount, number.*

off of Use *off* without *of. The spaghetti slipped off* [not *off of*] *the plate.*

OK, O.K., okay All are acceptable spellings, but avoid the term in academic and professional discourse.

on account of Use this substitute for *because of* sparingly or not at all.

one another See *each other, one another.*

or See *nor, or.*

outside of See *inside of, outside of.*

owing to the fact that Avoid this and other wordy expressions for *because.*

per Use the Latin *per* only in standard technical phrases such as *miles per hour.* Otherwise, find English equivalents. *As mentioned in* [not *As per*] *the latest report, the country's average food consumption each day* [not *per day*] *is only 2,000 calories.*

percent, percentage Use *percent* with a specific number; use *percentage* with an adjective such as *large* or *small. Last year, 80 percent of the members were female. A large percentage of the members are women.*

plenty *Plenty* means "enough" or "a great abundance." *They told us America was a land of plenty.* Colloquially, it is used to mean "very," a usage you should avoid in academic and professional writing. *He was very* [not *plenty*] *tired.*

plus *Plus* means "in addition to." *Your salary plus mine will cover our expenses.* Do not use *plus* to mean "besides" or "moreover." *That dress does not fit me. Besides* [not *Plus*], *it is the wrong color.*

precede, proceed *Precede* means "come before"; *proceed* means "go forward." *Despite the storm that preceded the ceremony, it proceeded on schedule.*

pretty Avoid using *pretty* as a substitute for "rather," "somewhat," or "quite." *Bill was quite* [not *pretty*] *disagreeable.*

principal, principle When used as a noun, *principal* refers to a head official or an amount of money; when used as an adjective, it means "most significant." *Principle* means "fundamental law or belief." *Albert went to the principal and defended himself with the principle of free speech.*

proceed See *precede, proceed.*

quotation, quote *Quote* is a verb, and *quotation* is a noun. *He quoted the president, and the quotation [not quote] was preserved in history books.*

raise, rise *Raise* means "lift" or "move upward." (Referring to children, it means "bring up.") It takes a direct object; someone raises something. *The guests raised their glasses to make a toast. Rise* means "go upward." It does not take a direct object; something rises by itself. *She saw the steam rise from the pan.*

rarely ever Use *rarely* by itself, or use *hardly ever. When we were poor, we rarely went to the movies.*

real, really *Real* is an adjective, and *really* is an adverb. Do not substitute *real* for *really.* In academic and professional writing, do not use *real* or *really* to mean "very." *The old man walked very [not real or really] slowly.*

reason is because Use either *the reason is that* or *because*—not both. *The reason the copier stopped is that [not is because] the paper jammed.*

reason why This expression is redundant. *The reason [not reason why] this book is short is market demand.*

regardless See *irregardless, regardless.*

respectfully, respectively *Respectfully* means "with respect." *Respectively* means "in the order given." *Karen and David are, respectively, a juggler and an acrobat. The children treated their grandparents respectfully.*

rise See *raise, rise.*

set, sit *Set* usually means "put" or "place" and takes a direct object. *Sit* refers to taking a seat and does not take an object. *Set your cup on the table, and sit down.*

should of See *could of.*

since Be careful not to use *since* ambiguously. In *Since I broke my leg, I've stayed home, since* might be understood to mean either "because" or "ever since."

sit See *set, sit.*

so In academic and professional writing, avoid using *so* alone to mean "very." Instead, follow *so* with *that* to show how the intensified condition leads to a result. *Aaron was so tired that he fell asleep at the wheel.*

someplace Use *somewhere* instead in academic and professional writing.

some time, sometime, sometimes *Some time* refers to a length of time. *Please leave me some time to dress. Sometime* means "at some indefinite later time." *Sometime I will take you to London. Sometimes* means "occasionally." *Sometimes I eat sushi.*

sort See *kind, sort, type.*

sort of See *kind of, sort of.*

stationary, stationery *Stationary* means "standing still"; *stationery* means "writing paper." *When the bus was stationary, Pat took out stationery and wrote a note.*

subsequently See *consequently, subsequently.*

supposed to, used to Be careful to include the final *-d* in these expressions. *He is supposed to attend.*

sure, surely Avoid using *sure* as an intensifier. Instead, use *certainly. I was certainly glad to see you.*

take See *bring, take.*

than, then Use *than* in comparative statements. *The cat was bigger than the dog.* Use *then* when referring to a sequence of events. *I won, and then I cried.*

that, which A clause beginning with *that* singles out the item being described. *The book that is on the table is a good one* specifies the book on the table as opposed to some other book. A clause beginning with *which* may or may not single out the item, although some writers use *which* clauses only to add more information about an item being described. *The book, which is on the table, is a good one* contains a *which* clause between the commas. The clause simply adds extra, nonessential information about the book; it does not specify which book.

theirselves Use *themselves* instead in academic and professional writing.

then See *than, then.*

to, too, two *To* generally shows direction. *Too* means "also." *Two* is the number. *We, too, are going to the meeting in two hours.* Avoid using *to* after *where. Where are you flying* [not *flying to*]?

two See *to, too, two.*

type See *kind, sort, type.*

uninterested See *disinterested, uninterested.*

unique *Unique* means "the one and only." Do not use it with adverbs that suggest degree, such as *very* or *most. Adora's paintings are unique* [not *very unique*].

used to See *supposed to, used to.*

very Avoid using *very* to intensify a weak adjective or adverb; instead, replace the adjective or adverb with a stronger, more precise, or more colorful word. Instead of *very nice*, for example, use *kind, warm, sensitive, endearing,* or *friendly.*

way, ways   When referring to distance, use *way*. *Graduation was a long way [not ways] off.*

well   See *good, well*.

where   Use *where* alone, not with words such as *at* and *to*. *Where are you going [not going to]?*

which   See *that, which*.

who's, whose   *Who's* is the contraction of *who* and *is* or *has*. *Who's on the patio? Whose* is a possessive form. *Whose sculpture is in the garden? Whose is on the patio?*

would of   See *could of*.

yet   See *but, yet*.

your, you're   *Your* shows possession. *Bring your sleeping bag along. You're* is the contraction of *you* and *are*. *You're in the wrong sleeping bag.*

yourself   See *herself, himself, myself, yourself*.

Photo credits: **p. 28**, Courtesy www.adbusters.org; **p. 31**, Environmental Protection Agency; **p. 32**, *Business Week*, The McGraw-Hill Company, NY; **p. 33**, Photo by Thememoryhole.org via Getty Images; **pp. 44–46**, From *Persepolis: The Story of a Childhood*, by Marjane Satrapi, translated by Mattias Ripa & Blake Ferris, copyright © 2003 by L'Association, Paris, France. Used by permission of Pantheon Books, a division of Random House, Inc.; **p. 52**, Centers for Disease Control and Prevention (upper image); United States Postal Service (lower image); **p. 56**, (cartoon) Douglas Fowler; (photo) Michael Enright/www.menright.com; **p. 179**, (upper left) Michigan Quarterly Review; (lower left) Courtesy of Business and Politics Journal; (upper right) Scientific American, Inc.; (lower right) Salon.com; **p. 187**, Mark Ungar. "Prisons and Politics in Contemporary Latin America." From *Human Rights Quarterly* 25 (2003) 909–14. © The Johns Hopkins University Press. Reprinted with permission of The Johns Hopkins University Press; **p. 189**, Courtesy of the Nieman Foundation for Journalism at Harvard University; **p. 191**, Photograph by H. Frederick Koeper. Courtesy College of Architecture and the Arts, University of Illinois at Chicago; **p. 221**, James B. Twitchell. *Living It Up—America's Love Affair with Luxury.* Title and copyright page. Copyright © 2002 by Columbia University Press. Reprinted by permission of the publisher; **p. 227**, Lucas Marcoplos. "Drafting Away from It All." Photo: Douglas Conway. From *Southern Cultures* 12.1 (2006) 33–41. © Center for the Study of the American South; **p. 231**, (text) Maurice Wallace. Excerpt from "Richard Wright's 'Black Medusa.'" Copyright © 2003 for the Study of Afro-American Life and History, Inc. Reprinted with permission; (database) From *InfoTrac* by Thomson Gale. Reprinted by permission of the Gale Group; **p. 237**, Article courtesy of The Nobel Foundation; Stamp: Topham/The Image Works; **p. 265**, William Tsutsui. *Godzilla on My Mind* title and copyright pages. Copyright © William Tsutsui 2004. Reprinted with permission of Palgrave Macmillan; **p. 267**, Reprinted with permission of New York Review of Books. Copyright © 2008 NYREV, Inc. Photo: Hasan Sarbakhshian/AP Images; **p. 271**, (text) Rebecca M. Chory-Assad and Ron Tamborini. Excerpted text, posted on EBSCOhost Research Databases, from "Television Sitcom Exposure and Aggressive Communication: A Priming Perspective." From *North American Journal of Psychology*, vol. 6, issue 3. Copyright © 2006. Reprinted by permission; (database) EBSCOhost; **p. 275**, (article) Meredith Alexander. "Thirty Years Later, Stanford Prison Experiment Lives On," *Stanford Report* (August 22, 2001). © Stanford University. (photo) Courtesy of Philip Zimbardo; **p. 291**, Howard Schuman, Barry Schwartz, and Hannah D'Arcy. "Elite Revisionists and Popular Beliefs: Christopher Columbus, Hero or Villain?" From *Public Opinion Quarterly*, volume 69, #1, April 2005 issue, page 2. Copyright © 2005 by Howard Schuman, Barry Schwartz, and Hannah D'Arcy. Reprinted by permission of Oxford University Press via Copyright Clearance Center; **p. 295**, (text) Douglas O. Linder, *Tennessee v John Scopes* ("The Monkey Trial"), *Famous Trials* (a site maintained at the UMKC School of Law) http://www.law.umkc.edu/faculty/projects/ftrials/scopes/scopes.htm. (photo) Bettmann/Corbis; **p. 309**, Apurva Narechania. "Hearing Is Believing." Masthead page from *The American Scholar*, Volume 74, No. 3, Summer 2005. Copyright © 2005 by the author and the Phi Beta Kappa Society. Reprinted by permission of *The American Scholar*; **p. 313**, (article) Alan L. Miller. Excerpt from "Epidemiology, etiology, and natural treatment of seasonal affective disorder." From *Alternative Medicine Review*, March 2005, v. 10 il. P. 5 (9). Abstract text and two lines from the Introduction. Copyright © 2005 by Thorne Research, Inc. Used with permission. All rights reserved. (database) From *InfoTrac* by Thomson Gale. Reprinted by permission of the Gale Group.

Index

a, an, 164–65, 331
abbreviations
 periods in, 118
 uses of, 133–34
absolute concepts, adjectives and adverbs, 75
abstractions, 153
abstracts
 APA style, 254, 281
 CSE style, 301
academic writing. *See also* writing projects
 authority, establishing in, 12
 directness, strategies for, 13
 in disciplines. *See* disciplines, writing in
 standard English for, 148
 U.S. academic genres, 159–60
 U.S. academic style, 13
accept, except, 331
active voice
 consistency in use, 103
 defined, 65, 319, 330
 versus passive voice, 100
addresses
 commas in, 113
 numbers in, 135
adjective clauses
 commas with, 107, 109
adjectives, 73–74
 absolute concepts and, 75
 adverbs versus, 73–74
 comparatives and superlatives, 74–75, 319
 compound, 138–39
 coordinate, 111
 defined, 319
 plural nouns and, for multilingual writers, 75
 proper, 131
adverb clauses, commas with, 109
adverbial particles, defined, 173, 319
adverbs, 73–74
 absolute concepts and, 75
 adjectives versus, 73–74
 comparatives and superlatives, 74–75, 319
 conjunctive, 86, 112, 116, 321
 defined, 319
advice, advise, 331
affect, effect, 331
African-American vernacular, spoken *be*, subject-verb agreement with, 72

aggravate, 331
agreement. *See* pronoun-antecedent agreement; subject-verb agreement
alignment, in document design, 52–53
ALL CAPS, avoiding, 39
all ready, already, 331
all right, alright, 331
all together, altogether, 331
allude, elude, 332
allusion, illusion, 332
already, all ready, 331
alright, all right, 331
altogether, all together, 331
AM, a.m., 134
among, between, 332
amount, number, 332
analogies, 154
AND, Boolean operator, 180, 320
and/or, 332
annotations
 critical reading and, 26
 sources and, 196
antecedents of pronouns. *See also* pronoun-antecedent agreement
 compound, 82
 defined, 78, 319
 unclear reference to, 83–84
any body, anybody, 332
any one, anyone, 332
anyplace, 332
anyway, anyways, 332
APA (American Psychological Association) style, 253–82
 content notes, 259
 digital object identifier (DOI), 269, 270, 273
 in-text citations, 255–58
 list of references, 259–78
  author listings, 259, 261–62
  books, 262–65, 268
  directory to, 260–61
  electronic sources, 269–76
  formatting, 263
  other sources, 276–78
  print periodicals, 266–69
 long quotations, format for, 122, 253
 manuscript format, 253–54
 past tense, using, 64–65
 signal verbs, tense of, 198, 255

APA style *(continued)*
  sources without models, 276
  student research essay example,
    280–82
  visuals, labeling, 254, 281
apostrophes, 119–21
  common errors, 8
  compound nouns and, 120
  in contractions, 120
  plurals with, 120–21
  possessive case, 119–20
appeals
  emotional, 28, 32–33
  ethical, 28, 31
  identifying, 28–29
  logical, 28–29, 32
applied sciences. *See* natural and
    applied sciences
appositive phrases
  fragments, 88
  restrictive and nonrestrictive, 110
appositives
  colon with, 128
  commas with, 110
  defined, 110, 319–20
apt, liable, likely, 332
arguable statements, criteria
    for, 30
arguments, 28–38
  appeals in, 28–29, 31–33
  arguable statement in, 30
  argumentative thesis, 30–31
  critical reading of, 25–26
  defined, 25, 320
  designing, 34–35
  organizing, 34
  student essay, 35–38
  Toulmin's framework, 29–30
  visuals in, 31–32
articles (in periodicals). *See*
    electronic sources;
    periodicals
articles (part of speech), for multi-
    lingual writers, 164–66
as, as if, like, 332
assignments
  analyzing, 50–51
  completing, factors to consider,
    14
assumptions, communicating in
    writing, 145–46
assure, ensure, insure, 332
as to, 332
at, 173
audience
  analysis, questions for, 14–15
  language and style for, deter-
    mining, 16
  visuals for, choosing, 27
audio, for Web texts, 41

authority, establishing, 12, 143
author listings
  APA style, 255–57, 259, 261–62
  Chicago style, 287
  CSE style, 304–5
  MLA style, 208–13, 217–19
auxiliary verbs
  defined, 320
  verb phrases, forming,
    166–68
awhile, a while, 333

bad, badly, 74, 333
bar graphs, 56
be
  and passive voice, 167–68
  spoken forms, subject-verb
    agreement with, 72
because of, due to, 333
being as, being that, 333
beside, besides, 333
between, among, 332
bibliographic entries, *Chicago*
    style, 286–96
bibliographic notes, MLA style,
    214
bibliographies, as library
    resource, 181
blogs. *See* Web logs (blogs)
body, in plan for writing, 19
bookmarking (online), 182
books, citing as sources
  APA style, 262–65, 268
  Chicago style, 287–88
    online, 292
    print, 287–88
  CSE style
    online, 311
    print, 304–6
  MLA style
    online, 233
    print, 208–13, 219–25
Boolean operators, in keyword
    searches, 180, 320
both, several, 163
both . . . and, 101–2
brackets, in quoted material,
    126–27, 193, 199
brainstorming, to explore topic,
    17
breath, breathe, 333
bring, take, 333
browsers. *See* Web browsers
business writing, 50–51
but, yet, 333
but that, but what, 333

can, may, 333
can't hardly, 333
can't help but, 333

capitalization, 130–33
　ALL CAPS, avoiding, 39
　common errors with, 6
　for multilingual writers, 132
captions, for visuals, 57
cartoons
　citing in MLA style, 242–43
　as visuals, 56
case, pronouns. *See* pronoun case
catalogs, library, 179–80
censor, censure, 333
cf. (compare), 134
charts
　citing, 242
　as visuals, 56
Chicago style, 283–300
　in-text citations, 284–85
　long quotations, format for,
　　122, 283
　manuscript format, 283–84
　notes and bibliographic entries,
　　286–96
　　books, 287–88
　　directory to, 286
　　electronic sources, 289–93
　　journals, 288–89
　　other sources, 293–96
　signal verbs, tense of, 198
　sources without models, citing,
　　292
　student research essay example,
　　297–300
　visuals, labeling, 283–84, 298
claims, in arguments, 29–30
classical system, arguments,
　　organizing, 34
clause fragments, 89–90
clauses. *See also* dependent
　　clauses; independent
　　clauses
　comma errors with, 85–87, 109
　comma with, 106–10, 116
　conditional sentences, 170–71
　defined, 320
　restrictive and nonrestrictive,
　　109–10
clichés, 154
clip art, 58
clustering, to explore topic, 18
coherence, in paragraphs, tech-
　　niques for, 21–22
collaborating, strategies for, 25
collective nouns
　defined, 320, 324
　pronoun-antecedent agreement
　　with, 9, 82–83
　subject-verb agreement with,
　　69–70
colloquial language, avoiding,
　　150–51

colons
　introduction to series or list,
　　117, 128
　preceding lists, 117, 128
　with quotation marks, 124, 128
　uses of, 128
color, in document design, 53–54
commas, 106–14
　addresses and, 113
　in compound sentences, 7,
　　107–8
　with contrasting elements,
　　interjections, direct
　　address, tag questions, 112
　editing for, 107
　with introductory elements,
　　3, 107
　with items in a series, 111
　with nonrestrictive elements,
　　7, 108–9
　with parentheses, 126
　with parenthetical expressions,
　　112
　with place names, 112
　with quotation marks, 113, 123
　with transitional expressions,
　　112
　unnecessary commas, 5–6,
　　113–14
comma splices
　defined, 85, 320
　revising, 8, 85–87, 116
common errors. *See* Find It. Fix It.
common nouns, 131, 324
comparatives
　adjectives and adverbs, 74–75,
　　319, 321
　double, 75
comparisons
　clear, in sentences, 94
　figurative language, 153–54
compass directions, capitalizing,
　　132
complement, compliment, 333
complements, subject and object,
　　321
complete predicates, 327
compound adjectives, hyphen in,
　　9–10, 138–39, 321
compound antecedents, pronoun-
　　antecedent agreement, 82
compound nouns
　hyphens in, 138
　possessive case, 120
compound predicates
　defined, 327
　fragments, 89
compound sentences
　commas in, 7, 107–8
　defined, 328

compound structures
  consistent, 93
  pronoun case in, 81
  unnecessary commas with, 114
compound subjects
  forming, 68–69
  subject-verb agreement with, 69
comprise, compose, 334
conciseness, in sentences, 98–100
conclusions
  arguments, 34
  oral presentations, 41
  plan for writing, 20
  research project, 203
conditional sentences, for multi-
    lingual writers, 170–71
conjunctions
  coordinating, 85, 95, 107, 115,
    321
  correlative, 101–2, 321
  defined, 321
  parallelism with, 101–2
  subordinating, 87, 89, 95, 321,
    329
conjunctive adverbs
  commas with, 112
  defined, 321
  fused (run-on) sentences, 85–87
  linking clauses with, 86, 116
connotation, 152–53
conscience, conscious, 334
consensus of opinion, 334
consequently, subsequently, 334
continual, continuous, 334
contractions, apostrophe in, 120
contrast, in document design, 51
contrasting elements, commas
    with, 112
coordinate adjectives, 111
coordinating conjunctions
  commas with, 107
  defined, 321
  for equal emphasis, 94–95
  linking clauses with, 85, 94–95,
    115
  list of, 85, 107
  unnecessary commas with,
    6, 114
coordination in sentences, 94–95
copyright, visuals, permission
    for, 200
correlative conjunctions
  defined, 321
  list of, 101–2
could of, 334
count nouns, 162–65
cover letter, for portfolio, 24
credibility, establishing
  in academic writing, 13
  in arguments, 31–32

and critical reading, 26
  of sources, 185, 186, 188
  of Web information, 186
credit, in collaborative projects, 25
criteria, criterion, 334
critical reading, 25–26
  guidelines for, 26
  of sources, 185
critical thinking
  arguments, 28–38
  critical reading, 25–26
  about visuals, 26–28
CSE (Council of Science Editors)
    style, 301–17
  citations, formats for, 302
  in-text citations, 302–3
  list of references, 303–14
    books, 304–6
    directory to, 303
    electronic sources, 310–14
    periodicals, 306–10
  long quotations, format for, 122
  manuscript format, 301–2
  signal verbs, tense of, 199
  student research essay example,
    315–17
  visuals, labeling, 301
cultural contexts for arguments,
    29

dangling modifiers, 78, 321
dashes
  to link clauses, 87
  with quotation marks, 124
  using, 127
data, 334
databases, library resource,
    180–81
databases, citing
  APA style, 269–71
  Chicago style, 289–91
  CSE style, 311–13
  MLA style, 230–32
dates
  commas in, 112
  numbers in, 135
definite article, with count and
    noncount nouns, 165
definitions, quotation marks with,
    123
del.icio.us, 182
denotation, 152–53
dependent clauses
  defined, 89, 320, 322
  as fragments, 89–90
  pronoun case in, 80–81
  subjunctive mood with, 66–67
  subordinating conjunction
    with, 87, 89–90
determiners, 163–64

CONTENTS

How to Use This Book *iii*
Find It. Fix It. *1*

WRITING

1 A Writer's Choices *12*
a Academic writing
b Assignments and purposes
c Topic
d Audience
e Stance and tone
f Medium, genre, and formats
g Visuals
h Language and style

2 Exploring, Planning, and Drafting *17*
a Exploring a topic
b Developing a working thesis
c Gathering evidence and doing research
d Planning and drafting
e Developing paragraphs
f Reviewing
g Revising
h Editing
i Reflecting
A STUDENT'S PORTFOLIO COVER LETTER (EXCERPT)
j Collaborating

3 Critical Thinking and Argument *25*
a Reading critically
b Thinking critically about visuals
c Identifying basic appeals in an argument
d Analyzing the elements of an argument
e Making an argument
f Organizing an argument
g Designing an argument
h A STUDENT'S ARGUMENT ESSAY

4 Writing for Other Media *38*
a Electronic communication
b Web texts
c Oral and multimedia presentations
d A STUDENT'S POWERPOINT SLIDES AND SCRIPT (EXCERPT)

5 Writing in the Disciplines *46*
a Academic work in any discipline
b Writing in the humanities
c Writing in the social sciences
d Writing in the natural and applied sciences
e Writing for business

6 Designing Documents *51*
a Understanding design principles
b Choosing appropriate formats
c Using headings effectively
d Using visuals effectively

SENTENCE GRAMMAR

7 Verbs *60*
a Regular and irregular verb forms
b *Lie* and *lay*, *sit* and *set*, *rise* and *raise*
c Verb tenses
d Verb tense sequence
e Active and passive voice
f Mood

8 Subject-Verb Agreement *67*
a Words between subject and verb
b Compound subjects
c Collective nouns as subjects
d Indefinite-pronoun subjects
e *Who*, *which*, and *that* as subjects
f Linking verbs and complements
g Subjects with plural forms but singular meanings
h Subjects that follow the verb
i Titles and words used as words
j Agreement with spoken forms of *be*

9 Adjectives and Adverbs *73*
a Adjectives versus adverbs
b Comparatives and superlatives

10 Modifier Placement *76*
a Misplaced modifiers
b Disruptive modifiers
c Dangling modifiers

11 Pronouns *78*
a Pronoun case
b Pronoun-antecedent agreement
c Clear pronoun reference

12 Comma Splices and Fused Sentences *85*
a Separating the clauses into two sentences
b Linking the clauses with a comma and a coordinating conjunction
c Linking the clauses with a semicolon
d Rewriting the two clauses as one independent clause
e Rewriting one independent clause as a dependent clause
f Linking the two clauses with a dash

13 Sentence Fragments *87*
a Phrase fragments
b Compound-predicate fragments
c Clause fragments